The Origins of Modern Irish Socialism, 1881–1896

Poster advertising Labour Day in Dublin, 3 May 1891
(courtesy National Archives, Dublin; ref. SPO, CSORP 1891/12408)

The Origins of
Modern Irish Socialism,
1881-1896

FINTAN LANE

CORK UNIVERSITY PRESS

First published in 1997 by
Cork University Press
Crawford Business Park
Crosses Green
Cork
Ireland

British Library Cataloguing in Publication Data
A CIP catalogue record for this book is available from
the British Library.

ISBN 1 85918 151 1 hardcover
1 85918 152 X paperback

Typeset by Tower Books, Ballincollig, Co. Cork
Printed by Hartnolls Ltd, Cornwall

Contents

Acknowledgements

I have incurred many debts during my research for this book. First of all, I would like to extend my gratitude to the staff of the following institutions: Boole Library, University College, Cork; International Institute for Social History, Amsterdam; National Archives of Ireland; National Library of Ireland; Library of Trinity College, Dublin; British Library; Linen Hall Library, Belfast; New York Public Library; British Library of Political and Economic Science; and Cork City Library.

More specifically, I would like to thank Professor Tom Dunne, who supervised the doctoral thesis on which this book is based, for his support and continuing encouragement. Also, thanks are due to my parents, Jim and Maura Lane, for their support and encouragement. I am particularly grateful to my good friend, Andreas Schwalm, who loaned me his flat in Bochum while I wrote chapter 4 and pondered chapter 5. Another friend, Dominic Carroll, typed the various drafts of this book and I would like to both thank him for an excellent job and apologize to him for my perpetual harassment as the typing was in progress. I would also like to thank Patrick Varian of I.S. Varian Brushes (Dublin) for supplying me with information on his family.

Fintan Lane
January, 1997

Introduction

In September 1888 a reporter from the *New Yorker Volkszeitung* asked Friedrich Engels if there was any hope for socialism in Ireland. 'A purely socialist movement', replied Engels, 'cannot be expected in Ireland for a considerable time.'[1] He went on to remark that the Irish people were engrossed in the struggle against landlordism and, in terms of social reorganization, wished for nothing more than to become peasant proprietors. William Morris, the English socialist, had said much the same thing just two years before when he lamented the possibility that the Irish might have to travel 'the dismal road of peasant proprietorship' before socialism would have any chance of real success among them.[2] Moreover, contended Morris, the Irish 'will not listen to anything except the hope of independence as long as they are governed by England'.[3]

William Morris, however, was less pessimistic than Engels when it came to socialist organization in Ireland. He had, after all, made his cautionary comments on Irish politics following a visit to the Dublin branch of the Socialist League. Undoubtedly, Morris would have agreed with Engels that an Irish socialist *movement* (in the substantive sense of that term) was unlikely in the short term but he was concomitantly aware that Dublin socialists had already managed 'to place the red flag on Irish soil'.[4] In fact, modern Irish socialism (as an organized force) began with the inauguration of a Dublin branch of the Socialist League in December 1885 and not, as is popularly assumed, with the formation of the Irish Socialist Republican Party (ISRP) in 1896. Moreover, the Socialist League was immediately preceded by the semi-socialist Dublin Democratic Association which had

1

strong links to the Social Democratic Federation (SDF) in Britain.

Irish historiography has traditionally been inadequate with regard to working-class political life and this is especially true for late nineteenth-century Ireland. For many historians the arrival of James Connolly in May 1896 has remained a seminal event when, in the view of F.S.L. Lyons, a spark was lit and Irish socialism began.[5] Kieran Allen contends that Connolly was 'the founder of the Marxist movement in Ireland' while Peter Collins claims that the Dublin Socialist Society which invited him to the city had been nothing more than a 'middle-class discussion group'.[6] Priscilla Metscher in her book, *Republicanism and Socialism in Ireland*, likewise casually asserts that before 1896 'one could not speak of the existence of any self-reliant socialist organisation in Ireland'.[7] There have been few serious attempts to probe beyond these assumptions or to interrogate Connolly's (consciously disingenuous) claim that the ISRP initiated the Irish socialist tradition.[8] This is all the more remarkable if we are alert to Connolly's propensity for using history and myth-making as political weaponry.

The English orthodox communist, C.D. Greaves, in his 1961 biography of Connolly, was the first historian to offer a sketch of modern Irish socialism prior to 1896. However, in two pages, Greaves presented a picture that cannot survive close scrutiny.[9] There is no evidence, as yet, of the Bakuninist influence that he suggests permeated Dublin socialism in the 1870s and it is possible that Greaves over-extrapolated from Engels's letters of 1882 where he wrote rhetorically of a Bakuninist influence on Fenian strategy. Greaves, moreover, proceeds from an invisible Bakuninism to a section of the SDF which, in fact, never existed. Certainly, Dublin socialists in the 1880s and 1890s had close connections with the SDF (and there were some individual members in the city) but a branch was never established. John W. Boyle and Emmet O'Connor in their studies of Irish labour have repeated this mistaken claim.[10] Greaves also names Thomas Fitzpatrick and Michael Canty as old members of the SDF by 1896.[11] Again, these are mistaken designations: Fitzpatrick had been a member of the Socialist League and his politics were anarchist while there is no clear evidence that Canty was an active socialist in Ireland. Greaves also seems to conflate Thomas Fitzpatrick with John Fitzpatrick of the Dublin Trades Council.[12] Nonetheless, for many years, Greaves's cursory and flawed account of the evolution of Irish socialism was all that was available to academics and the public.

In 1988, John W. Boyle, in *The Irish Labor Movement in the Nineteenth Century*, produced the first serious survey of Irish socialism in the years before Connolly arrived.[13] In a book scanning the labour movement and its development through an entire century such a survey must necessarily be abbreviated but, despite this, he presented a largely well-focused delineation of the socialist organizations that existed in Ireland from 1885 onward.

He does, however, misidentify the Dublin Democratic Association as an SDF section when it in fact maintained a distance from that organization despite close affinities.[14] Likewise, he infers that the Dublin Socialist Union survived until 1894 when the evidence would suggest otherwise.[15] Nonetheless, Boyle unearthed a series of left-wing organizations which had previously remained buried in history. The purpose of this present study is to make available for the first time a detailed history of the beginnings of modern Irish socialism along with a concurrent exposition of the ideas that motivated the activists who made those beginnings. The picture that emerges is one of a tradition more diverse and more vibrant than previously believed. Moreover, socialism in Ireland between 1885 and 1896 can largely be seen as an outpost of the British 'socialist revival' and it is within this wider movement that we can locate the origins of modern Irish socialism. Connolly was not the Patrick of Irish socialism as he has been consistently presented. The importance of the ISRP lay in the ideas of socialist republicanism rather than in organizational factors.

As well as examining Irish socialism in the 1880s and 1890s (which is contextualized by a chapter on early Irish socialism) this book will reassess the beginnings of the British 'socialist revival'. This is necessary in terms of understanding socialism in Ireland but also because of the profound impact Irish politics had on the early development of the Democratic Federation which later became the SDF. Historians of British socialism have previously recognized the importance of the Irish question but no serious attempt has been made to explore the interaction. One of the formative influences on British socialism, aside from the Irish question, was the American agrarian radical, Henry George. In a separate chapter on social radicalism in Ireland between 1881 and 1885 George and his connections with Ireland are outlined and assessed. In the early 1880s, George, with the assistance of Michael Davitt, made an attempt to persuade the Land League movement to adopt the policy of land nationalization. He failed; but disciples of his and of Davitt joined with socialists in 1885 to form the Dublin Democratic Association. This organization was closely linked to the SDF and, importantly, among those involved were former members of the Land League. Later, in 1887, a prominent Land Leaguer, James Bryce Killen, emerged as a socialist agitator and revolutionist. Undoubtedly, George (and the Land League agitation itself) had some radicalizing impact. The first manifestation of socialism in Belfast came from among supporters of Henry George.

In a more general sense, this book is intended as a contribution to the growing literature on the Irish working class. In the past two decades labour history has established a firm foothold in Ireland, although it remains conspicuous by its absence from undergraduate courses within Irish academia. *Saothar*, the journal of the Irish Labour History Society, has contributed immensely to the extension of interest but much work still needs to be done and many areas (such as the impact of early 'new unionism') remain badly under-researched. We have yet to finish building the skeleton on which we can construct a generalized socio-political history of the Irish working class. This process has not been helped by the complete absence of a rigorous Marxist historiographical tradition in this country. Where are our Thompsons, Hobsbawms, Hills, Rudés, Savilles or Masons? The commitment that such historians bring to the study of working-class life and organization should not be underestimated.

The assault on nationalist historiography, began in earnest by the revisionists of the 1970s, forced the acknowledgement of a more complex social reality. However, the idea that class occupies a central role in the lives of Irish people has collected few adherents. As Kevin Whelan has pointed out, the revisionists, in the main, have treated class as a 'minor variable' seen as 'peripheral to the central concern of revisionist history'.[16] There is a sense in which labour history has been asked to wait while revisionism and its opponents reassess Anglo-Irish relations. However, politics did exist in Ireland in the late nineteenth century outside of the traditional blocs of nationalism and unionism. There were socialists and social radicals who saw their class interests as crucial factors in how they viewed the world. In many senses they ploughed a lonely furrow in a political nation primarily motivated by nationalist concerns but such social and political dissidents are worth examining. They were not entirely unsuccessful in their activities and they laid the foundations for what exists of socialism in modern Ireland.

NOTES AND REFERENCES

1   Interview with Friedrich Engels in *New Yorker Volkszeitung*, 20 Sept. 1888, republished in Karl Marx and Friedrich Engels, *Ireland and the Irish Question: A Collection of Writings* (New York, 1972), p. 343.

2   *The Commonweal*, 8 May 1886.

3   *The Commonweal*, 1 May 1886.

4   *The Commonweal*, Dec. 1885.

5   F.S.L. Lyons, *Ireland Since the Famine* (London, 1973), p. 273.

6   Kieran Allen, *The Politics of James Connolly* (London, 1990), p. ix; Peter Collins, 'Irish labour and politics in the late nineteenth and early twentieth centuries', in Peter Collins (ed.), *Nationalism and Unionism: Conflict in Ireland, 1885–1921* (Belfast, 1994), p. 126.

7   Priscilla Metscher, *Republicanism and Socialism in Ireland* (Frankfurt am Main, 1986), p. 256.

8   See Connolly's comments in the American edition of *Erin's Hope: The End and the Means*, quoted in R.M. Fox, *James Connolly: The Forerunner* (Tralee, 1946), pp. 31–2. Connolly would have been aware of the existence of a socialist tradition in Dublin: he knew both George King and John O'Gorman who had been

involved in socialist politics in the city since 1872. Moreover, at least one member of the ISRP, Arthur Kavanagh, had been active since 1885.

9 C.D. Greaves, *The Life and Times of James Connolly* (London, 1961), pp. 58–9. Greaves also misnames the Dublin Socialist Society as the Dublin Socialist Club (p. 57). Others who have repeated this error include Kieran Allen, op. cit., p. 13; Ruth Dudley Edwards, *James Connolly* (Dublin, 1981), p. 14; and Samuel Levenson, *James Connolly: A Biography* (London, 1973), p. 43.

10 John W. Boyle, *The Irish Labor Movement in the Nineteenth Century* (Washington, 1988), pp. 172–3; Emmet O'Connor, *A Labour History of Ireland, 1824–1960* (Dublin, 1992), p. 62.

11 C.D. Greaves, op. cit., p. 59.

12 ibid., pp. 59, 70. Greaves lists both Fitzpatricks under 'T. Fitzpatrick' in his index while he used no forenames in the text.

13 John W. Boyle, op. cit., pp. 171–91.

14 ibid., pp. 172–3.

15 ibid., p. 179.

16 Kevin Whelan, 'Come all you staunch revisionists: towards a post-revisionist agenda for Irish history', *The Irish Reporter*, no. 2, 1991, p. 26.

1.

Socialism in Ireland before the 1880s

The progression of socialism in Ireland largely complies with its evolution elsewhere in Europe and was particularly enmeshed with ideological developments in Britain. 'Utopian socialism', of the British strain, found a fragile space for its experimentation and Ireland produced one of that tradition's most interesting thinkers. 'Utopian socialism' is a loosely defined term but it commonly refers to the pre-Marxian socialist thought that existed in the gap between the Napoleonic wars and the revolutions of 1848. Marx and Engels derided the utopian socialists for their pan-class approach to social transformation. In Marxist terms, they were guilty of imagining the possibility of a complete social transformation without recognizing the necessity of 'class struggle'. These pre-Marxian socialists did not view life in terms of a conflict between an abused working class and its oppressors. Rather, society suffered from aberrant afflictions which could be resolved by voluntaristic action. In their opinion, wrote Friedrich Engels, 'it was necessary to discover a new and more perfect system of social order and to impose this upon society from without by propaganda, and, wherever it was possible, by the example of model experiments'.[1] The utopian socialists evinced a paternalism that revealed little, if any, confidence in the ability of the working class itself to act as an agency for social change. This paternalism reinforced their concomitant faith in the efficacy of education as a means of correcting perceived societal disorders. Their project, nonetheless, represented a disaffection with societal inequity and sought the eradication of individualism, competition and the domination of private property.

Robert Owen (1771–1858) has customarily been accepted as Britain's first prominent socialist. Owen argued that the system of unrestricted competition had moral implications in that it promoted individualism and, consequently, a lack of community. He suggested that external social factors were decisive in shaping the human character and, as such, an association had to be developed between the prevailing ascendancy of competition and individualism and the unhappiness of many human beings. Such an association, he concluded, would rupture the tenuous consensus that maintained the interior structures of the existing social formation and would impel people to consider the option of co-operativism. The industrial revolution, wrote Owen, 'created an aggregate of wealth, and placed it in the hands of a few, who, by its aid, continue to absorb the wealth produced by the industry of the many'.[2] He was strident in his indictment of those industrialists who were not content with a modest dividend. His personal philanthropy was palpable at his extensive New Lanark cotton mill and, later still, in his attempts to create co-operative communes in both Britain and America. Owen urged the establishment of 'villages of co-operation', both industrial and agricultural, which would be self-governing and networked together on an associational basis. Such communal socio-economic structures, he said, would 'give a contrary direction to the new scientific power which undirected eats up and destroys that prosperity which, in a high degree, by its nature, it is so well calculated to promote'.[3] Moreover, he invested much hope in these communities' putative capacity to alter the human character and produce a more social animal. The Owenite proposition was, in essence, social amelioration which sought to internally remodel, rather than overturn, the existing socio-economic system.

EARLY SOCIALISM IN IRELAND

In the autumn of 1822, Robert Owen visited Ireland where he discovered much interest in his theories. The welcome he received was curiously civil considering the widespread disquiet generated by his repudiation of organized religion just a few years earlier. Indeed, his religious dissidence was scarcely used against him during his visit, although individual Catholic clerics did speak out at his first Dublin lecture against the purported irreligion of his schemes. The *Freeman's Journal*, however, promptly dismissed these detractors as 'illiberal and unfair' and commented:

> It is very gratifying to find the better classes of society anxious for the adoption of some measure which should convince Mr Owen that . . . no doubt of the purity and philanthropy of his intentions is entertained by anyone whose opinion is worth a moment's regard, and that however unblushingly his sentiments may be misrepresented, the Public will do him justice.[4]

The relative quietude of the Irish clergy was later attributed to Owen's reported visit to Maynooth where he supposedly declared his disinterest in the spread of Protestantism in Ireland.[5] According to W.L. Sargant's 1860 biography of Owen, he was invited to Maynooth by the president, Dr Crotty, who declared at the end of Owen's two-hour lecture to the students and staff that the philanthropist 'would be secure from any further opposition on the part of the Catholic clergy' at his future meetings.[6]

Owen had been persuaded to visit Ireland by Captain Robert O'Brien, an avid enthusiast, who later joined the Owenite Orbiston community in Britain.[7] Lord Cloncurry played host to Owen during some of his Irish sojourn. Their impulse for inviting him was almost certainly provided by the threatening upsurge in agrarian violence caused by the famine crisis of 1822–23. Owen, himself, later made mention of seeing landlords who 'deemed it necessary to barricade the houses which they occupied, as though a powerful enemy surrounded their dwellings, and threatened a nightly attack'.[8] It was hoped that Owen's recommended reforms would be acted on by the government's Select Committee on Employment of the Poor in Ireland and, as a result, social tension could be dissipated. From the outset, Owen's exertions were reported by the country's main newspaper in an unambiguously favourable manner. The *Freeman's Journal*, which then had a pro-government orientation, referred warmly to his attempts 'to interest the Nobility and Gentry in favour of his plans for the amelioration of the people of Ireland by means of an improved system of employment and instruction'.[9] During his first weeks he busied himself inspecting institutes for education and meeting people of influence. He dined with the Bishop of Down and spent some days with the Duke of Leinster. He also had an interview at the Vice-Regal Lodge with the Lord Lieutenant which the *Freeman's Journal* optimistically surmised 'will lead to important and beneficial changes in the condition of our unfortunate countrymen'.[10] Owen went back to Britain for the Christmas period but he remained in touch with Lord Cloncurry who, on 2 January 1823, informed him that his Irish supporters had met 'some extraordinary instances of good sense and zeal among the middle and lower orders' but made no new recruits among the nobility. Cloncurry went on to bemoan the state of Ireland: 'Not a penny is expended to educate the ignorant Papist unless he is first converted — not a penny to promote industry or useful labour . . . You know I am in less danger than most others, yet I am full of fears, if not for myself, at least for my children and grandchildren.'[11] Robert Owen returned to Ireland later in January. On 18 January he addressed a meeting of seventy to eighty men at the Chamber of Commerce rooms in Limerick city. Presumably, women were excluded from this meeting which ended with an announcement of a further lecture at a different venue, 'where the presence of any Ladies who may be desirous of attending will be particularly acceptable'.[12]

Owen's purpose was to explain his economic theories and relate them to the current distress in Ireland. There existed, he argued, a striking contrast of excessive production and increasing immiseration. Overproduction, as a result of an unfettered industrial revolution, was deemed the root cause of poverty and distress in society. His reductive argument went on to suggest that scientific improvements had diminished the value of manual labour 'rendering the mass of society unable to obtain, under present arrangements, those commodities which they wanted, and which they now could so easily produce in superfluity'.[13] Having explained the problem, he suggested that the solution lay in the co-operativism practised at New Lanark where he had created model workers out of people who 'a few years ago were the very dregs of society'.[14] His plan would rebalance the economy and, at the same time, generate social harmony. His audience was appreciative and Owen agreed to lecture again the following week.

Owen's Limerick lectures occurred during an extensive tour of rural Ireland. At the end of February he returned to Dublin where on 1 March he issued an open letter, 'To the Nobility, Gentry, Clergy and Inhabitants of Ireland'. This letter accentuated the benign nature of his proposed social amelioration and his insistence on exonerating the wealthy classes of culpability for poverty and social unrest. They, he claimed, were victims also. In his letter Owen admitted that during his journeys through the country he 'saw many living under circumstances so wretched that, had I not been an eye-witness of their sufferings, I should have doubted whether human nature could support life under the privations which they experienced'. He continued:

> I saw the towns occupied by crowds, whose poverty is hourly increasing, while they live amidst dirt and disease . . . I saw the merchants and manufacturers living upon hope, and the remains of their former gains . . . I saw the landed proprietor and the landholder, after they had employed their capital, and exerted their industry with skill and ability, by these means, bring more speedy distress upon themselves and their families . . . I heard the Clergy in many districts declare, that the poverty of the farmers was so rapidly increasing, that they knew not how hereafter the tithes could be collected.[15]

The nobility and gentry, Owen asserted, were 'really desirous' of improving the condition of those around them but their efforts invariably ended in defeat. Properly organized, however, he contended that the natural resources were such that the country could comfortably sustain a population of fifty million. So, what was wrong?

> Why then are not its invaluable natural advantages applied for the benefit of its inhabitants? Why are its proprietors compelled to seek peace and

enjoyment in other countries, or to remain at home to witness poverty and
discontent around them, and feel no security in their situations? Who is
to blame? Who inflicts this misery upon the entire population of Ireland?
I am now enabled to reply with confidence — NO ONE. The existing
distress and suffering are the natural and necessary consequences of modern
inventions under a system which cannot derive benefit from them . . . It
is true, all parties in Ireland blame each other for the misery with which
it is afflicted. But this proceeds from error — from all parties being
really ignorant of the cause of the distress, and of the only means of
relieving it.[16]

The determinism embodied in Owen's polemic was, for the wealthy classes,
quite seductive. With social unrest increasing, Owen struck the right note
when he suggested that 'the first step to a permanent improvement is the
forbearance of all parties . . . It is absolutely necessary, for the future peace
and well-being of society, that the upper and lower classes should now immediately unite'.[17] Owen, however, presumed a unity of interests that never
existed and, in any case, such 'forbearance' implied continued poverty and
subordination for the lower classes. In essence, it was an exercise in attract-
ing the support of the wealthy in Irish society.

In his letter, Owen declared his intention to hold a public meeting in
Dublin on 18 March. This lecture, which was to be the first in a series,
was staged in the Rotunda and was prominently commended and advertised
in the *Freeman's Journal*. The attendance on the day was reported as a 'vast
assemblage of rank, fashion, intelligence, and talent' and those present
included the Duke and Duchess of Leinster, Lady Rossmore, the Earl and
Countess of Meath, Lord Cloncurry and other wealthy landowners.[18] The
Lord Mayor of Dublin took the chair. Robert Owen outlined his plan which,
he said, aimed 'to remove the afflictions of our fellow creatures, and our
own sufferings too'.[19] In his Dublin lectures Owen repeated the theme
enunciated in Limerick and went on to carefully detail the mechanisms of
co-operativism and its benefits in terms of increased prosperity and social
rapport. His lectures exuded paternalism and largely articulated the fears
of a class confronting possible social turmoil. There was harsh criticism,
particularly from clerics in the audience, but his propositions were, by and
large, well received. Daniel O'Connell attended the lectures and later wrote:
'I shall become a subscriber to Owen's Society. He may do some good and
cannot do any harm.'[20] The society to which O'Connell alluded was the
Hibernian Philanthropic Society which was established in the wake of the
Dublin lectures on the lines of the British and Foreign Philanthropic Society. Its object was, in the absence of government support, to collect funds
to promote co-operative experiments. Sympathetic individuals, such as
General Browne and Lord Cloncurry, contributed large sums but the society remained as ineffectual as its British counterpart.[21]

THE RALAHINE EXPERIMENT

John Scott Vandeleur, an affluent landowner from Clare, was among those inspired by Robert Owen's Dublin lectures. During Owen's stay in Ireland Vandeleur had frequent discussions with him on the topic of co-operativism and emerged profoundly impressed. John Finch, who visited Vandeleur's Ralahine estate in the early 1830s, later wrote that Vandeleur became convinced 'that it was perfectly practicable to cultivate land . . . in such a manner as to secure better rents to landowners, more interest for capital, and ten times more and greater advantages and enjoyment to labourers than can possibly be obtained by any mode at present adopted'.[22] Vandeleur joined the Hibernian Philanthropic Society and, following its collapse, maintained contact with the Owenite movement in Britain.[23] In common with the other landowning members of the society, Vandeleur made no immediate effort to transform into co-operatives either of his two large estates in County Clare. He did, however, set about improving and modernizing on his Ralahine estate and built a weaving factory, flax scutching mill, bleaching works and proper housing for his workforce. It was a new outbreak of agrarian violence at the beginning of the 1830s that finally pushed him to establish an Owenite community on his lands.

An observer in April 1831 described Clare as an area whose peasantry 'defied the government, whose military display had little terror for starving men, while catholic priesthood had no moral control over discontented people made furious by famine'.[24] Out of a total population of 250,000, the county contained an estimated 80,000 landless labourers and an equal number who held insufficient land for subsistence.[25] A shortage of conacre, short-term rented land, in the early 1830s ensured trouble. Moreover, a shift from tillage to grazing reduced employment prospects and caused pasture land to become a target for an enraged and frustrated peasantry. E.T. Craig later recalled: 'Men and women armed themselves with their agricultural implements and, in open day, in savage desperation, dug up the grass-lands, levelled the wall fences, and turned the cattle adrift.'[26] Wages for farm labourers, which varied between six pence and eight pence a day, were challenged and the *Clare Journal*, in late April 1831, reported: 'Notices cautioning the peasantry not to work for less than one shilling a day were posted in almost every district of the County.'[27] These notices were erected by the resurgent agrarian secret societies who, in Clare, traded under the titles of 'Terry Alts' and 'Lady Clare's Boys'.

Nocturnal attacks, killings and beatings became commonplace as the secret societies pursued their objectives. In some instances the intimidation proved successful. On 2 May 1831 a large crowd of peasants invaded the property of Denis McCormick at Artclony and demanded that he lower his rent from the £12 an acre he had charged the previous year. Confronted by an angry mob he relented and agreed to reduce his rent to £8 an acre for good land and £6 an acre for the rest. He also agreed to manure the land at no extra cost.[28] Not all landlords, however, conceded that easily. At the end of April 1831 Vandeleur was touched by the violence when his land steward, Daniel Hastings, fell victim to the 'Terry Alts'. Hastings, who was considered despotic by those he managed, was shot dead by an assassin as he bolted his door for the night.[29] Frightened by this incident, Vandeleur's wife and five children went to Limerick for refuge while he headed for Manchester. His mansion at Ralahine was left under armed police guard.[30]

Before the death of his land steward Vandeleur had already given serious consideration to initiating an Owenite community on his Ralahine estate, and Hastings's violent demise convinced him to accelerate his plans. In England he explained his intentions to John Finch, a Liverpool iron merchant and Owenite, who suggested that he approach Edward Thomas Craig, editor of the *Lancashire Co-operator*. Craig was born in Manchester in 1804 and had trained as a fustian cutter. At the age of fifteen he had witnessed the 'Peterloo' massacre where armed troops killed ten demonstrators and injured hundreds of others in Manchester. He became deeply involved in the co-operative movement and by 1830 he was president of the small Owenian Co-operative Society. Craig remained interested in socialism throughout his life and in the 1880s he became a member of the Social Democratic Federation and, later, the Socialist League. Vandeleur met him in a Manchester hotel and invited him to Ireland to manage the proposed experiment. Craig accepted the offer, and in a letter to Robert Owen enthused: 'Mr J.S. Vandeleur of Ralahine has invited me to Ireland to assist in his arrangements. I shall go there with pleasure, as my whole heart is with the cause.'[31] In later years he recalled his anticipation, 'that if successful in Ireland, the example would exercise some influence over the movement'.[32] In short, if co-operativism could succeed in tumultuous Ireland it could succeed anywhere.

In September 1831, Craig took a ship to Dublin and from there went by stagecoach to Limerick city. When he arrived in Ralahine he discovered that the estate had already been partially adapted for use as a co-operative farm. Nonetheless, he noted: 'Although much gratified with the capabilities of the land and the position and surroundings of the estate, the condition and prejudices of the people in the neighbourhood were not encouraging, and soon became a source of anxiety as to the possibility of success in organising a system of mutual co-operation among them.'[33] Craig, himself, was received with suspicion as it was widely thought he might be a police spy or, at best, sympathetic to the landlord class. His lack of the native language in this Irish-speaking district also proved a disadvantage: 'My attire was in marked contrast with that of their home-spun frieze coats; my language was to them a foreign tongue, and proved me to be a *Sassenach*; and their traditionary histories of the Saxon are but dark memories of conquest, confiscations, ejectments, injustice, and tyranny.'[34] The suspicion led to violence and Craig was struck by a stone from behind on one occasion. In addition, he discovered an antipathy among Vandeleur's family to the proposed experiment, and the 'servants in the hall knew that the "new system" was not desired by the family or the gentry, and their vulgar jests and coarse humour had to be tolerated with the best grace possible'.[35]

Despite the negative apprehensions Craig and Vandeleur persisted and on 6 November those employed on the estate were called together for a meeting where Vandeleur put his proposal. The penury of this initial group of members was remarked on by John Finch:

> Mr Vandeleur called a meeting of those persons from among whom he wished to form the Society . . . [These consisted] of the very poorest persons in the neighbourhood, many of them his former workpeople, without cottage, no other employment than his, not a shilling of capital . . . His reason for choosing such was, that, should the experiment fail, none of them might hereafter have cause for reproaching him with having made their condition worse than it was before.[36]

The Ralahine Agricultural and Manufacturing Co-operative Society was formed with an initial membership of fifty-two (twenty-eight men, twelve women and twelve youths and children). They were largely reluctant members and Craig recognized that 'some of them viewed their entering into the Society . . . as a disgrace to their family, owing to an opinion abroad that it was to be conducted upon a plan similar to the "Mendicity Houses" or refuges for the poor'.[37] The inauguratory meeting adopted a comprehensive forty-eight clause constitution and appointed a nine-person management committee. In line with the constitution Vandeleur automatically became president of the management committee and he was given the right to select the secretary, treasurer and storekeeper for the society. E.T. Craig was appointed secretary. The secretary and the treasurer sat on the management committee which left six places to be filled by election. At Ralahine women were, unusually for the period, eligible to vote. The day-to-day running of the co-operative was the chief concern of the management committee which was assisted in its work by five sub-committees. Vandeleur also retained the right, for the first twelve months of the co-operative, to dismiss any member deemed to be misbehaving. In addition, all prospective members had to be acceptable to Vandeleur before their application to join could be laid before the society. According to Finch, 'King Vandeleur had a power which we would by no means entrust to the governor of a community . . . but he never used it'.[38]

On 10 November, Vandeleur entered into a formal agreement with the society in which he agreed to lease 618 acres of his Ralahine estate for a period of twelve months. The paddock, woods and mansion house were excepted. Rent was fixed at £700 per annum and an interest charge of £200 per annum was put on the livestock. This sum was to be paid in the form of farm produce which the society agreed to deliver to the market free of charge. The fixed rental exceeded the total gathered in rent by Vandeleur in the previous year. Craig was of the opinion that 'had the rent been £100 less it would have made a vast improvement in the condition of the members. The landlord admitted that the rent was too high. It was very evident, also, that if the land had been the property of the members they would have become very prosperous and wealthy'.[39] The livestock, farm equipment and land were to remain the property of Vandeleur until sufficient funds were accumulated to pay for them, at which stage they would become the joint property of the members. R.G. Garnett was unquestionably correct when he commented:

> The community dwellers at Ralahine were in effect licensed residents with a contractual obligation to pay rent in perpetuity. Ralahine was a most successful experiment in communal living and social equality, but it was not a self-generated co-operative, and it is unlikely that the successors of John Scott Vandeleur would have conceded their land entitlement to erstwhile peasants . . . The distinction between governor and governed was too wide for Ralahine to be a true example of co-operative ownership.[40]

Life did undoubtedly improve for those who joined the Ralahine community. Wages, to begin with, remained at the low level of eight pence for a twelve-hour day for men and five pence a day for women but the members, at least, were sure of their employment and, by the time the experiment collapsed, individual members had accumulated savings of between one pound and five pounds.[41] On the other hand, the regime was harsh and 'vices' such as smoking, using snuff, and drinking alcohol were forbidden. The ban on alcohol failed, however, to prevent members imbibing outside the community and Ralahine's blacksmith was transported to Australia for seven years following a drunken brawl in which he killed a man. Robert Owen was pleased with the success of Ralahine and he complimented Vandeleur for being

> The only gentleman in Ireland who has made experiments on a large scale to try the effect of our principles . . . Mr Vandeleur is quite pleased with his tenants, and on both sides they confess to be doing much better by these plans of co-operation than they could otherwise do.[42]

Vandeleur's social experimentation remained, nonetheless, only a part of his life. After his marriage he had joined the Kildare Street and other Dublin clubs and enjoyed wagering for high stakes. In November 1833 he gambled his Ralahine estate and lost. Vandeleur was declared bankrupt and a warrant was issued for his arrest although by then he had absconded. His debts amounted to some £9,360.[43] The Vandeleur family took possession of the Ralahine estate and the co-operative was disbanded. It had lasted two years and was, incontrovertibly, the most progressive and innovative attempt to deal with the land and social crises of early nineteenth-century Ireland.

WILLIAM THOMPSON

Ireland's connection with utopian socialism extends far beyond the Ralahine co-operative. Among the visitors to Ralahine, during its brief existence, was William Thompson, a Cork landlord and left-wing disciple of Jeremy Bentham. John Stuart Mill, who debated with the Owenites in the late 1820s, described Thompson as 'the principal champion on their side' and 'a very estimable man'.[44] E.T. Craig, who had met Thompson before his visit to Ralahine, referred to him as 'one of the most earnest advocates of mutual co-operation'.[45] In point of fact, Thompson is widely accepted to have contributed more than Robert Owen to the political and economic theories of co-operativism.[46]

William Thompson (1775–1833) was the son of Alderman John Thompson, a wealthy Cork city merchant, who had served as Speaker and Mayor of the municipality, and as High Sheriff of the county. When his father died in 1814 Thompson took over the extensive family assets including a 1,400-acre estate near Rosscarbery in west Cork. He retained his house in the city, however, and was a prominent member of the local Philosophical, Scientific and Literary Society. In politics, despite his membership of the Protestant élite, he gave his support in the elections of 1812 and 1826 to Christopher Hely-Hutchinson, an advocate of Catholic emancipation.[47]

Bentham's doctrine of utilitarianism attracted Thompson and he carried out a careful study of the philosopher's writings on education with the intention of establishing an educational institute in the city. He entered into correspondence with Bentham who later wrote that 'a Chrestomathic School in everything but name is about to be set on foot by a disciple in Cork. It was necessary that the name (which would have connected it with my name) should be kept out of sight'.[48] Thompson visited Bentham in early October 1822, and remained on as his guest until February 1823, discussing ideas and meeting many of the leaders of English utilitarianism. It was about this time that Thompson first came into contact with Robert Owen although his initial reaction was one of caution as he saw Owen's ideas as little more than 'an improved system of pauper management'.[49] Thompson was immediately distrustful of the apparent incongruity in Owen's overtures to royal and aristocratic figures. He 'turned away with disgust from a system which then seemed to me to court the patronage of non-representative lawmakers'.[50] Despite this initial reticence, however, Thompson was quickly won to the co-operative movement, and he began to view co-operativism as 'the best and the only yet devised mode of free exertion affording you any chance of enjoying the products of your labor'.[51]

In 1824 he published the conclusions of a lengthy study into the distribution of wealth as *An Inquiry into the Principles of the Distribution of Wealth most conducive to Human Happiness, applied to the newly proposed System of Voluntary Equality of Wealth.* This book revealed Thompson as an impressive theoretician of a decidedly democratic strain. Distribution, he argued, was the fundamental problem within the existing socio-economic order. It was not, he contended, 'the mere possession of wealth, but the right distribution of it, that is important to a community'.[52] Condemning this 'vicious distribution of wealth', he wrote:

> The tendency of the existing arrangement of things as to wealth, is to enrich a few at the expense of the mass of the producers; to make the poverty of the poor more hopeless, to throw back the middling classes upon the poor, that a few may be enabled, not only to accumulate in perniciously large masses the real national, which is only the aggregate of individual, capital, but also, by means of such accumulations, to command the products of the yearly labour of the community . . . Who is not alarmed at the everyday increasing tendency to poverty on the part of the many, to the ostentation of excessive wealth on the part of the few?[53]

Thompson agreed with the Ricardian belief that the value of a commodity was equal to the value of the labour that produced it, but he went beyond that precept to argue that labour should possess the whole product of its exertions (albeit, collectively in communities). Owen, in contrast, claimed that the labourer was entitled only to 'his fair proportion'.[54] Thompson also contested the Owenite contention that the state occupied a neutral position. Apoliticism, as shown clearly by the following 1840 Owenite statement, remained a hallmark of the movement:

> The plans of the Socialists will be carried on under entire obedience to the laws of the State . . . The Socialists take no part in the agitation for political changes, as they are convinced that permanent prosperity and happiness can be gradually secured for every human being under any form of government which recognises the principle of toleration.[55]

Conversely, Thompson believed that there was 'some sense' in demanding political reform within the existing system as this would smooth the way to a co-operative commonwealth.[56] For him political power was a requisite for true freedom: 'Added to knowledge, the Industrious Classes must also acquire power, the whole power of the social machine in their own hands.'[57] He did, however, share Owen's unwavering faith in the curative capacity of education and example. In his 1827 book, *Labor Rewarded*, Thompson held that, 'If Co-operative Industry tend more to human happiness than Competitive Industry, its supporters are confident it will be adopted when understood. On no other ground would they wish it to be adopted'.[58] This somewhat naïve perspective reflected an earlier rejection of force which he described as 'the instrument employed by ignorance . . . But no sooner was force made use of than security fled, and, with security, production and consequently the means of happiness'.[59] Thompson was not a revolutionist, in spite of his recognition of the institutional nature of class inequality. He maintained that: 'When happiness, the child of knowledge, becomes the lot of the industrious, the idle will become ashamed of their unenvied and unhappy idleness, and will join the ranks of the industrious, the active and useful in mind or body.'[60]

His democratic values came into open conflict with Owen at the first Co-operative Congress in 1831. Thompson did not agree that Owen's plans for immense communities were financially feasible and argued for small-scale communities such as Ralahine with its system of democratic committee rule. Owen replied that such committees created confusion and that he 'had found by thirty years' experience, that people could not act for themselves in a Community. There must be some conducting head'. Such a society as they conceived 'could only be effected by the direction of one mind'. Thompson retorted by asking Owen 'if he had taken care to give to the world, after his own death, the valuable knowledge he possessed'.[61] At this congress Thompson also announced his willingness to make 600 acres of his estate available, at a low rent, for a prospective co-operative community. He himself would pay a contribution and would join the community, but he wished for no privileges.[62]

During the course of a speech at the 1831 congress Owen remarked that 'if we were resolved to go into a community upon Mr Thompson's plan we must make up our minds to dissolve our present marriage arrangements, and go in as single men and women'.[63] This sarcastic quip was a reference to Thompson's known progressive views on the institution of marriage and women's oppression. Thompson had opined: 'Were the influential males really bound by the laws of marriage which they imposed on the females, the institution would not remain in its existing state another year.'[64] Likewise, he accused religious people of creating 'blind and undistinguishing dogmas' and of suffering from an 'early mental association of vice with freedom of sexual intercourse', and of failing to comprehend that it would have been 'happy for the human race had the increase of numbers been left to individual regulation, protecting only the weak from the oppression of the strong' rather than 'depriving one of the contracting parties of all rights, self-control and independence'.[65] Thompson's advocacy of women's emancipation was grounded in his support for 'the claim of every rational adult, without distinction of sex or colour, to equal political rights'.[66] His indignation at the subjugation of women was intensified by his close friend-ship with Anna Wheeler, the daughter of a Protestant cleric. Wheeler's own experience of marriage, at fifteen, to a brutal drunkard, had convinced her of the inimicability of the social order towards women. She immersed herself in a study of social and political philosophy including the controversial work of the feminist Mary Wollstonecraft.[67] In 1825 Wheeler and Thompson's collaboration bore fruit in the publication of his book, *Appeal of one Half the Human Race, Women, Against the Pretensions of the Other Half, Men, to Retain Them in Political, and Thence in Civil and Domestic Slavery*. The tone and theme can be gleaned from the title. He argued:

> Women may be eligible by law to the situation of professors; the law may protect them when married from the personal violence or constraint of any kind of their husbands . . . but if none but men are to be the electors, if none but men are to be jurors or judges when women complain against men of partiality and injustice, is it in human nature that a sympathy from old habit, from similarity of organisation and trains of thought, from love of domination, should not have a tendency to make men swerve from the line of justice and the pretensions of women, and be lenient to the errors of men?[68]

Thompson's resolute promotion of the claim of 'every rational adult' to 'equal political rights' also impelled him to participation in the struggle for Catholic emancipation. Daniel O'Connell visited Cork in August 1828 and spoke at a meeting in the South Parish Chapel organized by the 'Friends of Catholic Emancipation'. The meeting was described by the unionist *Cork Constitution* as being 'as usual, inflated, bombastic and clamorous about rights, liberties and so forth'.[69] Among those 'clamouring' for 'rights' was William Thompson who proposed a vote of thanks to O'Connell for his attendance. The meeting ended, in the view of Cork unionism, 'little enlight-ened by the inflated and unconnected bombast of the evil-minded demagogue'.[70] In fact, O'Connell attended another meeting at the Cork Chamber of Commerce rooms, chaired by Thompson, and from which a County and City of Cork Liberal Club was formed.[71] This Liberal Club was, in essence, the Cork branch of the Catholic Association and among its tasks was the collection of the Catholic Rent. This 'rent', which was widely collected, was used to fund the political campaign for emancipation. Over one hundred members enrolled at the initial Cork meeting and a committee was formed to make preliminary arrangements for the club. Thompson was appointed chairman of this temporary committee and, from there, involved himself in the practical work of the movement.[72]

Towards the end of his life Thompson began work on the formation of a community on his west Cork estate and a constitution was drafted on his democratic principles. However, he died on 28 March 1833 before he could complete his plans. When his will was read it was discovered that he had bequeathed most of his estate to the co-operative movement but his relatives, not surprisingly, contested and, following a twenty-five-year legal squabble, they retained the estate.

In later years it was claimed that Marx plagiarized Thompson when writing *Das Kapital*. The accuser was Anton Menger, a professor at Vienna University, who contended in 1886: 'In Thompson's views one immediately recognises the mode of thinking, indeed even the forms of expression, that are later found in so many socialists, particularly Marx and Rodbertus.'[73] He also expressed a conviction that Thompson was the 'foremost founder of scientific socialism'.[74] Engels, in reply, offered a convincing refutation of Menger's thesis and provided examples of errors in his delineation.[75] It is unquestionably true that Thompson's import has been exaggerated in terms of his influence on Marxian socialism. At the same time, he certainly constitutes the most advanced thinker to emerge from the Owenite movement.

MARX, THE FIRST INTERNATIONAL AND IRELAND

After 1833 socialism in Ireland received a shallow burial. Unlike the British, the Irish Owenites had accrued no significant following among urban or rural workers and the liberal landowners had done little more than faint-heartedly dabble with the new ideas. Working-class radicals contributed their energy to the development and struggles of the evolving trade unions which had been decriminalized since 1824. These labour organizations, significantly, were drawn towards the Repeal and home rule campaigns but their political opinions, for the most part, strayed no further than the nationalist agenda.[76] Nonetheless, during the late 1830s and 1840s a Chartist movement materialized in Ireland, its most notable evocation being the establishment of the Irish Universal Suffrage Association in 1841.[77] The Chartists contained a vocal and capable left wing but the movement as a whole could only superficially be characterized as socialist. Properly speaking, Chartism can be located within the British Radical tradition. Indeed, Eric Hobsbawm has dismissed the political kernel of Chartism as 'little more than a handful of traditional and radical slogans'.[78] Chartism in Ireland was noted for its moderate tone.[79] A group of artisan socialists did exist in Dublin in 1841–43 but disbanded following concerted attacks from supporters of Daniel O'Connell. Vincent Geoghegan, in a seminal article, names the leaders as John Elliot and Michael Graves.[80]

Ireland's evident incuriousity with regard to socialism failed, however, to ward off the affections of foreign socialist theoreticians. The defeat of the revolutions of 1848 across Europe had ushered in a decade of retrenchment for the socialist movement but the 1863 Polish national rising caused working-class activists in London and Paris to form, in 1864, an international federation of working-class organizations.[81] This federation, the International Working Men's Association (or First International), soon captured the interest of Friedrich Engels and also that of Karl Marx who was to draft almost all the documents issued by its general council in its early years.

Karl Marx, and his collaborator Friedrich Engels, reshaped socialist politics in the late nineteenth century. Marx, the son of a middle-class German lawyer, had begun his career in politics as a Young Hegelian and as editor, in Cologne, of the influential *Rheinische Zeitung* which was subsequently closed down in 1843 by the government because of its liberal politics. Marx emigrated to France, following the closure of his newspaper, and rapidly made contact with French and *émigré* German socialists. In Paris he met Engels, the son of a textile manufacturer, and when expelled from France they moved to Brussels. Marx and Engels joined the shadowy Communist League and soon became its foremost theoreticians. Over the next four decades Marx produced an enormous body of work including his *magnum opus, Das Kapital*. Marx was a revolutionist who argued that the existing socio-economic order had to be completely overthrown and a new system built which centred on the needs and wants of the working classes. He contended that life involved a perpetual class struggle between the oppressed workers and the oppressing capitalist and landowning classes. A resolution to this conflict could only be found in a participatory democracy based on equality and community. Unlike the utopian socialists Marx predicted the necessity for violent revolution as he believed that the ruling classes would not willingly relinquish their power. By the 1860s both Marx and Engels were resident in England.

Marx's first comments on Ireland evinced little enthusiasm for the issue of Irish independence which O'Connell had revived with his Repeal agitation. Engels had, in 1843, denounced O'Connell's 'miserable, petty middle class objectives which are at bottom of all the shouting and agitation for Repeal'.[82] Engels objected to O'Connell's 'two-faced Whig' leadership, and argued that his aims were too limited and that he was likely to disappoint the 'millions of militant and desperate Irishmen' whom he had mobilised.[83] By 1848 he did, however, see hope in the Chartist movement. He wrote: 'Henceforth the mass of the Irish people will undoubtedly unite ever more closely with the English Chartists and will act in accordance with a common plan. This will bring the victory of the English democrats, and hence the liberation of Ireland, considerably nearer.'[84]

Before the 1860s Marx and Engels presumed that the 'Irish Question' would be resolved in the wake of a socialist revolution in Britain. Marx viewed Irish separatism with a jaundiced eye and 'believed that it would be possible to overthrow the Irish regime by English working class ascendancy'.[85] By 1867, however, he was writing to Engels: 'Previously I thought Ireland's separation from England impossible. Now I think it inevitable, although after separation there may come federation.'[86] Marx and Engels's interest in Ireland was heightened by the growth of the Fenian republican movement in the 1860s. Marx saw a revolutionary potential in the militant separatism advocated by the Fenians and was attracted by its apparent anti-clericalism, its 'socialistic tendency (in a negative sense, directed against the appropriation of the soil) and by being a lower orders movement'.[87] His enthusiasm, nonetheless, did not extend to supporting the Fenian dynamite campaign in Britain. He deplored the Fenian explosion at Clerkenwell in December 1867 in which twelve people died as 'a very stupid thing'.[88] His opposition was political rather than moral. He wrote to Engels about the affair:

> The London masses, who have shown great sympathy for Ireland, will be made wild by it and driven into the arms of the government party. One cannot expect the London proletarians to allow themselves to be blown up in honour of the Fenian emissaries. There is always a kind of fatality about such a secret melodramatic sort of conspiracy.[89]

Between 1867 and 1870 Marx developed an analysis that placed Ireland, and Poland, at the centre of the European revolutionary vortex. Engels later wrote to Karl Kautsky declaring that these were two nations which had 'not only the right but even the duty to be nationalistic before they became inter-nationalistic'.[90] In September 1869, Engels travelled to Ireland with Lizzy Burns and Eleanor Marx and visited Dublin, the Wicklow mountains, Killarney, Cork and Queenstown*.[91] Though this was not Engels's first time in Ireland (he had previously visited in 1856) his holiday increased his interest in the country and he began compiling a study on Irish history. In addition, two months after Engels's visit, a jailed Fenian Jeremiah O'Donovan Rossa was elected as a member of parliament for Tipperary in a by-election. Despite being immediately disqualified, this electoral victory gave a tremendous boost to the Fenian movement. In an 1870 letter to the Lafargues, Marx, himself, affirmed:

> Here, at home, as you are fully aware, the Fenians' sway is paramount. Tussy [Eleanor] is one of their head centres. Jenny writes on their behalf in the *Marseillaise* under the pseudonym of J. Williams . . . You understand at once that I am not only acted upon by feelings of humanity. There is something besides. To accelerate the social development in Europe, you must push on the catastrophe of official England. To do so, you must attack her in Ireland. That's her weakest point. Ireland lost, the British 'Empire' is gone, and the class war in England, till now somnolent and chronic, will assume acute forms.[92]

---

*Queenstown is now known by its original name of Cobh.

Marx was clear as to what his analysis meant in terms of the work embarked on by the International Working Men's Association (IWMA):

> England, being the metropolis of capital, the power which has hitherto ruled the world market, is for the present the most important country for the workers' revolution, and moreover the only country in which the material conditions for this revolution have developed up to a certain degree of maturity. Therefore to hasten the social revolution in England is the most important object of the International Working Men's Association. The sole means of hastening it is to make Ireland independent. Hence it is the task of the International everywhere to put the conflict between England and Ireland in the foreground, and everywhere to side openly with Ireland. And it is the special task of the Central Council in London to awaken a consciousness in the English workers that for them the national emancipation of Ireland is no question of abstract justice or humanitarian sentiment, but the first condition of their own emancipation. [93]

At the inaugural meeting in 1864 of the IWMA, Ireland was listed as one of a number of countries in which British policy was to be condemned. [94] The arrest and mistreatment of Fenian activists, fifteen months later, was the first issue that provoked genuine interest by the IWMA general council. In May 1866 the council discussed joining an excursion party to Ireland which 'had at heart the amelioration of the relations between the English and Irish peoples'. [95] A few months earlier it had sent an appeal for funds for the relief of Irish prisoners to the *Workman's Advocate* for publication. [96] The general council also requested an audience with the Home Secretary to discuss the issue of Irish prisoners but this was refused. [97] The council's work, however, was noted by the Fenian leader Jeremiah O'Donovan Rossa who wrote to Peter Fox, an English member, expressing his thanks for articles published in the *Workman's Advocate* highlighting their plight. [98] In November 1867, the general council organized a public debate on the Irish question which extended over two of its weekly meetings. Eugene Dupont, the French delegate, argued that 'the Council would be wanting in its duty if it remained indifferent to the Irish cause. What is Fenianism? Is it a sect or a party whose principles are opposed to ours? Certainly not. Fenianism is the vindication of an oppressed people of its rights to social and political existence'. [99] John Devoy and James Stephens, both leading Fenians, joined the IWMA in the United States although neither participated to any appreciable extent in the work of the organization. Stephens, who signed up in 1866, was too immersed in Fenian internal squabbling to take his membership seriously. Devoy, who joined following his release from prison in 1871, became the delegate of the Irish section on the New York committee but, again, his immersion in Fenian activities precluded a more earnest involvement. The Irish section of the New York IWMA drew its membership primarily from the very large pool of *émigré* Fenians.[100] Irish branches of the International were also formed within the Irish community in Britain in the early 1870s. Joseph Patrick McDonnell, formerly a leading Dublin Fenian, was among those recruited in England, and was to prove an important acquisition. In 1868, after a period in jail, he arrived in London where he became an important organizer for the movement seeking an amnesty for those Fenians still incarcerated.[101] By 1871 McDonnell had become acquainted with many in the radical and socialist underground in London and he joined in the enthusiasm for the Paris Commune that swept through that milieu.[102] The Commune, however, was to give the International an undeserved notoriety and caused a widening of the political gap between it and the Fenians. In the popular mind, the IWMA had engineered the Paris uprising and was responsible for the deaths of members of religious orders. O'Donovan Rossa wrote in *The Irishman* in condemnation of the Communards after the death of the Archbishop of Paris and most Fenians recoiled from anything that appeared to support the Commune.[103] This fallacious linkage was to provide the IWMA with problems when it attempted to organize in Ireland.

Marx met McDonnell for the first time on 18 June 1871 and the following Tuesday he proposed him for membership of the general council.[104] In August McDonnell was appointed secretary for Ireland but he immediately came under attack from *The Irishman* which alleged that his reputation was 'that of an eccentric, agitating character, without steadiness or force'.[105] The vituperation from his erstwhile comrades, however, quickly subsided and no concrete allegations materialized. McDonnell went on to become one of Marx's most consistent supporters on the general council. McDonnell saw the organization of IWMA branches in Ireland as one of his main priorities and in January 1872 he informed the General Council of 'branches of the association being in the course of establishment in numerous localities'.[106] On 11 March *The Irish Times* reported that the International 'is about to establish itself amongst us' and that a preliminary meeting had taken place the previous day in an old loft in Chapel Lane in Dublin. A Frenchman, evidently sent from London, occupied the chair and speeches 'of the most revolutionary character, went so far as to justify the shooting of Generals Thomas and Clement in Paris'.[107] The Dublin branch was one of four sections established in Ireland in early 1872. The others were in Cork, Belfast and Cootehill. IWMA agents were also active in Ennis, Limerick and Tipperary.[108]

Little is known of the Belfast or Cootehill sections although Canon Maguire, a Cork cleric, noted with satisfaction that 'those wretched people had been expelled from Belfast'.[109] The antipathy shown towards the IWMA was no less virulent in Dublin and Cork. In Dublin, the section was formed sometime in mid-February and made its first public appearance on 10 March. The central character in the Dublin branch was Richard McKeon, a cabinet-maker in his forties, who the police described as 'a troublesome character, and a regular fanatic in politics, having been a Chartist, a Young Irelander, a member of the National Brotherhood of St Patrick, and a Fenian'.[110] McKeon was an old friend of McDonnell. A Frenchman named Charles Wery delivered a paper for the group at a meeting on 24 March, attended by twenty-five to thirty people, on the 'History of the International'.[111] The next public meeting on 29 March was the first to receive extensive press coverage. It turned out to be a farcical affair which a hostile press capitalized on. The meeting was organized for 8 p.m. above a public house in the neighbourhood of the North Union workhouse. The chairman, a man called Williams, failed to show, and according to the *Freeman's Journal*:

> The audience waited for his arrival for a full hour. It was suggested to club for a drink to beguile the time, but this proposition one of the elderly politicians — who himself was far from sober — indignantly denounced as calculated 'to give a handle to the enemy'. His remonstrance turned the tide of opinion, and the project was abandoned, but there was a lively exodus from the apartment to the shop beneath, and the members returned, wiping their mouths with a prolonged back-handed motion, suggestive of heavy drinks out of pewter.[112]

Eventually, one of the Internationalists stood up 'and termed Williams a coward and traitor for having been afraid to come forward after having organised the meeting'.[113] The gathering then quickly degenerated into a vicious argument, as to whether the International supported the Paris Commune, before the owner of the public house burst into the room demanding to know who dared use his premises as a meeting place for 'blackguards and murderers'.[114] The Internationalists were ordered from the building.

The difficulties endured by the Dublin Internationalists were increased when Fr Patrick Lavelle issued an appeal to the 'young men of Ireland' to shun the IWMA:

> I . . . write this hurried word adjuring you, as you value your sacred faith — that holy religion for which your fathers suffered, were exiled and died — as you value the honour and hope for the liberty of your prostrate country; to shun that ill-omened organisation as you would Satan himself, to flee from it as 'from the face of thunder'. I now avoid all reference to the connexion with or approval of the infamous Commune of Paris, against which the blood of a noble archbishop, eminent priests, and brave, greyhaired soldiers cry to heaven. Enough for me, for you, that Garibaldi is its prophet.[115]

On 7 April the Dublin section held its final public meeting at McKeon's premises in Chapel Lane. Before the appointed hour a mob gathered in the laneway and, as a consequence, the attendance didn't rise above twenty. A man called Flanagan took the chair but within minutes the anti-internationalists interrupted the meeting and according to the *Irish Times* correspondent: 'The defenders of the Communists of Paris were set upon, and a hand-to-hand encounter ensued . . . Chairs and tables were upset, the glass was smashed in the windows, and every stray piece of wood was availed of as a weapon for attack or defence . . . Several members of the detective force were in the room at the time, but exercising a wise discretion, allowed the parties to fight it out.'[116] The IWMA meeting was broken up and its members chased down the stairs and up the street by an incensed mob. This debacle effectively marked the end of the International in Dublin. According to police reports, the members were primarily 'used-up Fenians' and the attendance at meetings was drawn entirely from the labouring and artisan classes.[117]

The Cork section fared somewhat better. Founded on 25 February, its first meeting was held in the home of John de Morgan on Pope's Quay. De Morgan, originally from Belfast, taught elocution and oratory in a number of academies around Cork. He was described as 'a man of great keenness and fluency', and was, unquestionably, the guiding force behind the group.[118] In early March the Cork branch issued a declaration of principles in which it stated:

> That all Societies, and all individuals adhering to it will acknowledge truth, justice, and morality as the basis of their conduct towards each other, and towards all men without regard to colour, creed or nationality; that we as Irishmen believe it our duty to advocate the principle, and aid the cause of the political and social revolution throughout the world, and that the International is one of the best mediums by which that assistance can effectively be given.[119]

This declaration, which was widely published, lucidly illustrated the revolutionist character of the International and caused much concern among the clergy and middle classes of the city. At a Sunday service on 16 March at St Peter and Paul's Church, Canon Augustine Maguire, brother of the sitting MP, J.F. Maguire, denounced the IWMA as antagonistic to religion and the existing social order and called on working men to crush the Cork organization.[120] The Cork Internationalists, however, had already met with some moderate success. De Morgan and four other IWMA members, one of them a foreigner, had made contact with the trades in Cork. On 16 March a general meeting of the coachbuilders was convened to receive a delegation from the International. The coachbuilders, at this time, were engaged in a dispute for a nine-hour day and the IWMA's promise, 'that trades entering the organisation, in the event of a strike, would be supported for a period of two years if necessary', seemed quite appealing.[121] At the end of the meeting many joined and the *Freeman's Journal* noted that the Cork branch had accrued a membership of at least three hundred within weeks of its formation.[122] At this stage, the *Cork Examiner*, which was owned by J.F. Maguire, augmented the clerical onslaught with a series of items attacking the International.

On 22 March notices were posted throughout Cork city addressed to the 'working men of Cork':

> The apologist of the Communists of Paris is amongst you. The apologist of those who murdered the Archbishop and priests of Paris is amongst you!! Beware of those who ask you to connect yourselves with the International Society.[123]

The posters advertised a public meeting to be held in the Atheneum on the following Sunday, 24 March at 3.30 p.m., to denounce the International and to distance the city from its local branch. The organizers included leading members of the Cork Working Men's Society, temperance societies and various trades. The Internationalists immediately responded with their own poster which called on working men to 'attend in your thousands and let your cry on Sunday be "Nine hours and Liberty"'.[124] Over three thousand people turned out for the meeting but, shortly before it commenced, John de Morgan arrived with 'a body of men, perhaps about one hundred in number, composed in part of working men, and in part of roughs, nearly all of whom wore green neckties'.[125] These men positioned themselves behind and on top of the platform. Almost immediately the meeting began to collapse into disorder and within half an hour the Atheneum was engulfed in a full-scale riot as Internationalists battled with the promoters and supporters of the meeting. The *Freeman's Journal* reported:

> They rallied at both sides repeatedly, and the taking and retaking of the platform was conducted by leaders who were armed with bludgeons . . . There is no doubt but the International had organised a party to break up the meeting, and the result proved that they were the stronger party. The building was very much damaged. The stools were smashed, cornices torn down, and even some of the flooring was pulled up to make weapons of.[126]

The riot lasted several hours with the Internationalists emerging the clear victors. Canon Maguire was outraged. In a sermon the following night he declared that 'Cork stood disgraced before the Christian world . . . [having been] triumphed over by a few men, the emissaries of that devil's legion . . . The working men of Catholic Cork . . . have brought disgrace upon themselves by tolerating for a single day the presence of such a body amongst them'.[127] Again, he called for the organization to be crushed. John de Morgan became the victim of the greatest animosity as a 'red scare' swept the city. He had publicly identified himself as the leader of the Cork International. He lost his teaching post and many of his private pupils withdrew from his tuition. McDonnell, in London, issued an appeal for funds to keep him active in Cork but eventually de Morgan was forced to leave the city and move to England. The Cork branch could not withstand the clerical and press hostility and it soon dispersed. Even the coachbuilders issued a denial that they had ever been involved with the Internationalists.[128]

The IWMA was, itself, also encountering problems and in September 1872 it was agreed to transfer the general council from London to New York. This move precipitated the decline of the International which officially ended as an organization in 1876. Joseph McDonnell had emigrated to the United States in late 1872 where he subsequently became involved in American labour politics. De Morgan involved himself in English republican politics. The Internationalists who remained in Ireland faded from view, although some were later to participate in the 'socialist revival' of the 1880s.

NOTES AND REFERENCES

1 Friedrich Engels, *Socialism: Utopian and Scientific* (New York, 1985), p. 36.
2 Robert Owen, 'Report to the county of Lanark' (1820), in G.D.H. Cole (ed.), *A New View of Society and other Writings of Robert Owen* (London, 1927), p. 258; R.G. Garnett, *Co-operation and the Owenite Socialist Communities in Britain, 1825–45* (Manchester, 1972), p. 6.
3 'Address to the electors of the Burghs of Lanark, Selkirk, Peebles and Linlithgow' (24 Apr. 1819), in Robert Owen, *The Life of Robert Owen with Selections from his Writings and Correspondence*, vol. 1A (London, 1857), p. 332.
4 *Freeman's Journal*, 20 Mar. 1823.
5 Vincent Geoghegan, 'Ralahine: an Irish Owenite community (1831–1833)', *International Review of Social History*, vol. xxxvi, no. 3, 1991, pp. 378–9; R.G. Garnett, op. cit., pp. 102–3; J.F. Hogan, 'Early modern socialists, II', *Irish Ecclesiastical Record*, vol. xxvi, 1909, p. 24.
6 William Lucas Sargant, *Robert Owen and his Social Philosophy* (London, 1860), p. 177.
7 J.F.C. Harrison, *Robert Owen and the Owenites in Britain and America* (London, 1969), p. 30.
8 *Freeman's Journal*, 2 Mar. 1823.
9 *Freeman's Journal*, 4 Nov. 1822.
10 ibid.
11 Lord Cloncurry to Robert Owen, 2 Jan. 1823, published in W.J. Fitzpatrick, *The Life, Times and Contemporaries of Lord Cloncurry* (Dublin, 1855), pp. 341–2.
12 *Freeman's Journal*, 22 Jan. 1823.
13 ibid.
14 ibid.
15 *Freeman's Journal*, 2 Mar. 1823.

16   ibid.

17   ibid.

18   *Freeman's Journal*, 19 Mar. 1823.

19   ibid.

20   Quoted in Vincent Geoghegan, op. cit., p. 380.

21   ibid., p. 380; R.G. Garnett, op. cit., p. 102.

22   Quoted in Vincent Geoghegan, op. cit., p. 381.

23   David Lee, *Ralahine: Land War and the Co-operative* (Dublin, 1981), p. 30.

24   Quoted in Vincent Geoghegan, op. cit., p. 383.

25   R.G. Garnett, op. cit., p. 104.

26   E.T. Craig, *An Irish Commune: The Experiment at Ralahine, County Clare, 1831–33* (Dublin, 1983), p. 4. This is an abridged edition of his *The Irish Land and Labour Question Illustrated in the History of Ralahine and Co-operative Farming* (London, 1882).

27   *Clare Journal*, 28 Apr. 1831, cited in David Lee, op. cit., p. 18.

28   ibid., p. 29.

29   E.T. Craig, op. cit., pp. 11–12.

30   Patrick Bolger, *The Irish Co-operative Movement: Its History and Development* (Dublin, 1977), p. 14.

31   Quoted in R.G. Garnett, op. cit., p. 106.

32   E.T. Craig, op. cit., p. 8.

33   ibid., pp. 10–11.

34   ibid., p. 20.

35   ibid., pp. 21–2.

36   Quoted in Vincent Geoghegan, op. cit., p. 388.

37   ibid., p. 389.

38   R.G. Garnett, op. cit., p. 116.

39   Quoted in David Lee, op. cit., pp. 37–8.

40   R.G. Garnett, op. cit., p. 123.

41   ibid., p. 120.

42   ibid., p. 117.

43   ibid., pp. 118–19.

44   John Stuart Mill, *Autobiography* (New York, 1924), p. 87.

45   E.T. Craig, op. cit., p. 125.

46   R.G. Garnett, op. cit., pp. 47–8; Sidney and Beatrice Webb, *The History of Trade Unionism* (London, 1920), pp. 162–3; Richard Pankhurst, *William Thompson, 1775–1833* (London, 1954), pp. 23–4; Patrick Lynch, 'William Thompson and the socialist tradition', in John W. Boyle (ed.), *Leaders and Workers* (Cork, 1966), p. 14.

47   Richard Pankhurst, op. cit., pp. 4–5.

48   Bentham to William Plumer, 17 Oct. 1819, in Stephen Conway (ed.), *The Collected Works of Jeremy Bentham, Volume 9* (Oxford, 1989), p. 360.

49   William Thompson, *Labor Rewarded: The Claims of Labor and Capital Conciliated or How to Secure to Labor the Whole Product of its Exertion* (London, 1827), p. 98.

50   ibid., p. 99.

51   ibid., p. 117.

52 William Thompson, *An Inquiry into the Principles of the Distribution of Wealth* (London, 1824), p. ix.
53 ibid., pp. xvi–xvii.
54 J.F.C. Harrison, op. cit., p. 71.
55 Quoted in R.G. Garnett, op. cit., p. 26.
56 ibid., p. 50.
57 William Thompson, *Labor Rewarded*, p. 73.
58 ibid., p. 100.
59 William Thompson, *An Inquiry*, pp. xiii–xiv.
60 William Thompson, *Labor Rewarded*, p. 101.
61 R.G. Garnett, op. cit., p. 59.
62 Richard Pankhurst, op. cit., pp. 158–9.
63 Quoted in R.G. Garnett, op. cit., p. 60.
64 Quoted in Richard Pankhurst, op. cit., pp. 63–4.
65 ibid., p. 64.
66 William Thompson, *Appeal of one Half the Human Race, Women, Against the Pretensions of the Other Half, Men, to Retain Them in Political, and Thence in Civil and Domestic Slavery* (London, 1825), p. 9.
67 On Anna Wheeler, see Dolores Dooley, *Equality in Community: Sexual Equality in the Writings of William Thompson and Anna Doyle-Wheeler* (Cork, 1996), *passim*, but esp. pp. 56–103.
68 William Thompson, *Appeal*, p. 172.
69 *Cork Constitution*, 26 Aug. 1828.
70 ibid.
71 Fergus O'Ferrall, *Catholic Emancipation: Daniel O'Connell and the Birth of Irish Democracy, 1820–30* (Dublin, 1985), pp. 223–5.
72 ibid., p. 225.
73 Quoted in Friedrich Engels, 'Lawyers' Socialism', in Karl Marx and Friedrich Engels, *Collected Works*, Volume 26 (London, 1990), p. 608.
74 ibid., p. 608.
75 ibid., *passim*.
76 For a discussion of the engagement between Irish labour and nationalism through the nineteenth century, see Emmet O'Connor, *A Labour History of Ireland, 1824–1960* (Dublin, 1992), pp. 20–2, 200–1, and *passim*. Also, see Rachel O'Higgins, 'Irish trade unions and politics, 1830–50', *Historical Journal*, vol. iv, 1961; Fergus D'Arcy, 'The artisans of Dublin and Daniel O'Connell, 1830–47', *Irish Historical Studies*, no. 66, 1970; Fergus D'Arcy, 'The National Trades Political Union and Daniel O'Connell, 1830–1848', *Éire-Ireland*, vol. xvii, no. 3, 1982.
77 On Chartism and Ireland, see Rachel O'Higgins, 'The Irish influence in the Chartist movement', *Past and Present*, no. 20, Nov. 1961; Rachel O'Higgins, 'Ireland and Chartism: a study of the influence of Irishmen and the Irish question on the Chartist movement', PhD thesis, Trinity College, Dublin, 1959; and Dorothy Thompson, 'Ireland and the Irish in English Radicalism before 1850', in James Epstein and Dorothy Thompson (eds.), *The Chartist Experience: Studies in Working Class Radicalism and Culture, 1830–60* (London, 1982).
78 E.J. Hobsbawm, *The Age of Revolution: Europe 1789–1848* (London, 1977), p. 261.

79 Emmet O'Connor, op. cit., p. 24.
80 Vincent Geoghegan, 'The emergence and submergence of Irish socialism, 1821–51', in D.G. Boyce, Robert Eccleshall and Vincent Geoghegan (eds.), *Political Thought in Ireland since the Seventeenth Century* (London, 1993), p. 100.
81 G.D.H. Cole has written that 'The 1850s were almost a dead period for Socialist thought. The defeat of the European Revolutions of 1848 and the repressive police regimes which thereafter re-established themselves over most of Europe left, for some time, little scope either for open agitation or even for free discussion of Socialist ideas'. See his *Socialist Thought: Marxism and Anarchism, 1850–90* (London, 1957), p. 1.
82 Quoted in John Newsinger, 'A great blow must be struck in Ireland: Karl Marx and the Fenians', *Race and Class*, vol. xxiv, no. 2, Autumn 1982, p. 153.
83 Quoted in ibid., p. 153.
84 Friedrich Engels, 'Feargus O'Connor and the Irish people' (9 Jan. 1848), in Karl Marx and Friedrich Engels, *Ireland and the Irish Question: A Collection of Writings* (New York, 1972), p. 50. Hereafter cited as *MEI*.
85 Marx to Engels, 10 Dec. 1869, *MEI*, p. 284.
86 Marx to Engels, 2 Nov. 1867, *MEI*, p. 143. For examinations of Marx's changing view on Ireland see John Newsinger, op. cit.; Fergus D'Arcy, 'Marx, Engels and the Irish question' in Kevin B. Nowlan (ed.), *Karl Marx: The Materialist Messiah* (Cork, 1984); Ian Cummins, *Marx, Engels and National Movements* (London, 1980), pp. 104–18; Ellen Hazelkorn, 'Marx, Engels and Ireland', *Teoric*, no. 10, Autumn 1980; and Ellen Hazelkorn, 'Karl Marx and Friedrich Engels: the Irish dimension', DPhil thesis, University of Kent, 1980.
87 Marx to Engels, 30 Nov. 1867, *MEI*, p. 147.
88 Marx to Engels, 14 Dec. 1867, *MEI*, p. 149.
89 ibid.
90 Quoted in Ian Cummins, op. cit., p. 104. For a discussion of Marx's posited parallel between Poland and Ireland see Nigel Harris, *National Liberation* (Harmondsworth, 1990), pp. 40–8.
91 Engels to Marx, 27 Sept. 1869, *MEI*, p. 273.
92 Marx to Paul and Laura Lafargue, 5 Mar. 1870, *MEI*, p. 290.
93 Marx to Meyer and Vogt, 9 Apr. 1870, *MEI*, p. 294.
94 John W. Boyle, *The Irish Labor Movement in the Nineteenth Century* (Washington, 1988), p. 75.
95 Minutes of General Council meeting, 15 May 1866, *Documents of the First International* (Moscow, 1964), vol. 1, p. 191. Hereafter cited as *DFI*.
96 Minutes of General Council meeting, 2 Jan. 1866, *DFI*, vol. 1, pp. 151–2.
97 Minutes of General Council meeting, 20 Feb. 1866, *DFI*, vol. 1, pp. 166–7; also, Minutes of General Council meeting, 6 Mar. 1866, *DFI*, vol. 1, pp. 168–9.
98 Minutes of General Council meeting, 16 Jan. 1866, *DFI*, vol. 1, p. 159.
99 Minutes of General Council meeting, 19 Nov. 1867, *DFI*, vol. 2, pp. 175–6.
100 Seán Daly, *Ireland and the First International* (Cork, 1984), pp. 17–19.
101 ibid., pp. 48–50.
102 ibid., pp. 62–3.
103 Ellen Hazelkorn, 'Marx, Engels and Ireland', p. 15.
104 Seán Daly, op. cit., p. 63.

105 John W. Boyle, op. cit., p. 81.
106 ibid., pp. 82–3.
107 *Irish Times*, 11 Mar. 1872.
108 Seán Daly, op. cit., pp. 130–1; Minutes of General Council meeting, 4 May 1872, *DFI*, vol. 5, p. 176; *Freeman's Journal*, 1 Apr. 1872, commented on efforts to form a Limerick section: 'There is not much possibility of the society making anything like a head here, as the influence of the clergy, would in itself, be almost sufficient to prevent the doctrines from taking any hold on the bulk of the citizens.'
109 *Freeman's Journal*, 26 Mar. 1872. On the Belfast branch, also see John W. Boyle, op. cit., pp. 88–9.
110 Seán Daly, op. cit., p. 133.
111 ibid., pp. 133–4.
112 *Freeman's Journal*, 30 Mar. 1872.
113 *Irish Times*, 30 Mar. 1872.
114 ibid.
115 *Freeman's Journal*, 29 Mar. 1872.
116 *Irish Times*, 8 Apr. 1872.
117 Seán Daly, op. cit., p. 137.
118 *Freeman's Journal*, 20 Mar. 1872.
119 *Irish Times*, 15 Mar. 1872.
120 *Freeman's Journal*, 18 Mar. 1872.
121 ibid.
122 *Freeman's Journal*, 19 Mar. 1872.
123 *Cork Examiner*, 25 Mar. 1872.
124 ibid.
125 ibid.
126 *Freeman's Journal*, 25 Mar. 1872.
127 *Freeman's Journal*, 26 Mar. 1872.
128 John W. Boyle, op. cit., p. 86.

2.

British Socialism and
Irish Politics, 1881-85

The political intercourse between Ireland and British socialism during the 1880s is an area that has stimulated little discussion among historians. From 1867 until 1923 the Irish question played an important, and energizing, role in British politics but, as D.A. Hamer has indicated, the period between 1880 and 1893 saw Ireland assume the status of the predominant issue.[1] Those thirteen years were crucial years in the history of British socialism. The 'socialist revival' of the 1880s marked an escape from the obscurity and extraneousness which the socialist movement had endured since the demise of Owenism.[2] The Social Democratic Federation and its splinter, the Socialist League, were organized by the middle of the decade and, despite an unimpressive membership, they acquired considerable influence. In 1893 the emergence of the Independent Labour Party signalled the profound alteration that was about to occur in British parliamentary politics.

In an important article on the Irish in Britain, Steve Fielding has suggested that the campaign for home rule 'forced the Irish into wider political sympathies which embraced radical Liberalism and Labour'.[3] This inclination to reach out to potential allies on the left in British politics is a phenomenon that can be traced back to the United Irishmen at the end of the eighteenth century.[4] Irish separatists, home rulers and Land Leaguers operated in a largely hostile political environment and were routinely located outside the mainstream of constitutional politics because of the perceived revolutionary implications of their demands. The post-1867 Fenian movement, in particular, found its British allies primarily in the working-class Radical clubs and among the socialists of the International Working Men's

32

Association. The image promoted by the Fenians, and later by many activists in the Land League, was one of the 'Irish people' against a miscreant state. This dichotomy appealed to many working-class Radicals and socialists. In a similar vein the Irish 'land war' of 1879–82 proved a decidedly invigorating period for those interested in excoriating government misbehaviour. John Bruce Glasier, the leading Scottish socialist, remembered his membership of the Irish Land League with enthusiasm when in 1900 he recalled a visit he had made to Ireland almost twenty years before:

> It was an enchanting experience . . . There is nothing save love comparable to the joy of revolutionary ardour, and happily they are not infrequently mutually convertible emotions. We went through the country fairly revelling in sedition! We drank the health of the Irish Republic on the topmost battlement of the tower of Sligo Cathedral. We renounced the British government on the highways, and shrieked treason from jaunting cars across the fields to the startled peasantry. We jeered the constabulary at their barrack doors, and on one occasion were chased by a carload of them half-way from Drumihair into the town of Carrick-on-Shannon. We attended secret conventions of moonlighters among the hills, and we visited suspects in Kilmainham Gaol . . . Altogether my sensations during that excursion were of almost ideally perfect revolutionary delight.[5]

COERCION AND OPPOSITION

In April 1880 the Irish vote in Britain was mobilized in a concerted manner to assist the eviction of Benjamin Disraeli's Conservative government because of its pronounced aversion to the home rule movement. In the immediate prologue to the election Disraeli accentuated his animus by declaring that the movement represented a danger 'scarcely less disastrous than pestilence and famine'.[6] The Irish parliamentary party's response, not unnaturally, was to urge support for the more sympathetic Liberal Party. Justin Huntly McCarthy, son of the leading Irish MP, reported that the 'appeal was eagerly responded to: in almost every case the Irish vote was all but unanimously given to a Liberal candidate, and in not a few constituencies the Irish vote was big enough to turn the balance one way or the other'.[7]

The new administration under William Gladstone did indeed display less obduracy on the issue of home rule and it tentatively began to feel its way toward the introduction of reforming legislation to deal with the land question. On the other hand, the Liberals, in common with the Conservatives, were intrinsically offended by the agrarian agitation which had begun in 1879. The propertied classes in Britain and Ireland were alarmed by the Land League's extraparliamentary campaign and the increased level of agrarian 'outrages' in late 1880 did little to calm their fears.

The Chief Secretary for Ireland, W.E. Forster, began in the autumn of 1880 to pressurize the Cabinet to bring in coercive legislation to deal with the Land League and its supporters. The effective use of communal ostracism and threats of retributory violence had acutely undermined the land system in Ireland. Landlords, bailiffs and landgrabbers were systematically resisted. Attempts to prosecute key Land League organizers foundered when it became clear that no Irish jury was inclined to deliver a conviction.[8] Ireland's magistrates called on the government to bring in coercion but Forster's efforts to introduce a coercion bill were initially checked by ministerial opposition led by the Birmingham capitalist Radical, Joseph Chamberlain.[9] By January 1881, however, the coercionists had won the argument within the Cabinet and mainstream Radicalism acquiesced. On 24 January Forster introduced his first coercion measure to parliament by arguing that existing law was incapable of dealing effectually with the situation as it stood. The Protection of Person and Property (Ireland) Act 1881, otherwise known as the Coercion Act, gave the Lord Lieutenant of Ireland power 'by warrant to arrest any person reasonably suspected of treason, treasonable felony, or treasonable practices, and the commission, whether before or after the Act, of crimes of intimidation or incitement thereto'.[10] Less grandly put, it allowed internment without trial of suspected Land League activists and it meant the suspension of habeas corpus. The bill passed through all its stages and received the royal assent by commission on 2 March.

It had encountered a stormy reception in the House of Commons from members of the Irish parliamentary party, and quite a few Radicals, such as John Morley, were deeply displeased. While accepting that the disturbed situation in Ireland was 'obviously intolerable', Morley, who was later to become Chief Secretary for Ireland, insisted that 'there was more than one way of setting about the restoration of order'.[11] He continued:

> You may by suspending *Habeas Corpus*, and garrisoning his country with thirty thousand troops, frighten him into mechanical quiet for a year or two, but this is not teaching him respect for law, nor instilling habits or order in him, in the sense of breeding in his mind a spontaneous loyalty to what is ordained, or of attracting any real moral strength to our government. The thing has been tried often enough for us to know what comes of it. The moment the prison door is unlocked, and the gag is removed, we find that our precious device for making Irishmen respect laws has only embittered their hatred for us and our law a thousandfold . . . As for the propriety of teaching the Irish that they will never gain anything by violence, such a lesson may be as proper as we please, but it is unfortunately not true. The Irish know much better. They know that they have never gained anything without violence.[12]

Friedrich Engels, in a letter to the German socialist Eduard Bernstein, took a more sanguine view of the new legislation. 'The Irish', he wrote, 'have forced Gladstone to introduce continental regulations in Parliament and thereby to undermine the whole British parliamentary system. They have also forced Gladstone to disavow all his phrases and to become more Tory than even the worst Tories.'[13] Engels predicted the emergence of a new conservative party centred on the landowning Whigs and moderate Tories which, in turn, would be faced by a new bourgeois Radical party. But 'so as to avoid any humbug and trickery . . . a proletarian Radical party is now forming under the leadership of Joseph Cowen (MP for Newcastle) who is an old Chartist, half, if not entirely, Communist and a very worthy chap. Ireland is bringing all this about, Ireland is the driving force of the Empire'.[14] The new advanced Radical party to which Engels referred was the Democratic Federation, later to become Britain's first modern socialist party.

THE DEMOCRATIC FEDERATION AND IRISH POLITICS

Conor Cruise O'Brien is mistaken when he suggests that the Anti-Coercion Association developed directly into the Democratic Federation; nonetheless, the Irish agitation undoubtedly played a significant role in the formation of the federation and, more importantly, provided a focus for its early activities.[15] Ernest Belfort Bax, a leading member, later remarked that the new organization was 'largely occupied' with Ireland in its formative years.[16] H.M. Hyndman, president of the Democratic Federation, explained the interaction in an interview with Henry George:

> A good many advanced politicians in London and the provinces have long desired a central nucleas of agitation which would be available at all times in the interest of the working classes against measures which might be brought on to their injury, or in order to forward reforms against which there was a conspiracy on both sides of the House. What gave an impetus to the formation of the Federation, and is at present the principal cause of its existence, was the action of the government in relation to Ireland. The Liberal Government came into office pledged to the greatest consideration in regard to Ireland; in point of fact it was pledged to undo the wrongs of centuries and to make Ireland as contented as Scotland. But instead of carrying out its pledges, this Liberal Government has launched into a career of brutal tyranny such as not even a Tory Government could have successfully attempted. And when the Liberal Party thus took upon itself the carrying out of Tory policy, there was no English organisation in or out of Parliament which could offer or organise resistance in England.[17]

Hyndman discerned the Irish question to be the underlying motor in the early development of the Democratic Federation. Moreover, he argued that the support for coercion from middle-class Radicals, as well as the Whigs, within the Liberal Party had divided Radical opinion and had unfortunately forestalled the support of many working men's organizations for the Irish agitation.[18] It forced the latent division, agreed *The Radical*, that imaginatively titled organ of advanced Radicalism, between the 'real Radicals' and the 'sham Radicals'; in other words, between those disillusioned with the investment in Liberalism and those who supported the prolongation of the Liberal parliamentary alliance and the policy of political and social moderation.[19] Ambrose Barker, in 1880 a member of Charles Bradlaugh's National Secular Society and later a socialist, recalled the disappointment in his memoirs. There was, he wrote, 'great satisfaction generally that a great majority had overthrown the Tory Government in 1880. But that satisfaction was soon to be shattered. Reaction had ruled so long that great things were expected of the Radical–Liberal Government. But the people were soon to be disillusioned. They were looking to the Government to bring forward social reforms, instead of which a most stringent coercion bill was introduced'.[20]

The founding conference of the Democratic Federation was held in London on 8 June 1881. Prior to the conference three meetings were held to discuss the possibilities and programme of a new advanced Radical organization. Joseph Cowen, whom Engels expected to lead the new grouping, presided at the second of these preliminary meetings and joined a subcommittee established to draft a programme. Also on this committee were Professor E.S. Beesly, the positivist, H.A.M. Butler-Johnstone, a former Conservative MP from Canterbury, and H.M. Hyndman, who had been a radical Conservative.[21] Hyndman soon emerged as the central figure. In a letter to Karl Marx he explicitly envisaged the meetings as a coming together of 'the members who have opposed the Coercion Bill and some representative working men'.[22] In Ireland, J.J. Louden (just returned from a speaking tour in Britain) briefed the Central branch of the Land League on these developments on 22 March. Like Engels, he expected Joseph Cowen to lead the new grouping and facilitate the creation of an advanced parliamentary party. Louden called on the Land League to support the emerging movement and, in fact, members of the league watched the Democratic Federation with some interest. Cowen failed, however, to attend the inaugural conference and his connection with the Democratic Federation remained marginal. Two radical Parnellite MPs, Justin McCarthy and Lysaght Finigan, did attend but they were present for sectional reasons and not from any desire to affiliate to the federation.[23] Rev. Harold Rylett, a Protestant and leading Land Leaguer, was also present. Rylett had a history of involvement with British Radicalism. In the early 1870s he had been an associate of Joseph Arch and involved with the National Agricultural Labourers' Union.[24]

Hyndman presided at the conference which he began by censuring the lack of unity among British democrats and Radicals. This, he claimed, had allowed the Liberal government to combine 'practically with the Conservatives in carrying measures intensely conservative and despotic. This was a state of things which all Democratic organisations ought to help to put a stop to, even at risk of splitting the Liberal or all other parties'.[25] The conference passed a motion in favour of adult suffrage and other issues discussed included the necessity for triennial parliaments, equal electoral districts, payment of members and election expenses, the abolition of the House of Lords, and nationalization of the land.[26] With the exception of the call for land nationalization all the adopted objectives were political rather than social.[27] Ireland was discussed at length and Hyndman declared that

> the Irish people were now engaged in fighting the battle of the English as well as their own with reference to the land. It was time for the English people to refuse to have their money and the blood of their soldiers spent in carrying out a system of evictions which the Government only a short time ago, had declared iniquitous and villainous, although they were now enforcing it.[28]

Justin McCarthy 'who was received with loud cheers' argued that what Ireland needed was a domestic parliament and he warned that the country was 'within measurable distance of civil war'.[29] A resolution in favour of legislative independence for Ireland was moved and unanimously carried whereupon it entered the programme of the federation.[30]

Before the conference concluded Rev. Harold Rylett invited the new organization to send delegates to Ireland to examine the tumult for themselves.[31] The Democratic Federation gladly accepted this invitation and six members were dispatched to Dublin at the beginning of July. W. Sabin Fredericks, who had been involved in the Anti-Coercion Association, telegrammed the Land League on 28 June to arrange matters for the delegation and later that day at a Central branch meeting Thomas Sexton MP requested the officers of every branch throughout the country to facilitate the English visitors. Jessie Craigen, Finlay Finlayson and Alfred Winks landed on 1 July and went immediately to the offices of the Land League where they had an interview with Thomas Sexton who, at this stage, was acting head of the Land League.[32] (Michael Davitt, John Dillon and many others had already been jailed as government repression gathered pace.)

After their discussion with Sexton, Winks and Finlayson travelled to Naas in Kildare to address a public meeting organized 'to protest against the injustice of rack-renting landlords'.[33] Finlayson announced that he came there 'as the representative of a new English party, to see if it were not possible that the people of England and Ireland could not coalesce in a glorious movement to wrest the land from tyranny and oppression'. Winks, articulating Democratic Federation policy, told the meeting that legislative independence 'was their right just as much as it was his right to breathe the air' and he advised those assembled 'to stick to the League. If they did not kill landlordism it would kill them (cheers)'. The following morning two more delegates from the federation, William Saunders and W. Sabin Fredericks, arrived in Dublin and Saunders called on Sexton.[34] Meanwhile, Finlayson left for Mitchelstown in County Cork where he began a tour of the south-west and obtained eye-witness evidence of violent evictions; he later appalled a London audience with a graphic description of the eviction 'of one Hanrahan, at Mitchelstown, against whom marched two hundred constabulary, a cavalry regiment, and portions of two infantry regiments'.[35] On 3 July Saunders, Fredericks and Winks attended and spoke at a mass Land League demonstration at New Ross in County Wexford.[36] From there Fredericks and Winks travelled to Maryborough in Queen's County* to be present at a 'Sheriff's Sale' of tenant interest on farms vacant because of evictions. The proceedings were over by the time the Englishmen arrived but the local Land League quickly organized a meeting where speeches were made by both men.[37]

On 5 July Saunders, Winks and Fredericks attended their first meeting of the Central branch of the Land League. They were joined by Dr G.B. Clarke, also of the Democratic Federation.[38] (Clarke, who had been a member of the International, was later elected in 1885 as a Liberal MP for Caithness.[39]) Thomas Sexton welcomed the English delegation, referred to the Democratic Federation's support for land nationalization and home rule, and opined that it was 'a deputation the most remarkable in social position, intelligence, and political experience which . . . had ever come to this country from England'.[40] In terms of 'social position' the delegation, with the exception of Jessie Craigen, was undoubtedly middle class. Craigen, who was an active trade unionist, was seemingly alone in promoting class politics and, importantly, she pursued her inquiries under the guidance of members of the Ladies' Land League.[41] This effectively kept her outside the hallowed corridors of the male Land League. She never attended a meeting of the Central branch of the league which is scarcely surprising as women rarely did. The male members of the delegation, however, attended the Central branch meetings regularly during their time in Ireland and through these meetings would have come into contact with the most active leaders of the land agitation.[42]

Jessie Craigen headed south to Cork and on 8 July travelled to Kilmallock in Limerick where, in the company of Anna Parnell, she attended the trial of four women who were charged with 'obstructing the streets' during a Land League protest.[43] Clarke, Winks and Fredericks left for the west of Ireland on 6 July, although it appears that Clarke soon returned to Dublin

---

*Maryborough is now known as Portlaoise; Queen's County as Laois.

where he spent most of his Irish visit.[44] Winks and Fredericks addressed a series of public meetings in the west and it is interesting to note that they never strayed outside the contours of advanced Radical politics despite the vigour of some of their speeches. At Boyle, Fredericks observed:

> With their Irish hearts they would discriminate between the man who earned a livelihood by oppressing their Maker's image and those who earned a livelihood by honest toil. The death knell of that animosity which the landlords and the Conservative press laboured so assiduously to create had sounded . . . The blood of Irish patriots had often been shed in the cause of freedom, often for England on a foreign battlefield, and now they should not flinch to make any sacrifice which would help to gain them justice, a feeling which was growing up in England despite the influence of Gladstone and Harcourt (groans). Let them stick to their nationality, and Ireland would soon be once more a free and happy nation (loud and continued cheering).[45]

At a demonstration in Loughrea, Winks and Fredericks struck a republican note which would have been agreeable music to Fenian ears:

> Mr Winks said that the spirit of Emmet, Fitzgerald and Tone conjured the Irish people to strike for their just rights, and he trusted they would persevere until Ireland would have, if not its freedom, at least its own legislation (cheers). Mr Fredericks was handed a glass of water, and said: 'Friends, I am going to drink to the health of the Irish Republic' (tremendous cheering). If there was a Jeremiah Stringer in the crowd, he trusted he would take a note of this, as he would not be surprised if he was a comrade of John Dillon before he went back to England. He would not be afraid to take up a rifle in defence of Ireland's rights (cheers).[46]

Addressing a rally of some three thousand people in Clare, Jessie Craigen was keen to embrace issues other than home rule and land reform. Class divisions provided the central motif for her speech:

> My dear friends, I wish you to understand that I have come to you on behalf of England — on behalf of that England which you have never known; for there are two Englands. There is one England of landowners and griping capitalists, and there is another England of the working classes, and the latter is entirely distinct from the former. It is on behalf of that second England — it is on behalf of the working classes that I am here. I am myself a working woman — I am a representative of the Trades Union Congress from London . . . We were slaves practically in England till the year 1868. In that year household suffrage was granted, but we are still in a minority, and we mean to have the agricultural labourers to help us, for that which we ask for ourselves we desire you to gain, and we mean to help you to

get it. Every woman ought to have a voice through the vote in the spending
of the money. If we work for the money ought we not have a voice in the
spending of it? (Applause.)[47]

Craigen's speech was exceptional for its feminism and its strong class
politics but, by and large, the Democratic Federation delegates perceived
their function as the extension of solidarity to the agrarian and home rule
agitations. This solidarity would, they suggested, prove mutually beneficial
if it led to the destruction of the landed élite. Dr Clarke, who was later
a member of Henry George's reception committee in Britain, said that he
'trusted the democracy of Ireland would co-operate with the democracy of
England, and that together they would settle the land question for ever. That
settlement must be "the land for the people and all monopolies for the state".
The English people were not responsible for English tyranny — a selfish
oligarchy ruled both England and Ireland'.[48] This was the lexicon of
advanced Radicalism and Clarke's interest in the land question was to lead
to his election to Westminster as a crofter's candidate in Scotland four years
later. He never went beyond land reform to socialism but he was a strong
advocate of land nationalization. At a Newry Land League conference,
presided over by Rev. Harold Rylett, Clarke, on 11 July, admitted that he
did not completely approve of the league's programme because he
was in favour 'of the resumption of the land by the State' and its subsequent letting by the state at a fair rent.[49] In short, he opposed peasant
proprietorship.

It is clear that the leaders of the Land League appreciated, and held in
high regard, the Democratic Federation's investigative delegation — in 1881
allies in Britain were few and cherished. Moreover, it was encouraging and
heart-warming to hear Englishmen profess to be embarrassed by their
nationality because of the policy of coercion in Ireland.[50] On 12 July
the league hosted a dinner for the delegation in the European Hotel in
Dublin. Thomas Sexton presided and many leading Land Leaguers were
present. In an after-dinner speech Dr Clarke expounded his view on land
rights:

Landlordism is dead (cheers) — 'twill soon be buried (cheers) . . . Landlordism, he believed, had no more right to the land than the burglar who
choked a person and then took his watch had a right to stolen property.
He believed, however, in private property — nothing as much developed
the virtues of a race as the belief that one can hold what he had created
— but there must be some limit to private property. After the people had
become possessed of the land there must, to prevent a return to the present difficulties, be a limit to the amount of land any man can hold, as
well in tillage as in pasturage (applause). No man ought to hold more than
he can work (hear, hear).[51]

Shortly after this speech Clarke returned to Britain. Winks, Fredericks and Finlayson, on the other hand, were the main speakers the following day at a mass meeting in the Dublin Rotunda organized on their behalf. Once again, Sexton presided and in his opening remarks warmly applauded the Democratic Federation as a party of English democrats 'who had raised the banner of the rights of peoples against the privileges of class, and who on the question of the land asserted . . . that the land of a country should not be used for the profit or the privilege of any class of men, but should be so disposed of as to be turned to the best account for the general advantage of the people'.[52] Sexton also commended their 'manly superiority to the evil traditions of the relations between England and this country' in their support for legislative independence for Ireland. The English delegates followed Sexton with reciprocal praise for the Land League and entreaties not 'to yield until their will was accomplished. There must be no making of terms with Landlordism. They must give it no quarter'.

The Rotunda public meeting signalled the high point of the Democratic Federation's visit but Winks and Fredericks remained in Dublin for some time longer. On 14 July they addressed a meeting of the Ladies' Land League where Winks praised its members who 'were engaged in a most womanly and humane task' and he hoped they would carry on 'disregarding alike sneers and calumnies, and intent only on the good that must result from the exercise of benevolence, consideration and kindness in mitigating human misery'.[53] Anna Parnell, in thanking the federation for its support, referred also to Jessie Craigen whom she said 'if not an Irish woman, ought to be one'.[54] Winks and Fredericks attended a meeting of the St James's branch of the Land League on 17 July where they were proposed and accepted as members.[55] Clarke and Finlayson, *in absentia*, were also nominated as members of the Irish Land League.

The league organized a mass demonstration of strength in Dublin's Phoenix Park on 24 July and both Winks and Fredericks were present as prominent speakers. This rally in the Phoenix Park was the culmination of a march through the city centre which attracted tens of thousands of participants and spectators. The presence of 100,000 people, claimed Thomas Sexton, 'proved beyond denial that even under the shadow of Dublin Castle, and even in the citadel of class domination, the cause of the Irish people lives and thrives'.[56] It was an emotional demonstration tempered by the knowledge that Dublin was a proclaimed district and that many Land League leaders remained interned under the Coercion Act. Aside from Winks and Fredericks, the Democratic Federation was represented by H.M. Hyndman who had travelled from London to speak. (Hyndman joined the Land League and served as an active member of the executive of the Land League of Great Britain.[57]) Introduced as the president of the Democratic Federation, Hyndman marvelled that a Liberal Government, placed in power largely by Irish votes, should have carried a Coercion Act contrary not only to the first principles of Irish but of English liberty (hear, hear). He did not come here to denounce his own country, but he knew they had done wrong in Ireland, and he had seen enough to explain to him why it was the Irish distrusted England and often distrusted people who would gladly serve them . . . It was to do something to prevent this race hatred in the future that he had come here, because the people of England and Ireland were one (applause). He did not speak of the landlords — they were linked together in both countries for a common cause; let the people link together in a similar manner (applause). What the Irish people were doing now . . . the English people would have to learn to do; they were fighting a struggle which was a lesson to the world. There had been, no doubt, in the struggle certain things done which all reprobated, but never had a great social revolution been carried through with so little outrage and bad feeling as had this struggle under the Irish National Land League (applause).[58]

Hyndman's argument for internationalism in a popular movement against landlordism reinforced the delegation's earlier propaganda. His sentiment also neatly connected with Charles Stewart Parnell's 13 February proposal to widen the agitation by including the English masses. Interestingly, however, Hyndman did not make a similarly determined reference to legislative independence for Ireland. Indeed, some of his comments arguably implied a preference for a continued union. He did lambast the Liberals and protested at their imprisonment of John Dillon and Michael Davitt:

Under these circumstance, any man who called himself a Liberal or a Radical took shame to himself. But the English people did not know what was being done in Ireland; they were kept in ignorance by a combination of a landlord Parliament and a capitalised Press. The time would come when the English and Irish would join hands across the Irish Sea and acknowledge that the cry of the 'land for the people' applied to England as well as to Ireland; when these mists of prejudice and passion which had been purposely started up between them would have faded away, when no longer should it be merely the disunited kingdom where men distrusted each other, but a common truce and a common welfare should embrace and welcome all (applause).[59]

The rally was a considerable success for the Democratic Federation. Three of its members had spoken and it was clearly held in high esteem by the Land League in Ireland. Later that evening the Commercial branch of the league, of which Sexton was president, entertained Hyndman, Winks and Fredericks at dinner in the European Hotel. Toasts, including one to 'Democracy', were drunk and Amos Varian, president of the Davitt branch, enlivened the evening with songs.[60] Hyndman had reason to feel satisfied by the time he left Ireland: the Democratic Federation was beginning to make a name for itself.

HYNDMAN, IRELAND AND SOCIALISM

Henry Mayers Hyndman dominated the Democratic Federation and later the Social Democratic Federation into which it evolved in 1884.[61] He was a curious recruit to the socialist cause but he is now popularly recognized as the 'father' and 'founder' of the modern socialist movement in Britain. Karl Kautsky echoed common opinion in 1912 when he wrote that to Hyndman 'belongs the credit that he was the first to unfold the red banner of Socialism in England'.[62] Kautsky's hyperbole was based on Hyndman's unquestionably pivotal role in establishing Britain's first nationwide socialist organization. As an activist, however, he provoked mixed reactions from those he worked with. John E. Williams, a decided Hyndmanite, first met him during the course of the anti-coercion agitation and later noted that many socialist activists in London 'were a bit suspicious of him as a middle-class man at first'.[63]

Such suspicions were aroused by more than Hyndman's wealthy lifestyle and fondness for the frock-coat and top hat.[64] His first public political manifestation had been as a radical Tory and his formative intellectual environment had been one of conservatism.[65] Indeed, in March 1880 he went forward as an 'Independent' candidate for Marylebone and was attacked by Gladstone as a Tory.[66] His published programme was for 'wide, steady, progressive Liberalism' in Britain and imperialism abroad.[67] This was Tory Democracy. On Ireland, he was a resolute unionist and he asserted that he was 'altogether opposed to Home Rule'.[68] During his candidature Hyndman met the London working-class socialist Joseph Lane who later worked with him in the Social Democratic Federation. Lane was unimpressed: 'Land nationalisation he thought too extreme; was opposed to Home Rule; on the suffrage question he made a remark I have never forgotten or forgiven. He asked me if I meant to say that a loafer in the East End of London was to be placed on an equality with myself. No, the very farthest he would go was that every man who could read and write should have a vote.'[69]

In February 1880 Hyndman had written an article entitled 'Irish needs and Irish remedies' for *The Fortnightly Review*. It began with an expression of concern for 'the welfare of the Empire' which he felt was compromised by the Irish home rule movement.[70] But, although 'the hotter-headed agitators' might attempt a separatist rebellion, he consoled himself with the belief that the 'Protestants of the north and the well-to-do Catholics would soon put down any communistic insurrection'.[71] He took an antipathetic view of the land agitation and wrote: 'The right of a landlord to demand rent, so long as society remains what it is, cannot be disputed, nor of course his right to evict on non-payment'.[72] This was rationally anchored in his conviction that landlords 'are maintained in the peaceful enjoyment of their land because on the whole it has been found to the general advantage of society that they should be so'.[73] Likewise, his opposition to home rule was centred on a self-conscious class interest:

> An Irish Parliament is to sit in Dublin. Well and good. Under what fran-
> chise is its Lower House to be elected? What would be the case when a
> lowering of the qualification put the entire power of election for all local
> business in the hands of a poverty-stricken and uneducated peasantry? . . .
> The classes possessed of property and intelligence would be legally at the
> mercy of a body whose members had been elected by men holding views
> on the subject of the right of individual ownership, and the proper incidence
> of taxation, much at variance with what is at present supposed to be sound
> . . . Is Ireland fit for manhood suffrage?[74]

This pronounced fear of an extended suffrage was a theme common to late-Victorian British conservatism. Hyndman was to travel quite a distance intellectually between early 1880 and mid-1881. In a palpable sense he switched sides but it was not an unproblematic crossing or an immaculate intellectual reconstruction.

Hyndman, at this time, could not have been unaware of the growing strength of socialism in continental Europe, and this may have encouraged his interest in the still-extant intellectual leader of the socialist movement, Karl Marx. In the summer of 1880, having made Marx's acquaintance, Hyndman read a French edition of *Das Kapital*.[75] (It was still unavailable in English translation.[76]) In a letter to Marx, then resident in London, he disclosed his admiration for the work and claimed to 'have learned more from its perusal . . . than from any other book I ever read'.[77] The writings of Marx, in general, were little known in Britain in 1880 outside a few Radical clubs in London and those translated into English had reached a rather unvariegated audience.[78] In that context Hyndman's interest was undoubtedly unusual particularly for an individual from his political background.

Hyndman and Marx met for the first time in early 1880.[79] Hyndman perceived the imminence of profound political and social changes in Britain but, as he wrote to Marx in February 1880, he wished these alterations to occur 'without troublous, dangerous conflict'.[80] He wanted a peaceful social upheaval and he was mostly to maintain this position even after he became a convinced Marxist. His relationship with Marx himself was less than harmonic; Marx found him personally overbearing and suspected him of political opportunism. Engels, who never met Hyndman, took a consistently negative view of the Democratic Federation and its leader. In May

1882 he advised Eduard Bernstein not to be deceived by the emergence of the federation:

> So far it is of no account whatever. It is headed by an ambitious candidate
> for Parliament by the name of Hyndman, an ex-Conservative, who can
> get together a big meeting only with the help of the Irish and for specifically
> Irish purposes. Even then he plays only a third-rate part, otherwise the
> Irish would give it to him.[81]

Engels's Cowen-led party had failed to materialize in the form he had envisaged and as the federation progressed he became increasingly dismissive of its potential to become a real working-class movement. He attributed this inability to an unwillingness among British socialists to effectively merge theory and action:

> The people who more or less have the correct theory as to the dogmatic
> side of it, become a mere sect because they cannot conceive that living
> theory of action, or working with the working classes, at every possible
> stage of its development, otherwise than as a collection of dogma to be
> learned by heart and recited like a conjuror's formula or a Catholic prayer.
> Thus the real movement is going on outside the sect and leaving it more
> and more.[82]

Engels had a reputation for acerbity and harsh judgement but his assessment of Hyndmanite Marxism as sectarian and dogmatic rings true.[83] Friedrich Engels and his London coterie, however, invited disappointment if they truly expected a speedy replication, or near-reproduction, of the German socialist movement in Britain from such slender beginnings.

Hyndman was neither a subtle theoretician nor a charismatic agitator but he did develop a single-minded ambition to steer the Democratic Federation towards the politics of social democracy and Marxism. In order to do this he had first to overcome those who wished the organization to continue as merely a gathering of advanced Radicals and democrats. At the beginning of 1881 he had published an article in *The Nineteenth Century* which indicated a new-found interest in socialism:

> The social danger which underlies and intensifies the political is becom-
> ing more difficult of solution each day. These schemes for the reorganisa-
> tion of society which Fourier, Saint Simon, Owen, Lassalle, Marx and others
> propounded are no longer the mere dreams of impracticable theorists or
> the hopeless experiments of misguided enthusiasts; they have been taken
> down from the closet of the Utopian investigator into the street, and move
> vast masses of men to almost religious exasperation against their fellows
> . . . For the questions now being discussed by hundreds of thousands on
> the Continent go to the very foundations of all social arrangements. It is

> no longer a mere barren argument about the rights of man to political
> representation: it is a determined struggle to change the basis of agreements
> which have hitherto been considered absolutely essential to the prevention
> of anarchy.[84]

His reluctance to fully embrace socialism at this stage was reflected in his
reference to the 'fanatics of the new Socialist gospel'.[85] Hyndman criticized their haste and their alleged propensity to violence. 'The wiser heads',
he wrote, 'admit that the realisation of this their materialist Utopia must
be gradual.'[86] In fact, Hyndman went as far as to suggest that increasing
government involvement in social and economic matters marked a step in
an evolutionary process to a new social order.

> Thus whilst we are arguing about Communism, and in some directions
> upholding the old idea that competition, not State management, must be
> the rule, we ourselves are slowly advancing, without perhaps observing
> it, towards the system which when proposed in all its bluntness we de-
> nounce as a chimera under the present circumstances of mankind. Poor-
> law relief and the School-Board education are communistic in principle.
> The Post-Office, telegraphs and municipal management of gas and water
> involve the principle of State or Commune's control. Does not this, even
> in sober England, show the tendency of the time?[87]

This was mild stuff but the article, with its image of an ineluctable rising
tide, did send out a stark message that socialism was a doctrine to be taken
seriously. On Ireland, Hyndman bemoaned the proposed suspension of
habeas corpus but hardly in a manner favourable to the agrarian agitators:

> In the face of dangerous agitation, we, like others, find that the only sound
> means of maintaining order is by a combination of legal but almost revolu-
> tionary change with more or less pronounced despotism. The dangerous
> communism of the Fenians, who represent the extreme left wing of the
> Irish party, is as completely destructive of present arrangements as the purest
> socialism of Paris or Berlin . . . If only the plain-speaking about Ireland,
> which is now to be heard all round, had been in fashion a few years ago,
> we should not have to make up our minds to something not far short of
> a measure for compensated expropriation of landlords.[88]

Nonetheless, while Hyndman still argued that many Irish tenants had been
coerced into joining 'an agrarian strike aggravated by rattening and intimidation', he had by January 1881 come to accept poverty and injustice as the
root source of the conflict.[89]

His essay, 'The dawn of a revolutionary epoch', revealed a discernible
modification of Hyndman's Tory Democratic predilections. In his memoirs
he described it as 'the public beginning of my attempt to establish a really

independent democratic party of the people, apart from and opposed to the two capitalist factions'.[90] However, Hyndman's initial solicitation 'in favour of the policy which . . . could alone save this country and the empire from disastrous collapse' was to Disraeli.[91] Clearly, conservatism still held an attraction for him. He later claimed that it was Disraeli who convinced him of the impossibility of effecting change through the Conservative Party dominated as it was by the 'great families'. Certainly, the encounter pushed him further in the direction of Marxian social democracy. Early in 1881 he wrote to Marx of the emerging Democratic Federation initiative as the 'movement . . . for which you have so long waited'.[92] Hyndman's gradualist inclinations had been assuaged by Marx's letter of 8 December 1880 in which he had conceded the possibility of a peaceful revolution in Britain. Writing to Hyndman he evinced an uncommon determinism which neatly connected with Hyndman's evolutionism:

> I welcome the prospect of the journal you speak of. If you say that you do not share the views of my party for England I can only reply that that party considers an English revolution not *necessary*, but — according to historic precedents — *possible*. If the unavoidable evolution turns into a revolution, it would not only be the fault of the ruling classes, but also of the working class. Every pacific concession of the former has been wrung from them by 'pressure from without'. Their action kept pace with that pressure and if the latter has more and more weakened, it is only because the English working class know not how to wield their power and use their liberties, both of which they possess legally.[93]

Interestingly, this letter was one which Hyndman failed to destroy during his time of difference with Marx. It is clear that he valued its message. Replying to Marx he had written: 'Revolution is possible . . . But what I mean is I do not wish to push men on to what must be violence when they might easily attain their objects by peaceful action in common.'[94]

Hyndman had moved beyond democratic radicalism by the time he helped found the Democratic Federation in June 1881. While his socialism had yet to take a definitive shape the broad strokes were evident. At the founding conference on 8 June he presented each delegate with a copy of his book *England for All: The Textbook of Democracy*. Hyndman hoped, with this volume, to set the tone of the new organization but, as it transpired, some of its proposals fell short of the temper of the meeting. He fudged on the crucial issue of land nationalization, and legislative independence for Ireland was conspicuously absent from the first edition.[95] Moreover, his book advocated manhood rather than adult suffrage and he alluded positively to the 'high ideals of empire and greatness'.[96] Hyndman, nonetheless, made an effort to summarize Marx's *Das Kapital* in two chapters dealing with labour and capital, and in doing so provided Britain with its first popularization of Marxist economics. Tactlessly he omitted to credit Marx and this led to his personal split with the German socialist.[97] In a letter to F.A. Sorge in December 1881 Marx commented on Hyndman's 'textbook':

> The chapters on Labour and Capital are only literal extracts from, or circumlocutions of, *Das Kapital*, but the fellow does neither quote the book nor its author . . . Vis-à-vis myself, the fellow wrote stupid letters of excuse, for instance, that 'the English don't like to be taught by foreigners', that 'my name was so much detested etc'. With all that, his little book — so far as it pilfers *Das Kapital* — makes good propaganda, although the man is a weak vessel and very far from having even the patience . . . of studying a matter thoroughly . . . Many evenings this fellow has pilfered from me in order to take me out and learn in the easiest way.[98]

England for All was flawed but it introduced an economic critique of the existing social order that was to form the basis of an emerging political and intellectual dissidence.

His chapter on Ireland represented a substantive political shift. Hyndman's revised analysis built on his earlier admission of British stolidity and suggested that the British government was to a great extent culpable of creating, as well as aggravating, the turmoil in Ireland. His sympathies were thoroughly with the Irish. The Irish people, he wrote, had suffered from centuries of British misgovernment and in itself the injustice inflicted had done much to embitter relations between the two countries. But, he argued, enough had occurred within recent decades to explain the current crises. Significantly he blamed Britain and the landlord class, in equal measure, for the Famine. In Irish nationalist minds the Famine was seen as the supreme indictment of British rule and Hyndman's acceptance of the validity of this charge was important:

> The great catastrophe of 1847 ought to have opened our eyes to some portion of the truth — ought to have shown the people of England that here we had an exceptional problem to deal with, and that such dominance as had been established was discreditable to the rulers and ruinous to the ruled.
>
> That fearful famine formed the starting-point of the modern history of Ireland. It had been predicted by men of very different views and capacities. It came, as such cataclysms sometimes do come, in its worst possible shape, and was followed up by revolutionary legislation which all can now see was most unfortunate. Instead of accepting the wise recommendations of the Devon Commission — made, be it remembered, three years before the Famine — or the still wiser advice of Lord Beaconsfield, given about the same time, but later so unfortunately withdrawn — full rights were given to landlords, new and old, to uproot the population, tear down their miserable dwellings and hurry them across the Atlantic, famine fever wearing out their bodies, and fury at such injustice and tyranny rankling in

their minds. Who that has read through the details of that miserable time, when men, women and children were turned out of their holdings — as they are now being turned out, though happily in far fewer numbers — to wander in starvation, and misery along the highways, can wonder that a generation has grown up in Ireland and in the United States which regards with inextinguishable hatred England and all that belongs to her?[99]

And reversing his opposition to the land agitation he extolled it as 'justifiable and righteous' and went further to insist that 'no country could be peaceable under such a rule as we have inflicted upon the people of Ireland'.[100] His abhorrence of popular agitation had receded considerably and he was vocal in his support for the Land League. Indeed, the league had, in his opinion, carried on the agitation 'with surprisingly little bloodshed or bad action'.[101] More importantly, the Irish agitation convinced Hyndman of the political value of extraparliamentary movements:

> This, at least, is certain, that unless the Land League had been formed, and the Irish had stood together in a great economical movement, no such Land Bill as that of 1881 would have been brought before the English House of Commons at all. The Land League, whether it be called communistic, nationalistic, or what not, brought the first genuine attempt yet made at reform within the range of practical politics, and must be maintained to give it effect.[102]

The Irish provided Hyndman with his first example of the power of mass movements and had shown him the strength of collective action. Political power could be forged in the streets.

By June 1881, Hyndman had become an advocate of Irish home rule as well as a supporter of the land agitation. However, he viewed legislative independence as a necessary rather than a preferred option. He argued for an extension of local administration and responsibilities in order to stave off the dismemberment of the British state. He did not favour separatism. 'It is because separation would be injurious to both countries', he wrote, 'as mutual understanding would be beneficial, that Irishmen should at length be granted fair play and self-government.'[103] The Irish demand for home rule, he insisted, must be 'fairly' met 'without actual disruption of the Empire'.[104] Hyndman's imperialist predilections remained with him throughout his socialist career. Over thirty years later he supported Edward Carson and the Ulster Volunteers despite the opposition of the British Socialist Party executive on which he then served.[105] His socialism harboured a British nationalistic inclination.

THE TYRONE MANIFESTO

After the founding conference Hyndman and the Democratic Federation soon discovered that their staunch position on the Irish question discommoded the more sedentary Radicals who had initially sympathized with the federation's objectives. In fact, the Irish agitation was to play an unwitting role in the organization's progression to socialism. It helped, so to speak, to separate the wheat from the chaff. Having sent a delegation to Ireland the Democratic Federation organized public meetings on its return and the report of its members was distributed as a pamphlet. Hyndman, himself, joined the executive of the Land League of Great Britain and fancied (seriously) that 'among Irishmen my truly urbane disposition and peace-loving tendencies were at once appreciated at their real value'.[106] He, and the federation, became deeply involved in the British anti-coercion campaign, organizing conjoint demonstrations with the Land League in London after the arrest and imprisonment of Parnell in October 1881. By October many of the more moderate Radicals had quit the organization because of a direct intervention it had made in Ireland a month before.

In September a Westminster by-election occurred in County Tyrone and there were candidates representing both the Liberal Party and the Land League as well as the Conservative Party. The Land League candidate was Rev. Harold Rylett who a few months earlier had attended the inaugural conference of the Democratic Federation. His candidature was intended, in large measure, as a direct attempt to weaken the Liberal candidate, Thomas Dickson, and punish the Liberal Party for its coercion measures. Dickson, himself, was against coercion and he publicly recognized the inadequacy of the government's recent Land Bill. 'The coercive policy of the Government', he declared on 21 August, 'I opposed from the beginning, and will continue to oppose; and I shall always regret that Liberal statesmen resorted to such measures believing as I do that what Ireland requires is remedial and not coercive legislation.'[107] Nonetheless, the Land League and Parnell were determined to make a stand against the Liberals. The Newry branch of the league described it as an opportunity for 'squelching sham Liberalism in Ulster forever'.[108] Some local nationalists, including a number of priests, disagreed; they saw the policy as divisive and worried that it might lead to the election of Colonel William Stuart Knox, the Conservative candidate. Even the Land League had its dissenters and the Castlefin branch called on people to support Dickson. John Taylor, president of the branch, argued that Dickson 'is the only one of the popular candidates who can keep Tyrone from the disgrace of returning Knox'. He continued: 'With reluctance I disagree with Mr Parnell's policy in this matter . . . The result of Mr Parnell's present policy will be, I fear, to destroy for all useful purposes the Land League organisation in Ulster.'[109] It was clear, however, that the league was firmly disengaging itself and the Irish vote from British Liberalism. For Radicals associated with the Democratic Federation the election presented a dilemma but Hyndman, with his innate dislike of Liberalism, plumped immediately for Rylett. On 2 September the executive committee of the Democratic Federation issued an address to the electors of Tyrone:

Gentlemen — The Executive Committee of the Democratic Federation desire at this critical juncture in Irish politics to appeal through you to the electors of Tyrone to vote for the Rev. Harold Rylett at the approaching poll. We have seen in sadness the Prime Minister of Great Britain and Ireland, an old man of seventy-three, turn his back upon the enthusiasms of his youth, the convictions of his manhood, the teachings of his maturer years. We have watched with contempt the great men of the Liberal party forswearing their most cherished principles and accepting unchecked despotism for Ireland at Mr Gladstone's dictation. The hollowness and hypocrisy of capitalist Radicalism were surely displayed in all their revolting meanness when Mr Forster insisted on his right to arrest his fellow-citizens on suspicion, when Mr John Bright brought wavering members to the House of Commons to vote against their consciences for coercion, when Mr Joseph Chamberlain read at Birmingham his cowardly recantation of his protests to the Cabinet. Such men do not and cannot represent the true democracy of England. We, therefore, as Englishmen, call upon you as Irishmen to vote for our countryman, the Englishman, Harold Rylett, who comes forward in the days of darkness and depression to champion that personal liberty and individual freedom for which your fathers and our fathers fought and fell. We call upon you to return him to Parliament instead of the candidate of a party whose idea of justice is incarceration without trial, and whose conceptions of freedom are bounded by the walls of Kilmainham Jail. Men of Tyrone, two hundred prisoners accused of no crime but patriotism, guilty of no wrong but sympathy with the fatherless and the widows in their affliction, appeal to you to right and release them. Men of Tyrone, we Englishmen appeal to you to forget race hatred, class difference, religious prejudice and political jealousy in one solid protest against injustice and oppression. Vote for Harold Rylett, and show the doubtful and the time-serving that Englishmen and Irishmen can unite and conquer in a great cause.

For the Executive Committee of the Democratic Federation.
(signed) H.M. Hyndman, Chairman.[110]

The Tyrone manifesto, with its reference to 'the hollowness and hypocrisy of capitalist Radicalism', proved too much for many of the Radicals involved with the federation. The Democratic Federation, undoubtedly, had begun to portray itself as an alternative to Radicalism rather than as a ginger group on its periphery. The organization began to haemorrhage and it lost the support of all the London Radical clubs. Hyndman saw this leakage as a critical event in the political development of the federation:

> This pronouncement of the new advanced party was placarded all over Tyrone, and was published in the anti-coercion and anti-Liberal papers. Thereupon the Radical Clubs of London, and most of the Radicals, forsook us and fled. We all of us regretted this, but it was really the best thing that could have happened, and hastened our development towards clear-cut definite Socialism.[111]

In Ireland, the Parnellite *Freeman's Journal* published the federation statement. Again the group had shown itself to be a loyal ally of the Land League. Moreover, Alfred Winks had coincidentally arrived back in Dublin on 23 August and spoke for the Democratic Federation at a meeting of the Central branch of the Land League. He availed of the opportunity to criticize the government's Land Bill which he observed 'was only three pence in the pound of the debt due them'.[112] Likewise, he impugned the Liberals' repressive legislation which he said 'was not a law, but was simply codified robbery and murder, and not worthy of obedience'. Alfred Winks, in particular, was deeply concerned by the Irish question and in April he had been among a delegation of radicals that met Parnell in Manchester to offer support for the Land League movement. Winks's presence in Dublin underlined the earnestness of the British democrats' solidarity with the Land League while the Tyrone manifesto provided evidence of their willingness to eschew the half-hearted.

Winks attended a meeting of the John Dillon branch of the Land League while in Dublin. At this meeting he again enjoyed the company of Amos Varian who was to remain a prominent contributor to radical political debate in Dublin throughout the 1880s.[113] Varian, who had also attended the Central branch meeting with Winks on 23 August, was at the time in conflict with the executive of the league because of his attempts to decentralize the organization. At the Central branch meeting Thomas Sexton had upbraided Varian, as the leading Dublin activist, because of the decision taken the previous night at some meetings of the Dublin city branches to the effect that at their next meetings they should appoint delegates to form a central city executive which would have control of the local organization. The Dublin city branches were similarly discussing a proposal that they should meet at a regional convention *prior* to the imminent national Land League convention. Sexton pointed out that he had already intimated that county or regional conventions should be held *after* the national convention. Likewise, he argued that the constitution of the League 'never contemplated the erection of any other authority, be it intermediate or subsidiary, between the League and its representatives among the Dublin branches or elsewhere'.[114]

Sexton demanded that Varian report to the executive 'the object he had in view and take the opinions of the Executive upon it as to whether that object was consistent with the constitution of the League'. Amos Varian replied by stating that with regard 'to the proposed meeting of the city branches that they did not certainly wish to be hampered in their free judgement by any executive if that executive did not represent their views'. Moreover, he declared that the city branches were 'at liberty to hold any meeting we please'. In an indignant letter to the *Freeman's Journal*, Varian later expressed his exasperation at the attitude of the Land League leadership:

> Oh! Let the leaders think, but paralyse thought in the people, then it will be easy to guide them. Such doctrines may be acceptable in Russia or Prussia. May God help the people who submit to them! No, no. Let free discussion and public meetings be held prior to the convention. Let individual liberty exist and be promoted by the Land League, and we will have hope in the future of the movement, whatever may take place at the convention.[115]

The issue was one of democracy within the Land League, and the Dublin branches were clearly revolting against the authoritarian style in which the organization was run. They were demanding more responsive structures and an element of semi-autonomy. Interestingly, Varian, the presumed leader of the Dublin 'revolt', was also one of those Land League activists most in contact with the representatives of the Democratic Federation and later was a prominent member of the Dublin Democratic Association.

RADICALISM TO SOCIALISM

As the Democratic Federation counterposed itself more and more to Radicalism it gained recruits from the disordered and diffuse socialist community and from the ranks of dissident intellectuals. Hyndman maintained a running battle with mainstream Radicalism and used the lack of engagement with the anti-coercion campaign as his principal truncheon. In March 1882, in an interview for the *Irish World*, he accused the Radical societies of showing no sympathy for the victims of coercion:

> Firstly, to have protested against the action of the Liberal Government would have been to admit they had been completely deceived at the last general election by those who then came forward as the popular leaders. Secondly, the leaders of existing Radical organisations, or so-called Radical organisations, as well [as] trades unions, are to a large extent, absolutely in the hands of the capitalist class, who control their action to a very large extent.[116]

Charles Garcia of the Marylebone Central Democratic Association took issue with Hyndman's contention when the interview was republished in *The Radical*.[117] Garcia, who had helped to form the Anti-Coercion Association, protested that a number of clubs and associations in London had supported the anti-coercion agitation. He cited eight Radical organizations that had involved themselves, and continued:

> What then does Mr Hyndman mean by asserting that no Radical organisa-
> tion opposed Coercion? I attended very nearly every Anti-Coercion meeting
> held in London, but I do not remember hearing Mr Hyndman speak at
> any one of them, nor do I remember seeing his name attaching to any Anti-
> Coercion article in any newspaper, journal or magazine. No, Sir, it was
> not until the Coercion Bills became law that Mr Hyndman came forward.
> I yield to no man in my respect for Mr Hyndman's courage and in-
> dependence — I am willing to give him credit to any amount for the good
> work he has done in the cause of Democracy during the last twelve months;
> but I must protest strongly . . . in justice to the many earnest men who
> worked so hard before Mr Hyndman came forward.[118]

Garcia, however, was missing the point. The leaders of the Democratic Federation were correct when they castigated the Radical movement for its lack of organized action and Garcia's eight clubs were the exception that proved the rule. Moreover, all those cited by him were advanced Radical groups situated on the fringe of the greater movement. During the year since the introduction of coercion it was the Democratic Federation which had assumed a proactive role and which had become publicly identified as the leading anti-coercion organization in Britain. The Irish correspondent to *The Radical* reflected a popular perception on 24 June when he asserted the primacy of the Democratic Federation among the 'existing reform associations of the United Kingdom'.[119] The indefatigable, unbending ex-ertions of the federation in support of the Land League had immeasurably enhanced its political stature and public profile. These exertions had, of course, also driven out the Gladstonian Radicals.

By 1882 the balance within the Democratic Federation was beginning to tilt in favour of those who wanted to openly declare for socialism. Hynd-man had begun to articulate the Marxian economics that would come to underpin the politics of the organisation. In January 1882 he led a series of public discussions at London's Westminster Palace Chambers on 'Prac-tical Remedies for Pressing Needs'. The remedies advocated as 'stepping stones' included 'the feeding of children in the Board Schools; the organisa-tion co-operatively of unemployed labour; the Eight Hour Law; the na-tionalisation of railways and mines; and the construction and maintenance of wholesome homes for the people by public bodies, national and municipal, at public cost'.[120] These discussions brought Hyndman and the federation into contact with many activists and would-be activists previously unknown to them. Moreover, the focus on social issues demonstrated that the federation was more than a support group for the Irish Land League. 'Though overlaid in the early months by the Irish agitation', wrote Hyndman, 'the Socialist propaganda of the Democratic Federation went steadily on and we slowly gathered around us most of the abler young men of the advanced section.'[121] In fact, Hyndman was not averse to using the profile created by the Irish agitation to promote his wider politics. Hence, when replying to Charles Garcia on Radicals and coercion, he diverged into an exposition of historical materialism and a concomitant rejection of the alleged panacean qualities of land nationalization:

> Happily an exhaustive analysis of the historical development of our present industrial society has already been made for us by one of the greatest thinkers of modern times — Dr Karl Marx. He shows clearly that the capitalist class rob the working class by means of the surplus value which they get out of the labour of the 'free' workers, more than the landlord class do by their monopoly of land, and the consequent appropriation of agricultural rents, ground rents and royalties.[122]

He concluded his article with a lengthy translation from Engels's book *Socialism: Utopian and Scientific*.[123]

During 1882 the Democratic Federation collected some notable recruits. James Leith Joynes, who had been arrested with Henry George in Ireland and who had since converted to socialism, joined and played a prominent role. H.H. Champion, a former army officer, was recruited as were R.P.B. Frost and Ernest Belfort Bax. Bax, who had converted to socialism as early as 1879, was to serve as the movement's leading 'philosopher'.[124] Andreas Scheu, the leading Austrian Marxist, also joined. Scheu, along with his brothers Heinrich and Josef, had been a founding member of the Austrian Social Democratic Workers' Party and he was a formative influence on Karl Kautsky as his first real mentor. By 1882, Scheu was in exile in Britain and, while still a Marxist, was considered to lean towards anarchism.[125] In January 1883 William Morris, the poet and designer, became a member of the federation. Morris was an important acquisition and in the years ahead he proved a determined and effective apostle of socialism.

The new recruits included many attracted to politics by Henry George's propaganda tour of Britain. George had encouraged his listeners to question the landed élite and some of his audience found their appetite for social criticism merely whetted. Intellectual stimulation came also from a number of other sources and the increasing success of the socialists in Germany seemed to point to that movement as a viable medium to amplify dissent. However, the Radical exodus had ensured the contraction of working-class support for the Democratic Federation and most of the new recruits came from the middle class. Hyndman recognized this when he wrote to Henry George in March 1883: 'The common English workmen are more or less embittered against the Irish and at times I feel despondent. But Socialist ideas are growing rapidly among the educated class.'[126] The proportionate reduction of working-class members had both positive and negative consequences for the socialists in the federation. A positive consequence was that the socialist intellectuals who had come to dominate the leadership no longer faced a phalanx of working-class Radicals unwilling to change the organization's social objectives. Contrariwise, a negative consequence of the limited working-class base was the effect it had on the version of Marxism expounded by the federation. Dogma and political sectarianism became hallmarks of Hyndmanite Marxism. Trade unions, for example, were largely dismissed as inimical to the struggle for socialism and were viewed as organizations whose limited fight-back had to be superseded rather than developed.[127] Likewise, the federation adopted the Lassalean 'Iron Law of Wages' theory which implied that strike action could only affect the level of wages in the short term. Ultimately, so this theory ran, wages could not be increased relative to the standard of living. It is not surprising that British socialists adopted the 'Iron Law of Wages' theory as the Gotha Programme of the German Social Democratic Party included it despite Marx's objections. In 1891 Marx's *Critique of the Gotha Programme* pinpointed the pitfalls of the theory but by then it had almost become part of the staple diet of Marxian socialism in Britain. The 'Iron Law' was crudely popularized in the 1884 Democratic Federation pamphlet *The Socialist Catechism*. Written by J.L. Joynes it argued that capitalism 'constantly tends to a bare subsistence for the mass of the labourers' and that the capitalist 'agrees to return to them as wages about a quarter of what they have produced by their work, keeping the remaining three quarters for himself and his class'.[128] Also in 1884, Hyndman wrote an article for *Justice*, the organization's newspaper, on the 'Iron Law of Wages' in which he stated that to say 'that wages have risen even relatively during the last fifty years does not alter the fact that wages do tend in this country . . . towards the cost of subsistence'.[129] Such a doctrine inevitably led to an underestimation of the value of industrial action.

'Socialism is said to be everywhere', wrote Emile De Laveleye in April 1883.[130] 'The red spectre haunts the imagination of all, and it is a very general belief that we are on the eve of a great social cataclysm.'[131] Somewhat implausibly, he also asserted that the 'agrarian movement in Ireland . . . clearly owes to it its origin'.[132] Socialism across Europe was, in truth, experiencing something of a resurgence and in Britain the Democratic Federation mustered the self-confidence to issue its first fully socialist manifesto. *Socialism Made Plain*, published in June 1883, marked a major step in the federation's transition from Radicalism to socialism. Addressing workers, the manifesto advocated that they 'demand and obtain the full fruits of your labour and become your own governing class yourselves'.[133] It continued:

> So long as the means of production, either of raw materials or of manufac-
> tured goods are the monopoly of a class, so long must the labourers on
> the farm, in the mine or in the factory sell themselves for a bare subsistence
> wage. As land must in future be a national possession, so must the other
> means of producing and distributing wealth. The creation of wealth is
> already a social business, where each is forced to co-operate with his
> neighbour; it is high time that exchange of the produce should be social
> too, and removed from the control of individual greed and individual
> profit.[134]

William Morris wrote the following year that socialism 'was not dead in England in spite of all appearances to the contrary and the Democratic Federation by its outspoken resistance to coercion in Ireland . . . had earn-ed the right of being considered the one organisation which cherished the rights of the people'.[135] It was a natural progression, he argued, for the organization to openly proclaim for socialism and this had resulted in the publication of *Socialism Made Plain*.

In August 1884, the federation's annual conference formalized the developing adhesion to socialism and the organization was restyled the Social Democratic Federation (SDF). The programme adopted was explicitly socialist and demanded control of the means of production, distribution and exchange for the working class in a democratic state.[136] Moreover, the socialist London-based Labour Emancipation League finally threw its lot in with the federation and Joseph Lane, its most prominent member, joined the SDF executive. The organization also, in January 1884, had begun publication of a weekly newspaper, *Justice*. Engels grudgingly admitted in late 1883 that 'now at last they are obliged openly to proclaim our theory as their own, whereas during the period of the International it seemed to them to be foisted on them from outside, and . . . recently a lot of young people stemming from the bourgeoisie have appeared on the scene who, to the disgrace of the English workers it must be said, understand things bet-ter and take them up more enthusiastically than the workers themselves'.[137] His overall judgement, however, remained negative and he cautioned August Bebel against being 'bamboozled into thinking there is a real proletarian movement going on here'.[138] Whether or not Engels's pessimism was well grounded, a socialist organization had been crafted from the discontents of advanced Radicalism and the ranks of independent intellectuals. It began life with a membership of less than four hundred and was never to have more than a few thousand members.[139] However, as the Fabians discovered, a large membership is not everything and the SDF had an influence and political import that much exceeded its narrow membership base.

NOTES AND REFERENCES

1   D.A. Hamer, 'The Irish question and Liberal politics, 1886–1894', *Historical Journal*, vol. xii, 1969, p. 511.

2   Since the demise of the Owenite movement in the 1840s the only significant manifestation of socialism in Britain had been the isolated section of the International Working Men's Association. The 'socialist revival' of the 1880s created a modern socialist movement in Britain.

3   Steve Fielding, 'Irish politics in Manchester, 1890–1914', *International Review of Social History*, vol. xxxiii, no. 3, 1988, p. 261.

4   Marianne Elliott, 'Irish republicanism in England: the first phase, 1797–99', in Thomas Bartlett and David Hayton (eds.), *Penal Era and Golden Age: Essays in Irish History, 1690–1800* (Belfast, 1979), pp. 204–21; Marianne Elliott, *Partners in Revolution: The United Irishmen and France* (New Haven and London, 1982), pp. 144–50; Nancy J. Curtin, *The United Irishmen: Popular Politics in Ulster and Dublin, 1791–98* (Oxford, 1994), pp. 21, 94, 109, 191.

5   *The Clarion*, 17 Mar. 1900.

6   Lord Beaconsfield to the Duke of Marlborough, 8 Mar. 1880, quoted in Justin H. McCarthy, *England under Gladstone, 1880–1884* (London, 1884), p. 1.

7   ibid., p. 8.

8   Samuel Clark, *Social Origins of the Irish Land War* (Princeton, 1979), p. 248; Paul Bew, *C.S. Parnell* (Dublin, 1980), pp. 49–50.

9   *Cork Examiner*, 3 Jan. 1881; T.W. Moody, *Davitt and Irish Revolution, 1846–1882* (Oxford, 1981), pp. 428–9.

10 Justin H. McCarthy, op. cit., p. 119.

11 John Morley, 'England and Ireland', *The Fortnightly Review*, 1 Apr. 1881, p. 411.

12 ibid., pp. 413–14.

13 Friedrich Engels to Eduard Bernstein, 12 Mar. 1881, in Karl Marx and Friedrich Engels, *Ireland and the Irish Question: A Collection of Writings* (New York, 1972), p. 329. Hereafter cited as *MEI*.

14 ibid., p. 330.

15 C.C. O'Brien, *Parnell and his Party, 1880–1890* (Oxford, 1968), p. 62.

16 E.B. Bax, *Reminiscences and Reflexions of a Mid and Late Victorian* (London, 1918), p. 74.

17 *Irish World*, 18 Mar. 1882.

18 ibid. Only a sprinkling of leading Radicals openly opposed coercion. Henry Broadhurst, the trade unionist and Radical MP, confessed: 'As a working man he was always opposed to Coercion, but he was convinced that the present Government would not have advocated it had it not been a necessity. Therefore, he felt called upon to support them . . . As the results have shown, it was calculated to do an immense amount of good to the Irish people.' *Daily Press*, 8 Dec. 1881; *The Radical*, 10 Dec. 1881.

19 *The Radical*, 1 Apr. 1882. Commenting on *The Radical*, Hyndman wrote: 'It was to advocate real Radicalism in its better sense that at this period a little journal called *The Radical* was started by three able Scotsmen . . . and supported by others who afterwards did good service in different directions. It is not too much to say that though not Socialists, and indeed opposed to Socialism,

Messrs. Samuel Bennett, William Webster and Morrison Davidson, with them W.M. Thompson, did their full share by their work on *The Radical* to rouse a sense of independence among the workers, when the great majority of the Liberal Party were grovelling before Mr Gladstone and his pet Whig Coercionists.' H.M. Hyndman, *The Record of an Adventurous Life* (London, 1911), p. 223.

20 Quoted in John Quail, *The Slow Burning Fuse: The Lost History of the British Anarchists* (London, 1978), p. 18.

21 H.A.M. Butler-Johnstone to Karl Marx, 7 Mar. 1881, Marx Papers, IISH; *The Radical*, 12 Mar. 1881.

22 H.M. Hyndman to Karl Marx, 28 Feb. 1881, Marx Papers, IISH.

23 M.S. Wilkins, 'The non-socialist origins of England's first important socialist organization', *International Review of Social History*, vol. iv, 1959, p. 203.

24 ibid., p. 203.

25 *Daily News*, 9 June 1881.

26 ibid; *Times*, 9 June 1881; *Pall Mall Gazette*, 9 June 1881.

27 The object and programme of the Democratic Federation were published in full in *The Radical*, 16 July 1881:

Object:

To unite the various organisations of Democrats and workers throughout Great Britain and Ireland for the purpose of securing equal rights for all, and forming a centre of organisation in times of political excitement. To agitate for the ultimate adoption of the programme of the Federation. To aid all social and political movements in the direction of these reforms.

Programme:

1. Adult Suffrage.
2. Triennial Parliaments.
3. Equal Electoral Districts.
4. Payment of Members' and Officials' Expenses out of the Rates.
5. Bribery, Treating and Corrupt Practices to be made acts of Felony.
6. Abolition of the House of Lords as a Legislative Body.
7. Legislative Independence for Ireland.
8. National and Federal Parliaments.
9. Nationalisation of the Land.

28 *Daily News*, 9 June 1881. Samuel Bennett, proprietor of *The Radical*, echoed Hyndman's gratitude to the Irish people 'for beginning a revolution which, I trust, will never end until Landlordism . . . has been abolished, not only in Ireland, but also in England and Scotland' (*The Radical*, 29 Oct. 1881). Many saw Ireland as the cutting edge in the campaign for land nationalization and the consequent voiding of the landed élite.

29 *Daily News*, 9 June 1881.

30 ibid; *The Radical*, 16 July 1881.

31 Chushichi Tsuzuki, *H.M. Hyndman and British Socialism* (Oxford, 1961), p. 44.

32 *Freeman's Journal*, 2 July 1881.

33 ibid.

34 *Freeman's Journal*, 4 July 1881.

35 ibid; *The Radical*, 23 July 1881.

36 *Freeman's Journal*, 4 July 1881.

37 ibid.

38 *Freeman's Journal*, 6 July 1881.

39 E.P. Thompson, *William Morris: Romantic to Revolutionary* (New York, 1976), p. 352.

40 *Freeman's Journal*, 6 July 1881.

41 *Freeman's Journal*, 4, 20 July 1881.

42 *Freeman's Journal*, 6, 13, 20, 27 July 1881.

43 *Freeman's Journal*, 9 July 1881.

44 *Freeman's Journal*, 6 July 1881; *The Radical*, 16 July 1881.

45 *Freeman's Journal*, 11 July 1881.

46 *The Radical*, 16 July 1881. Constable Jeremiah Stringer was notorious at the time as a government 'note-taker' at Land League demonstrations. He had given evidence in court against prominent Land Leaguers on the basis of speeches they had made.

47 *Freeman's Journal*, 20 July 1881.

48 *The Radical*, 29 Oct. 1881; *Freeman's Journal*, 13 July 1881.

49 *Cork Examiner*, 12 July 1881.

50 *Freeman's Journal*, 11 July 1881.

51 *Freeman's Journal*, 13 July 1881.

52 *Freeman's Journal*, 14 July 1881.

53 *Freeman's Journal*, 15 July 1881.

54 ibid.

55 *Freeman's Journal*, 18 July 1881.

56 *Freeman's Journal*, 25 July 1881.

57 H.M. Hyndman, *Record*, p. 255.

58 *Freeman's Journal*, 25 July 1881.

59 ibid.

60 ibid.

61 The most successful biography of Hyndman is C. Tsuzuki, op. cit. Also see Mark Bevir, 'H.M. Hyndman: a rereading and a reassessment', *History of Political Thought*, vol. xii, 1991.

62 Karl Kautsky to Secretary British Socialist Party, 3 Mar. 1912, reproduced in H.M. Hyndman, *Further Reminiscences* (London, 1912), pp. 517–18.

63 *Justice*, 21 July 1894.

64 Hyndman, who earned his living on the stock exchange, addressed socialist meetings and sold the party newspaper attired in his frock-coat and top hat. In this he contrasted sharply with William Morris, another wealthy socialist, who famously sat on his top hat after resigning his directorship of the Devon Great Consuls Company and refused to ever wear one again. E.P. Thompson, op. cit., p. 192.

65 Mark Bevir, op. cit., p. 131.

66 C. Tsuzuki, op. cit., p. 30.

67 E.P. Thompson, op. cit., p. 293; E. Archbold and H.W. Lee, *Social-Democracy in Britain: Fifty Years of the Socialist Movement* (London, 1935), appendix i, *passim*.

68 E.P. Thompson, op. cit., p. 293.

69   Joseph Lane to Ambrose Barker, Mar. 1912. This was entitled *The 'Father' and 'Founder' of the Modern English Socialist Movement* and was published as a leaflet in 1912. Copy in the IISH.

70   H.M. Hyndman, 'Irish needs and Irish remedies', *The Fortnightly Review*, 1 Feb. 1880, p. 208.

71   ibid., p. 209.

72   ibid., p. 213.

73   ibid., p. 225.

74   ibid., pp. 216–17.

75   H.M. Hyndman, *Record*, p. 209.

76   Volume One of *Das Kapital* remained unavailable in English translation until Hyndman himself serialized the first ten chapters, beginning October 1885, in the periodical *Today*. A complete, and more substantial, translation was published in 1887. Edward Aveling and Samuel Moore translated and Engels oversaw the project. See Kirk Willis, 'The introduction and critical reception of Marxist thought in Britain, 1850–1900', *Historical Journal*, vol. xx, no. 2, 1977, p. 420; Yvonne Kapp, *Eleanor Marx. Volume II: The Crowded Years, 1884–1898* (London, 1976), pp. 120–2.

77   H.M. Hyndman to Karl Marx, 1 Oct. 1880, Marx Papers, IISH.

78   John Rae, 'The socialism of Karl Marx and the Young Hegelians', *Contemporary Review*, Oct. 1881, p. 586. Also see John Rae, *Contemporary Socialism* (London, 1884), pp. 111–12. In 1884, with an impressive disregard for the emerging 'socialist revival', Rae saw no inclination toward socialism in Britain (*Contemporary Socialism*, pp. 59–63). On the sparse availability of Marx's writings see also H.M. Hyndman, *Record*, p. 224; and Kirk Willis, op. cit., *passim*.

79   C. Tsuzuki, op. cit., p. 32; E.P. Thompson, op. cit., p. 292; H.M. Hyndman, *Record*, pp. 268–71.

80   H.M. Hyndman to Karl Marx, 25 Feb. 1880, Marx Papers, IISH.

81   Friedrich Engels to Eduard Bernstein, 3 May 1882, *MEI*, p. 333.

82   Quoted in Stanley Pierson, *Marxism and the Origins of British Socialism* (London, 1973), p. 182.

83   Hyndman, in the first volume of his memoirs, rather implausibly claimed that Engels retracted his assessment on his deathbed: 'At the close of his life, when he was dying of cancer of the throat at Eastbourne, he expressed his regret . . . that he had probably been mistaken as to the Social Democratic Federation and myself.' (*Record*, p. 253.) Hyndman, in his outraged vanity, was most probably attempting to counter the recently published letters from Marx and Engels to Sorge which were highly critical of both him and the SDF. Marx, according to Hyndman, similarly reversed his view 'shortly before his death' and reconciled with Hyndman. (*Record*, p. 251.) Again, Hyndman hardly constitutes a reliable voice on the matter.

84   H.M. Hyndman, 'The dawn of a revolutionary epoch', *The Nineteenth Century*, no. xlvii, Jan. 1881, p. 2.

85   ibid., p. 5.

86   ibid., p. 4.

87   ibid., pp. 12–13.

88   ibid., p. 16.

89 ibid., p. 15.
90 H.M. Hyndman, *Record*, p. 225.
91 ibid., p. 237.
92 H.M. Hyndman to Karl Marx, 15 Jan. 1881, Marx Papers, IISH.
93 Karl Marx to H.M. Hyndman, 8 Dec. 1880, Marx Papers, IISH.
94 H.M. Hyndman to Karl Marx, 13 Dec. 1880, Marx Papers, IISH.
95 A second edition published two months later included the demands for land nationalization and Irish home rule.
96 H.M. Hyndman, *England for All: The Textbook of Democracy* (London, 1881), p. 129.
97 Karl Marx to F.A. Sorge, 15 Dec. 1881, in Karl Marx and Friedrich Engels, *Selected Correspondence* (Moscow, 1965), pp. 345–6, hereafter cited as *Sel. Corr.*; Friedrich Engels to August Bebel, 30 Aug. 1883, in *Sel. Corr.*, pp. 364–5; H.M. Hyndman, *Record*, pp. 284–5. In any event Marx was publicly identified as Hyndman's inspiration within weeks of publication. See review in *The Radical*, 25 June 1881.
98 Karl Marx to F.A. Sorge, 15 Dec. 1881, *Sel. Corr.*, p. 346.
99 H.M. Hyndman, *England for All*, p. 114.
100 ibid., p. 119, pp. 117–18.
101 ibid., p. 119.
102 ibid., pp. 121–2.
103 ibid., p. 127.
104 ibid., p. 99.
105 C. Tsuzuki, op. cit., pp. 188–9.
106 H.M. Hyndman, *Record*, p. 255.
107 *Irish Times*, 22 Aug. 1881.
108 *Freeman's Journal*, 31 Aug. 1881. Ulster Liberals withstood the home rule onslaught longer than Liberals in the rest of Ireland. Indeed, the Liberals in Ulster won nine seats at the general election of 1880 — more than they had achieved since 1835. Irish nationalists, therefore, were particularly motivated when opportunities arose to destabilize the Liberals in Ulster. See K. Theodore Hoppen, *Elections, Politics and Society in Ireland, 1832–1885* (Oxford, 1984), pp. 264–73, esp. pp. 270-3.
109 *Freeman's Journal*, 6 Sept. 1881. In the event, Dickson won 3,163 votes against 3,034 for Knox and 907 for Rylett. (*Freeman's Journal*, 9 Sept. 1881.)
110 *Freeman's Journal*, 3 Sept. 1881.
111 H.M. Hyndman, *Record*, p. 295.
112 *Irish Times*, 24 Aug. 1881.
113 *Freeman's Journal*, 26 Aug. 1881.
114 *Irish Times*, 24 Aug. 1881.
115 *Freeman's Journal*, 9 Sept. 1881.
116 *Irish World*, 18 Mar. 1882.
117 The interview was republished in *The Radical*, 1, 8, 15 Apr. 1882.
118 *The Radical*, 8 Apr. 1882.
119 *The Radical*, 24 June 1882.
120 H.M. Hyndman, *Record*, p. 296.

121 ibid., p. 293.

122 *The Radical*, 15 Apr. 1882.

123 Hyndman's translation must have been made from the 1880 French edition of the book. A complete, and improved, English translation became available in 1892. See Introduction by Engels (1892), in Friedrich Engels, *Socialism: Utopian and Scientific* (New York, 1985), pp. 7–29. Engels's short survey, with its critique of pre-Marxian socialism, became a key text of classical Marxism.

124 C. Tsuzuki, op. cit., pp. 48–9.

125 Gary P. Steenson, *Karl Kautsky, 1854–1938: Marxism in the Classical Years* (Pittsburgh, 1991), pp. 37–8. See also Andreas Scheu, *Umsturzkeine* (Vienna, 1920).

126 H.M. Hyndman to Henry George, 14 Mar. 1883, Henry George Papers, NYPL.

127 On trade unions and the SDF see Henry Collins, 'The Marxism of the Social Democratic Federation', in Asa Briggs and John Saville (eds.), *Essays in Labour History, 1886–1923* (London, 1971), pp. 53–7.

128 J.L. Joynes, *The Socialist Catechism* (London, 1884), p. 2.

129 *Justice*, 15 Mar. 1884.

130 Emile De Laveleye, 'The progress of socialism', *Contemporary Review*, Apr. 1883, p. 561.

131 ibid., p. 561.

132 ibid., p. 561.

133 Democratic Federation, *Socialism Made Plain: Being the Social and Political Manifesto of the Democratic Federation* (London, 1883), p. 3.

134 ibid., p. 5.

135 *Justice*, 9 Aug. 1884.

136 E.P. Thompson, op. cit., pp. 344–5.

137 Friedrich Engels to August Bebel, 30 Aug. 1883, *Sel. Corr.*, p. 364.

138 ibid., p. 365.

139 P.A. Watmough, 'The membership of the Social Democratic Federation, 1885–1902', *Bulletin of the Society for the Study of Labour History*, vol. xxxiv, Spring 1977, pp. 35–40.

3.

Social Radicalism in Ireland, 1881-85

Irish socialists were unvarying during the 1880s in their acceptance of the seemingly Sisyphean nature of their task. The First International had encountered intractable and unremitting hostility the decade before and was, to employ a phrase, run out of town. The Catholic Church, in particular, nurtured a profound enmity to the politics of social radicalism and had frequently used the word 'communism' as an expletive when articulating its opposition to the Fenian separatist movement and its activities. Nonetheless, Irish history is one of colonialism and was characterized in the late nineteenth century as involving an alienation from the political structures of the British state. The aspiration for home rule was frustrated and this led to considerable irritation, with the idiom of separatism receiving much exercise. Dislocation from the existing state, whether through autonomy or absolute separation, was the fundamental demand in Irish politics. Ireland was a politically discontented country.

Moreover, the country was economically underdeveloped and, with a rural majority, the land system constituted a very real point of contention. Landlordism was doubly damned as it was popularly associated with both political and social injustice. Politically, the landlords were seen as the shareholders of colonialism. Their properties were commonly perceived as the ill-gotten gains of oppression and confiscation and they themselves were viewed as bulwarks of unionism. Likewise, the demand for peasant proprietorship was driven by a belief that landlordism was socially regressive and injurious to the economic condition of rural Ireland. There were solid premises for the disapprobation of the landlord system and the 'land war' of 1879–82 emphasized a smouldering social discontent. In the early 1880s the agrarian and home rule movements were closely linked and it is a commonplace to note that political life was certainly not pedestrian during this period. But, was Ireland amenable to social criticism that went beyond the objectives of peasant proprietorship and legislative independence?

HENRY GEORGE AND LAND NATIONALIZATION

The presence of Henry George in Ireland in 1881–82 has evoked remarkably little interest.[1] Rather surprisingly, both J.W. Boyle and Emmet O'Connor in their recent surveys of Irish labour in the nineteenth century fail to mention George's earliest Irish visit.[2] This is a regrettable omission because land nationalization, despite its limited constituency, was made available by both George and Michael Davitt as an alternative policy to peasant proprietorship while the agrarian movement was at its height.[3] Moreover, Henry George was an influential thinker who excited immense interest in the British socialist and labour movements.

Writing for *The Fortnightly Review* in 1897 J.A. Hobson, the radical economist, contended that Henry George 'may be considered to have exercised a more directly powerful formative and educative influence over English radicalism of the last fifteen years than any other man'.[4] The extent of his influence among those who initiated the 'socialist revival' has similarly been assessed as wide and deep.[5] Henry Pelling has suggested that George 'was naturally dismayed by the readiness of his supporters in England' to convert to socialism but until 1886 he co-operated amicably with socialist leaders.[6] Indeed, many leading socialists claimed him as a formative influence. George's book *Progress and Poverty*, Keir Hardie later recalled, led him, 'much to George's horror in later days when we met personally, into Communism'.[7] Andreas Scheu, a leading member of the Social Democratic Federation, informed a correspondent in 1884 that George 'through his lecturing tour has done admirable work in awakening the mind of the Nation to the fact that what we are pleased to call "progress" was not identical with the welfare of the masses'.[8] Henry George, above all, encouraged a critical review of classical political economy. Karl Marx, in a letter to F.A. Sorge, commented that *Progress and Poverty*, 'like the sensation it has created among you, is significant because it is a first though abortive effort at emancipation from orthodox political economy'.[9] The presumed linkage between George's agrarian radicalism and socialism was considered very real by John Rae who in his 1884 book *Contemporary Socialism* included a chapter on the agrarian radical because 'his doctrines are in many respects closely allied with those of socialism, and because he has done more than any other single person to stir and deepen in this country an agitation which, if not socialistic, at least promises to be a mother of socialism'.[10]

Henry George is now a name that has become obfuscated in the mists of history. During the final two decades of the nineteenth century, however, he enjoyed a formidable reputation as the principal and most articulate proponent of land nationalization. He was born in Philadelphia in 1839 and spent almost his entire political life in the United States until 1897 when he died while contesting the mayoralty of New York. George's best-known and defining work was *Progress and Poverty* which was first published in America in 1879. The following year an edition of his book appeared in Britain and 108,955 copies were sold during the 1880s.[11] It was a phenomenal success for a book of its type. In it, George delineated his argument for the extirpation of private ownership in land, and concurrently impugned the Malthusian doctrine that population tends to increase faster than subsistence. His assault on the Malthusian influence in political economy was important because the supposed foibles of economic life were then laid at the door of human agency. Once human culpability for social injustice was established it was a short step to agitation for social change. Henry George traced the unequal distribution of wealth 'which is the curse and menace of modern civilisation' to the 'institution of private property in land'.[12] Nationalization of all land, which was his proposed solution, was not only necessary as an economic reform but was ethically desirable. He wrote:

> The equal right of all men to the use of land is as clear as their equal right to breathe the air — it is a right proclaimed by the fact of their existence. For we cannot suppose that some men have a right to be in this world and others no right. If we are all here by the equal permission of the Creator, we are all here with an equal title to the enjoyment of His bounty — with an equal right to the use of all that nature so impartially offers.[13]

Socialists, of course, disagreed with George's advocacy of land nationalization in itself as a comprehensive remedy for social injustice but his interrogation of the prevailing social formation was welcomed. Indeed, in the early 1880s, many socialists would have seen George as an unwitting recruiting sergeant. James J. Shaw was undoubtedly correct when in 1884 he wrote in the *Journal of the Statistical and Social Inquiry Society of Ireland*:

> It is said that Karl Marx has denounced *Progress and Poverty* as the last ditch in which the institution of private property is driven to defend itself. Certainly no man can assert more strenuously than Mr George the rights of property in everything but land. But the rights of property will be in a bad way when they are driven to this last defence. For a very little consideration will show that this agrarian form of communism is most illogical, and cannot hold its ground against communism pure and simple. No communist would have any difficulty in showing that Mr George has totally

misapprehended and mis-estimated the relative strength of the various forces that work towards the unequal distribution of wealth.[14]

Shaw's point was well made and, in fact, the progression from Georgite land nationalization to socialism was a common sequence.

George visited Ireland four times during the 1880s. His last two appearances were to deliver single lectures on his way back to the United States from Britain in 1885 and 1889. In April 1884 he remained in the country for a week but his primary experience of Ireland was derived from his stay from October 1881 to October 1882 as a correspondent for the New York-based *Irish World*.[15] In *Progress and Poverty* George had used Ireland as an example of the negative consequences of the Malthusian theory of over-population. Allegedly overpopulated Ireland, claimed George, had been left to starve during the Famine while food continued to leave the ports.[16] The policy adopted by government had been informed by Malthusian theory while in truth, he charged, the misery and starvation had been produced by social conditions:

> No matter how sparse the population, no matter what the natural resources, are not pauperism and starvation necessary consequences in a land where the producers of wealth are compelled to work under conditions which deprive them of hope, of self-respect, of energy, of thrift . . . and when . . . a starving industry must support . . . landlords, with their horses and hounds, agents, jobbers, middlemen and bailiffs, an alien state church to insult religious prejudices, and an army of policemen and soldiers to overawe and hunt down any opposition to the iniquitous system?[17]

George wrote this in 1879 as the Irish land agitation, motivated by rural distress caused by a general agricultural depression, was beginning to mobilize.

In March 1881, seven months before his arrival in Ireland, he published *The Irish Land Question* which examined the current agrarian crisis in Ireland in an international context. He explained that while it was true that Ireland had been 'deeply wronged and bitterly oppressed' by Britain, it was not true that the country now suffered 'in an economic sense, at least' from any 'peculiar' oppression.[18] The Irish land system, he continued, which was so much talked of as if it were 'some peculiarly atrocious system' was the same system which 'all over the civilised world men are accustomed to consider natural and right'.[19] George's pamphlet properly controverted the notion of Irish exceptionalism although perhaps in a manner that bent the stick too far in the other direction. He compared, for instance, the rural distress to the constant drip of death from penury in all European countries as if the political and cultural impact of the Irish problem was based simply on a heightened national self-consciousness.[20] Likewise, Irish emigration was rather superficially equated with migration from the eastern to the western parts of the United States.[21] His point, however, was to illuminate the international necessity for land reform. He argued that, in common with other countries, the answer to poverty in Ireland lay in uncompensated land nationalization.[22] He wrote:

> There is in Ireland a large class now supporting the movement who are morbidly afraid of anything which savours of 'communism' or 'socialism', while in the United States . . . it is certain that many . . . would slink away from a movement which avowed the intention of abolishing private property in land . . . I understand all this. Nevertheless, I am convinced that the Irish land movement would gain, not lose, were its earnest leaders, disdaining timid counsels, to boldly avow the principle that the land of Ireland belongs of right to the whole people of Ireland, and, without bothering about compensation to the landlords, to propose its resumption by the people in the simple way I have suggested.[23]

George, furthermore, asserted that in assuming 'the radical ground' as he proposed, the Irish agitators would attract the support of their 'natural allies' in the English working class.[24] This was necessary as England not Ireland 'is the field where the struggle' would be won.[25] 'If the Irish leaders are wise', he commented, 'they may yet avail themselves of the rising tide of English democracy. Let the Land Leaguers adopt the noble maxim of the German Social Democrats. Let them be Land Leaguers first, and Irishmen afterwards'.[26]

SPREADING THE LIGHT

Henry George, of course, was not alone in his advocation of land nationalization as a solution for Ireland's agrarian troubles. Alfred Russel Wallace had made the same proposal in November 1880 and land nationalization as a policy had been a touchstone of British advanced Radicalism from at least the early 1870s.[27] Likewise, the Democratic Federation, which sent members to Ireland during the summer of 1881, argued for nationalization of the land and had strong links with the Irish Land League. Nonetheless, by the time George landed in Ireland in 1881 *Progress and Poverty* had established him internationally as the most cogent advocate of land nationalization. His reputation and writing, to some extent, had preceded him and modified versions of his theories were beginning to make converts in the Land League and elsewhere.

Indeed when George arrived at Queenstown in Cork harbour on 25 October 1881 a steamship agent, who was also a Land Leaguer, recognized his name on the passenger list and advised him to conceal his identity to avoid harassment when he disembarked.[28] The agent's concern proved unfounded and George, under his own name, booked his wife Annie and their daughter into a Cork hotel while he, with extreme difficulty, sought out local supporters of the Land League.[29] He did not stay in Cork but went on alone almost immediately to Dublin. He had arrived in Ireland at a dangerous time for supporters of the Land League. Twelve days earlier Charles Stewart Parnell had been arrested and interned without trial in Kilmainham jail and, as a result, Dublin had been rocked by two days of rioting. On 20 October the Land League had been declared a proscribed organization and suppressed. The business of state repression was in full swing.

George came to Ireland ostensibly as a correspondent for the *Irish World* which was owned by Patrick Ford, an advanced nationalist. Ford was a central figure in Irish-American politics and Michael Davitt was later to praise him above all others as having been 'actively and constantly the most powerful support of the struggle in Ireland on the American continent'.[30] Originally from Galway, Ford represented extreme nationalists who were willing to eschew conspiracy and support Davitt and Parnell's 'new departure' of 1879. His paper became the collection point through which Irish-American funds were funnelled to the Irish Land League. It was widely distributed in Ireland and exercised much influence.[31] The *Irish World*, to the consternation of many Irish parliamentary party members, was also strongly identified with the policy of land nationalization.[32] Both Ford and George were interested in effecting a radicalization of the Irish agrarian agitation. Indeed, shortly after his arrival in Ireland, George confirmed this shared desire when he wrote to Ford assuring him of his conviction 'that everything is working together to the end we both desire — the radicalisation of the movement and the people'.[33] George saw himself as a political missionary and his attitude to the Land League is made clear in his remark that 'at this time it is *extremely* important to get them into the right line'.[34] He was in Ireland to convert, not simply to cable first-hand reports to the *Irish World*.

George's first concern when he reached Dublin was to acquaint himself with the state of the movement and its personnel. 'I am inclined to think very highly', he commented, 'of the political sagacity of Parnell and the circle of leaders. I have some doubts though as to whether there is not too great a fear of delegating authority on the outside'.[35] Parnell and the other leaders, he revealed, still kept control of the movement from Kilmainham jail 'though communication with them is difficult' and '[William F.] Moloney is a sort of head centre outside the jail, with [John J.] Clancy for a sort of Lieutenant. The ladies run the whole business of relief and support, Anna Parnell is "boss". Of her order and grit there is no question, though I am not so sure about her judgement'.[36] The police, however, arrested Moloney on 25 November and Clancy was similarly interned as a 'suspect' shortly afterwards.[37] In the months after the suppression of the Land League the Ladies' Land League effectively carried on the agitation and George found himself working with them.[38] This experience had its effect on him and at a Dublin lecture in June 1882 he asked:

> Is it not blasphemy to say the Creator intended the state of things existing in this very city — poor girls stalking around making a living of dishonour — poor barefooted children coming at twelve o'clock at night to the Ladies' Land League (prolonged cheers for the Ladies' League). Since he came there and saw what these women had done he became a convert to female suffrage; and when the Irish people came to make their own laws they should give women a vote (cheers and laughter).[39]

Laughter at such a suggestion was scarcely uncommon in the 1880s and, in fact, the success of the Ladies' Land League made most members of the parliamentary party feel distinctly uncomfortable. Following the release of the male leadership it was quickly driven into extinction.[40] George was particularly impressed by Helen Taylor who he declared was one of, 'if not the most intelligent woman I ever met'.[41] Taylor, who was a stepdaughter of John Stuart Mill, was active in the Ladies' Land League and also a member of the Democratic Federation.

Not long after his arrival in Dublin George was asked to lecture in the city. E.D. Gray, the proprietor of the *Freeman's Journal*, and some others advised him not to speak there before speaking in England 'as they said I would have more influence there by speaking there first. I don't know but that the advice is sound; but my sympathies go so strongly with this people that it would seem to me cowardly to refuse anything that might encourage them'.[42] A lecture was arranged for the Round Room of the Rotunda for 14 November. In the meantime George went to Kilmainham jail where he visited Parnell. He also began arrangements for a trip to Britain where he intended to promote the Irish movement. In a letter to Thomas Briggs of the British Land Nationalization Society he expressed his feelings on Ireland:

> I find much here to interest me, and, to speak frankly, much that rouses my indignation. Surely the masses of the English people cannot understand the sort of Government that they are maintaining here, and how the first principles of human liberty are being trodden under foot by an irresponsible dictatorship wielded in the interests of a panic-stricken and maddened class.[43]

At the Dublin lecture he returned to this theme but his speech was largely a promotion of his policy of land nationalization. The meeting was well organized with the Young Ireland Society playing an important role. Likewise, the advertising was extensive and the *Freeman's Journal*, which described him as 'the distinguished American Political Economist', commented beforehand that *Progress and Poverty* was 'of world-wide fame' and that 'not a few who are competent to judge think it the ablest treatise ever written on the subject with which it deals'.[44] The financial proceeds of the lecture were to be donated to the Political Prisoners Aid Society. The Quaker and home ruler, Alfred Webb, presided in place of T.D. Sullivan MP, who was attending the funeral of the Archbishop of Tuam. A letter was read from Rev. Harold Rylett who expressed his disappointment at being unable to attend and he declared that he knew of no economist 'whose views on land and labour are more healthy and sound than his'.[45] Rylett, who was a Unitarian minister in County Down and a leading Land Leaguer, also related how the previous year Davitt had sent him a copy of *Progress and Poverty*. The platform attendance was impressive and it contained many leading Land League activists among whom were the radicals Amos Varian, J.B. Killen and R.J. Donnelly. The *Freeman's Journal* described the audience as 'vast and enthusiastic' and said it 'comprised a large number of ladies and several Catholic clergymen'.[46] The presence of a large number of women, unusual for political meetings at the time, might perhaps be indicative of the politicization engendered by the activity of the Ladies' Land League.

George's lecture is noteworthy for a number of reasons, not least of which is the newspaper coverage it generated. His searing criticism of British repression was nothing new but it won him the sympathy of his audience and allowed him pass on to a criticism that one would not have expected to be well received:

> The Land League had not gone in its demands . . . very much further than Mr Gladstone (hear, hear). They seemed to think it a very radical demand that they should ask for a peasant proprietorship. What did they want with a peasant proprietorship? What did they want with peasants of any kind? What they wanted was not peasants on one side and lords on the other side. What they wanted was free and equal and independent citizens (cheers). Peasant proprietorship, peasants of all kinds were . . . played out. Aristocracy was played out. In democracy was the hope of the people; and not merely a political democracy, but a social democracy — a democracy in which the equal right of every citizen was fully recognised — his equal right to his native soil and to natural opportunities . . . What was the true solution of the land question? Bishop Nulty (cheers) has said — 'The land, therefore, of every country is the property of the people of that country, because the real owner, the Creator who made it, has granted it as a voluntary gift to them'.[47]

George was careful to protect his critique of the Land League behind the names of Bishop Thomas Nulty of Meath and Michael Davitt whom he enlisted as his allies repeatedly throughout his speech. 'Not prison walls', he argued, 'nor armed policemen, nor fleets of ships, nor arbitrary laws, could put down the force of the great truth enunciated by Michael Davitt and Bishop Nulty (cheers).'[48] George walked a thin line in his conscription of Davitt and Nulty. Davitt had yet to publicly declare his conversion to land nationalization, although it was a policy he had privately supported for some time. Bishop Nulty was a stranger case. He had indeed issued a letter in which he arguably advocated land nationalization but his view of such a scheme was rooted in his conception of pre-feudal land rights in ancient Ireland. Moreover, he was unlikely to publicly endorse George's policy although he was close to George and in February 1882 he offered to write a commendation of *Progress and Poverty* which he said 'is the greatest book on political economy since Smith's *Wealth of Nations*'.[49] Nulty's name was frequently used in the *Irish World* to support Ford and George's wider understanding of the Land League slogan 'the land for the people'.

George was enthusiastically received and in rising to respond to a vote of thanks he provoked a chorus of 'renewed cheers and demonstrations of enthusiasm' which encouraged him to finish with a shout of 'God save Ireland'.[50] Afterwards he explained the acclaim to Patrick Ford as the result of the fact that it had been 'the only chance the Dublin people had had since the suppression of the Land League to show their enthusiasm'.[51] To Helen Taylor he wrote: 'Wish you could have heard my lecture in the historic Rotunda. I had an immense audience, and had them wild with enthusiasm. It was all I could do to prevent being dragged around the streets at its conclusion. I am sorry now that I did not let them do it, as it would have compelled the press agents to have taken more notice.'[52] Undoubtedly, George had received a tremendous reception and it must have strengthened his position in Dublin. In late November he was interviewed by the *Belfast Morning News*. In a lengthy interview he compared the government of Ireland to Russia and the South American republics and accused Gladstone of operating a 'reign of terror'. When asked about Davitt he replied that he had met him in New York 'and his idea of the ultimate solution of the question went as far as mine does — he wished to secure the land of Ireland, not for a class, but for the whole people'.[53]

By December 1881 George was beginning to develop a more informed understanding of the Land League and the Irish parliamentary party. He met Michael Boyton, a recently released 'suspect', who he assessed as 'the most intelligent and best informed man I have struck yet' and he confirmed his opinion 'that the movement has gone on by the force of innate ideas and not by good management. The loss of Davitt was enormous and has never been repaired. Parnell is a true man and a magnificent parliamentary leader, but he's not Davitt's grasp of detail, nor was he so advanced'.[54] Nonetheless, he was able to write in the *Irish World* that the lopping off of the head of the League was insufficient to kill the organization because 'the movement has gone too far for that . . . In every locality the people have become accustomed to act together and to stand together'.[55] Such sentiments aside, he was becoming aware of a deep antagonism towards his position:

There is a great amount of 'whiggery' in the Land League movement, more than I thought before coming here. And I think this is especially true of the leaders. With very many of them for whom it is doing the most the *Irish World* is anything but popular. And I have felt from the beginning as if there was a good deal of that feeling about myself. We are regarded as dangerous allies . . . But come what may this movement is going to assume a much more radical phase. In spite of everything the light *is* spreading.[56]

His unease was heightened by a trip to London in late December where he met leading members of the Land League. They informed him that the meetings protesting against Parnell's arrest in October had been primarily organized by the Democratic Federation and not by the Land League. Indeed, he discerned a policy 'not to have any co-operation with or aid from Englishmen'.[57] In London he also met H.M. Hyndman with whom he was impressed. Later he met Joseph Biggar MP who let him know that the Land Leaguers who had shifted to Paris to escape arrest had failed to make it the organizing centre that it was meant to be. He wrote to Ford:

The facts, as I gathered them from him, are that there is no more headquarters in Paris than in London. No reports are received there unless it be from Kilmainham and the ladies. The latter are doing all the real work that is being done.

I met, however, Biggar, Sexton, [F.H.] O'Donnell and [Richard] Lalor (or Lawlor) in the League rooms and took the liberty of telling them very frankly how things looked to me. I told them it seemed to me that there must necessarily be a waste of time and money when there was no central authority between Paris and Kilmainham, and no place where reports could be made and information got. I told them too that it seemed to me that the means of acting upon public opinion was very much neglected, and that the English people suffered to go crazy over misrepresentation, without any effort to correct them. I pointed to the piles of reports of the Democratic Federation, on the true condition of Ireland, which were lying in the next room because, as the Secretary told me, he had no time to send them out and no authority to employ any one; and to the fact that Bishop Nulty's letter . . . no effort had been made to distribute a single copy . . . With perhaps the exception of Biggar, the others seemed to agree with me, especially O'Donnell who said that with a very little management, a tremendous English movement can be started . . . that would be of enormous assistance. To sum up it seems to me that there is in many things a lack of management and consequently waste both of opportunities and resources. Sometimes it seems to me as if a lot of small men had found themselves in the lead of a tremendous movement and finding themselves being lifted into importance and power they never dreamed of are jealous of anybody sharing the honor. I do not refer to Parnell who I think from all I hear of him is a first class man though he lacks qualities and powers in which Davitt is strong.[58]

It was inevitable that George would encounter opposition to his attempt to open a debate on the objective of the Land League, and lecturing the leaders of the parliamentary party on their responsibilities was unlikely to make the situation any easier. George's chagrin, however, was genuine and impelled by what he saw as a disastrous dismissal of the British working class.[59] He made his criticism public in the columns of the *Irish World* which was widely read by activists in Ireland. His attack was pointed:

> That the Land League movement, which is largely analogous to trades union movements for shorter time and higher wages, should have as yet received so comparatively little support and sympathy from English working classes is, I think, largely due to the failure to properly present the Irish case, and to the failure on the part of the League leaders to take more radical ground . . . The fact is that the Land League movement, up to the present time, has definitely aimed at nothing more than class advantage . . . The truth is that there has been, and still is, much conservatism within the lines and in the management of the Land League many who would like to make the movement *a mere political and not a social revolution.*[60]

He also pointed out that the existence of Joseph Cowen, Helen Taylor and the members of the Democratic Federation showed the potential that existed in Britain.

On his return to Ireland he found, however, that he had other problems to deal with as the police were systematically attempting to disrupt distribution of the *Irish World*. Policemen had raided all the shops in Dublin where they believed the paper was sold and had informed the shopkeepers that they would not in future be permitted to sell the *Irish World*.[61] Catherine Keogh, the *Irish World*'s main distributor in Dublin, confronted the police because of their actions and issued a summons against them for seizing the papers. In January, however, a court dismissed her summons and the police celebrated this victory the following day by seizing a few thousand copies of the *Irish World* as they were landed on the North Wall Quay.[62] This was to be a recurring problem and the police even took to opening mail from the United States in order to confiscate copies of the paper.[63]

In early January 1882 George went to Donegal 'where some very extensive evictions are going on', and from there to Derry and Belfast.[64] His visits to Ulster, he later wrote, confirmed his belief 'that the agitation of the Land Question is not merely extending but is constantly becoming more and more radical'.[65] Certainly, his meeting with Rylett in Belfast would have encouraged George to believe this but the position in Donegal was anything but radical. He wrote privately to Ford that the 'no rent' strike (organized in reaction to government repression) was weakening in Donegal: 'That a good deal of the refusal to pay rent will not stand much strain I am convinced. A good deal of it, and this is the case in Donegal, is merely to get reductions, and the local clergy nearly everywhere seem to be throwing their influence on the side of compromise and rent-paying.'[66] George returned to Belfast on 27 January and delivered a lecture which he claimed 'was a great success', and the leaders there 'were enthusiastic about the new life it had put in the cause'.[67] Rev. Harold Rylett, John Ferguson and Charles J. Dempsey whom he met in Belfast were all sympathetic to his policy of land nationalization. All three were strong allies of Davitt: 'They all swear by Davitt and told me many things about him which I was glad to hear. They have all great confidence in Parnell's political sagacity and leadership, but Davitt was *the* organizer.' Moreover, they were capable of being highly critical of decisions taken by the national leadership and they complained to George that so far at least 'as Ulster is concerned it is a great mistake to forbid the reorganisation of the Land League under another name, as the farmers are being got hold of by the Liberal politicians through the Tenants' Defence organisations'. Ulster still retained a strong Liberal organization. Nonetheless, George wrote to Ford: 'Your name and that of the *World* were received most enthusiastically in Belfast, and the *radical truth* is spreading there.'

George's lecture in Belfast, 'Work and Wages', sought to demonstrate how all wealth could supposedly be traced back to the land which, as the creation of God, could not be coveted by individuals. In its essence his argumentation replicated that advanced in Dublin and both Bishop Nulty and Michael Davitt were again enlisted to support his proposition. This time, however, he also used the opportunity to introduce the name of Patrick Ford which evoked continued and noisy applause from his audience. He harshly condemned the landlord class as lazy and parasitical.[68] Likewise, he condemned the continued imprisonment of the five hundred or so 'suspects' and he attacked the low wages paid to Belfast millworkers whose working conditions he described as 'monstrous'.[69]

At the end of January 1882 George moved to London for the start of the new parliamentary session. He expected that 'the bringing together of the Irish members' would transform London into a focus for Irish news.[70] From February until May Henry George had little direct input into the conflict in Ireland other than through his weekly articles in the *Irish World*. On the other hand his time in London enabled him to meet many of the Irish MPs and form assessments of their possible political inclinations. He found little to encourage any hope that land nationalization was gaining ground in the Irish parliamentary party. He wrote to Ford:

> It is important that the influence of Davitt and Dr Nulty and yourself should be as strong as possible, for the parliamentary leaders are not radical at all. I doubt if there is a single Irish member of Parliament who has got beyond the idea of buying out the landlords and selling again to the tenants. And a good many of them I think look upon us really [as] going much

too far. But the light is spreading, and before the question is settled much more radical men will come to the front.[71]

If the light was spreading George was quite certain that Thomas Sexton, F.H. O'Donnell and Timothy Healy were not likely to be among those basking in its illuminating glory.

> Sexton is not a man of ideas. He is a good speaker, but I think not much more. O'Donnell is as he frankly admits at bottom a Conservative. So is Healy. The thing that seems uppermost in his mind . . . was that the 'radicals' or 'socialists' of the Irish party in America were hurting the cause by frightening men of means from it. I pointed out to him the fact that such Irishmen could not be counted on anyhow, either in Ireland or America but I think his notion of the *Irish World* is like that of most of the 'leaders' — that it is useful but dangerous.[72]

Healy, however, was not a stupid man and he understood that the *Irish World* had a substantial constituency. Indeed, in the same letter, George mentioned that Healy had agreed to write for the paper.

While some converts were made for land nationalization among Land League activists in Ireland, the national leadership was largely untouched. Davitt's position was known by few outside the Land League despite George's continued use of his name. The Catholic Church, paradoxically, seemed to George to provide one of the few advocates of social radicalism in Ireland. Soon after landing in the country he had been to see Bishop Thomas Nulty of Meath who had issued a pastoral letter which argued that land should be held by the people as common property. George was very impressed by Nulty and met him a number of times again to discuss the land question: 'I urged him all I know how to speak out, and I told him that his voice would not only sing through Ireland, but reach to the very verges of the civilised world.'[73] Bishop Nulty, however, had no intention of openly entering a political or social movement and he was quick to deny his alleged advocation of the 'no rent' campaign.[74] George believed, probably correctly, that Nulty felt 'under pressure' from Rome and other members of the Irish hierarchy.[75] Nonetheless, he wrote to Ford: 'The fact is that Bishop Nulty is in head and heart all right. He is as sound as you are.'[76] George also met Bishop Patrick Duggan of Clonfert and he informed Ford that Duggan had 'confirmed my opinion that absolute orders from Rome are holding back such men as he and Nulty'.[77] 'How this movement', he remarked, 'would flame up if men like Dr Duggan and Bishop Nulty could come right out and lead it.'[78] This is a view that Duggan may have held himself, and George reported the bishop's fears if the hierarchy continued to abstain from the struggle:

> He takes a gloomy view of the religious future. The present attitude of religious authority will, if persisted in, produce the same results as in France.

It will do what persecution could not do — divide the people from their Church. The only hope he said was that the people would force the Bishops along.[79]

Duggan was an admirer of Davitt. But admiration did not imply complete support for Davitt's social policies as Wilfred Scawen Blunt discovered when he met Duggan in 1886. Blunt quoted the bishop in his narrative of this period:

> You bring me an introduction from Davitt. It is the best you could bring. He is a holy man . . . Henry George came to see me — he explained to me his plan of Land Nationalisation. Davitt likes it. I don't agree with him. I said to George, 'This is beautiful, too beautiful. Is it not Utopia?' He said, 'Ah, that is the weak point'.[80]

Henry George should have heeded his own advice to Ford on Archbishop Thomas William Croke of Cashel and the other bishops: 'And as for the Bishops . . . the less prominence given to them the better as at the critical moment they cannot be relied on.'[81]

THE RELEASE OF MICHAEL DAVITT

Coercion failed to destroy the agrarian agitation in Ireland. In fact, the arrests of Parnell and the other leading members of the national movement seemed to encourage the agrarian 'outrages' that they were intended to curb. It was becoming clear by March 1882 that W.E. Forster, the Chief Secretary for Ireland, had been mistaken in his estimate of the efficacy of coercive legislation. Parnell, on the other hand, had little desire to remain in Kilmainham jail. Through intermediaries a deal, later known as the 'Kilmainham Treaty', was struck. The secretly negotiated agreement meant a change in policy for the Irish parliamentary party. As well as agreeing to use his influence to prevent further agrarian 'outrages' Parnell promised some support for the Liberal Party in the House of Commons. The British government, for its part, agreed to amend the 1881 Land Act and to deal fairly with the question of rent arrears. Moreover, those interned were to be released. Many of the prisoners, including Parnell and Dillon, were out by 4 May. Forster resigned in protest and was replaced by Lord Frederick Cavendish who was not, for the Irish party, an unpopular choice.

Michael Davitt had been in jail since early February 1881 and his absence had deprived George of his most influential confederate. H.M. Hyndman later described Davitt as a man 'worthy of the highest regard' who should be seen as 'one of the greatest men of the time'.[82] Such praise from a leading socialist was based on Davitt's practical and empathic identification with the British labour movement and with many struggles for social reform.[83] However, although close to socialism in some ways Davitt, as Francis Sheehy-Skeffington pointed out, was not a socialist.[84] In fact he had begun his political life as an advanced nationalist and, for Fenian activities, had spent some years in jail. In 1879 he was instrumental in initiating the Land League and he used his influence to secure support for this 'new departure' from Fenian elements who were wary of diluting the struggle for independence with social issues. Davitt was immensely popular in Ireland and he represented a radical nationalist tradition with its roots amongst the 'plain people'. George recognized the very real class difference between Davitt and Parnell:

> Mr Parnell and Mr Davitt represent two different types of men born in Ireland. The one is a landlord in the Pale; the other a child of those Irishy, who hunted 'to hell and Connaught', have preserved the old traditions. The one is by birth . . . a 'landed gentleman', words which have much meaning in Ireland; the other belongs of the class who had been trodden under the heel of the tenant farmer even more ruthlessly than the tenant farmer has been trodden under the heel of the landlord.[85]

It is unclear when, precisely, Davitt became a supporter of land nationalization. F.S.L. Lyons has suggested that a meeting between Davitt and Henry George in Patrick Ford's house in 1880 may have been important.[86] Henry George, himself, claimed that Davitt was a land nationalizer before they ever met and, moreover, in an 1882 letter to *The Nation* he contended that Davitt, Thomas Brennan and John Ferguson wanted to make land nationalization a part of the Land League's platform at its formation.[87] In some ways it is unimportant when exactly Davitt became a land nationalizer because until 1882 he loyally supported the Land League and its policy of peasant proprietorship. After his release from prison that was to change. Davitt had read George's book *Progress and Poverty* while in jail and he largely agreed with its analysis. On two points he did differ with George. Firstly, 'as a practical politician', he believed compensation to be necessary. Secondly, he did not accept that rent, or 'tax', on nationalized land should be set by the law of supply and demand. Government regulation was necessary if rents were to be kept at a fair and reasonable level.[88]

George was one of a select group, which included Sexton, Healy, A.M. Sullivan and Frank Byrne, that met Davitt at Vauxhall Station in London after his release from Portland prison on 6 May.[89] (Parnell and John Dillon had gone up to the prison to meet him as he was being released.) The celebration, however, was to be short lived. Early the next morning George received a telegram from Dublin informing him of the assassination in the Phoenix Park of Lord Cavendish and the Under-Secretary for Ireland, Thomas Burke. He went immediately to the Westminster Palace Hotel where

Davitt was staying and woke him up.[90] Davitt was shocked and later that day entered in his diary:

> The blackest day that has perhaps ever dawned for Ireland — or rather yesterday — only heard of atrocious occurrence this morning. Unless through providence of God all is lost for Ireland for a generation with frightful stain left upon its name. Parnell and everybody in despair . . . One act of hellish vengeance by unknown hands has undone the labour of the Land League and left it the victim of the crime.[91]

Patrick Ford was similarly horrified and denounced the 'horrible crime' that threatened to rob Ireland 'of the sympathy that has been of such incalculable assistance to her in her battle against landlordism'.[92] The killings had been carried out by a nationalist secret society which had apparently originally intended to assassinate Burke and W.E. Forster in revenge for the government's campaign of repression. The result was a stiff coercion bill and much anguish for members of the Irish parliamentary party.

ARGUING FOR LAND NATIONALIZATION

Within weeks of his release Davitt announced his support for the policy of land nationalization and he publicly allied himself with Henry George. John O'Leary, the Fenian, later remarked that Davitt, because of his adherence to this policy, could not really be considered a nationalist any longer but was 'some sort of an internationalist and socialist'.[93] This was a proposition that Davitt would have contested but it is undoubtedly true that O'Leary's response was not an uncommon one and Davitt was now aligned openly with what one correspondent to a provincial newspaper called the 'communistic web of the *Irish World* and their friends'.[94] His campaign for land nationalization arguably began at an inopportune moment for the Land League. The 'Kilmainham Treaty' was not universally welcomed and, as Lyons points out, Davitt's new position could be interpreted as a challenge to the Parnell leadership.[95] He, of course, vigorously denied that this was the case but he did leave himself open to the charge that he was damaging the national movement at a critical juncture.

On 21 May Davitt spoke alongside George at a meeting in Manchester. He told an Irish audience:

> Three years ago, when the cry of the 'land for the people' went up from a meeting in the west of Ireland, it was received with astonishment by our own countrymen, and branded at once as communistic and wicked in England . . . Those who believed with myself that peasant proprietary, immensely preferable though it be to landlordism, would not meet to the full the final solution of the Irish social problem, were two short years ago

put down as utopian dreamers, yet one of the most respected Bishops of Ireland has since proclaimed that 'the land of every country is the common property of the people of that country'. (Cheers.)[96]

Davitt also made a comment that he was to repeat in America a few weeks later: he claimed that he had 'never been a leader in Irish politics' but had been 'a free-lancer' who 'struck the enemy where he thought he was weakest'.[97] Such a remark would seem to indicate that Davitt was intent on striking out independently from Parnell and the Irish party. In Philadelphia on 26 June, while stating his support for Parnell, he said: 'I am compelled to state right out that I am no blind partisan of any man, or a slavish follower of any party, or section of party, within the Land League movement.'[98]

A more explicit exposition of land nationalization was delivered by Davitt in Liverpool on 6 June. 'The right of all men', he declared, 'to participate in the benefits of the soil . . . can be claimed from the fact that land is a natural agent, and that the value of land arises from and is maintained by aggregation of population and the exercise of industry by a people.'[99] Davitt was anxious to tackle one of the chief criticisms made of land nationalization in Ireland. Such a policy if enacted, he argued, would not imply a recognition of the British state's right to rule the country.

> I contend . . . that the nationalisation of the land under the existing political relationship of the two countries would be no more of an abandonment of national right or national honour than is involved in any transaction of the everyday political life of our country, while I claim for such a settlement more solid social advantages . . . than can be obtained under an improvement of the existing system or by the substitution of a peasant proprietary (loud cheers).[100]

The first part of this statement was more an assertion than an argument although he did state that his preferred option was land nationalization under self-government. Davitt would find it difficult to convince would-be peasant proprietors that they would be better off if the land was under British government control. This, and land hunger, were obstacles that land nationalizers in Ireland would always have to confront.

Davitt arrived in Cork on 8 June 1882 on his way to Queenstown from where he was to sail to the United States for a lecture tour. He had clearly been speaking with Parnell: 'In deference to a wish from him I have endeavoured to travel through Ireland without making any speech whatever at large or small meetings, and I would be the last man in the movement to do or say anything to embarrass Mr Parnell's work or action in the House of Commons.'[101] Nonetheless, speaking to a large crowd outside the Victoria Hotel, he asserted that 'what Ireland wants is the nationalisation of the land administered in Dublin by an Irish Parliament (great cheering)'.[102]

Two days later, as Davitt was *en route* to America, Henry George gave a lecture in Dublin on 'The Irish Land Question'. Anna Parnell and Thomas Sexton were among a crowded attendance at the meeting which was chaired by Dr Joseph Kenny, the leading home ruler. Also present were a large number of Ladies' Land League members.[103] George was exuberant:

> With Michael Davitt's liberty the true standard had been raised, 'The land for the people' (cheers). The land for the whole people, for every one of them, man, woman, and child, rich and poor, down to the humblest child (cheers). And now the question came up before the people of Ireland, and with them, and not with that Parliament over there, would rest the ultimate solution of the question (cheers). They would win what they wanted if they made up their mind to it.[104]

Sexton moved a vote of thanks at the end of George's lecture. However, he also made it clear that he personally was not a land nationalizer. A conflict was brewing. Michael Davitt's support for land nationalization was a serious matter because of his popularity and because of his influence within the nationalist and agrarian movements. The *Freeman's Journal* considered George's meeting 'remarkable' and commented that to his credit when he resumed his seat 'there were few in the Rotunda . . . who, if asked on the spur of the moment what it was Ireland now absolutely wanted, would have failed to answer, the nationalisation of the land'.[105]

Parnell was obliged to move before Davitt's campaign gathered more pace. In an interview with the *New York Herald* he attacked Davitt's new departure as impractical and argued that tenant farmers 'would have a smaller annual payment to make under our system than under that of nationalisation of the land'.[106] He also expressed his belief that Davitt was only testing public opinion and would soon realize that there was no substantial interest in his scheme. The interview was well timed as it was published on the day of Davitt's arrival in the United States.[107] Consequently, he was on the defensive from the moment he set foot in New York. Already the *Freeman's Journal* had reported that Land League leaders in America were refusing to endorse his new policy and that there was a quarrel between them and Patrick Ford about Davitt's reception. Ford, it was claimed, had Davitt's permission to organize the reception and this was 'putting him . . . into the hands of the Communist element of the Irish party' and would lead to the American Leaguers attending as private citizens rather than as formal representatives.[108] James J. O'Kelly MP, one of Parnell's lieutenants, had been very active in May and had turned many Irish-Americans against Davitt's new land policy.

In New York Davitt defended his plan for land nationalization and denied that he was advocating a 'new line'. Parnell, he claimed, had misinterpreted his Liverpool speech and referring to a charge that he was suggesting an alliance with English people he said that he did not believe 'that the democracy of England was blameable because the English aristocracy had wronged Ireland'.[109] Likewise, he refuted the suggestion that he 'favoured Communism or was trying to set himself up as a rival to Mr Parnell'. Davitt was clearly being put under immense pressure and Matthew Harris, the Galway Land League leader, added to this pressure with a lengthy letter which was published in the *Freeman's Journal* on 21 June. Harris accused Davitt of doing 'more damage to the cause of Ireland than a dozen Forsters with a dozen Coercion Acts at their backs could accomplish'.

Harris, who had been an important figure in the formation of the Land League, was worried that division would destroy the agrarian agitation. He wrote:

> It would be difficult to get abler men . . . or better material to float a move-ment than they possess. They have their bible, *Progress and Poverty*; their newspaper, the *Irish World*; and in their latest acquisition, Mr Davitt, the third great requisite, a popular leader, who in his own hive is not inferior to any of them. All of those men [Ford, George, Davitt] did good work in the land agitation, and deserve the gratitude of the Irish people . . . [But] they are attempting to destroy the great movement they themselves have helped to build up.[110]

Davitt, Harris contended, must think 'other people, Mr Parnell included, as possessing a very low degree of intelligence' when he asserted that there was little difference between himself and Parnell. In truth Davitt had made extremely weak attempts to underplay the gap between himself and Parnell. As regards the alliance with advanced Radicalism in Britain, Harris argued that the strength and importance of that movement was consistently over-rated: 'They make a great deal of noise and rattle, but are deficient in real power.'[111] It was a powerful attack which found an echo in James Daly's *Connaught Telegraph*. Daly was a conservative Land Leaguer who had told the Bessborough Commission that with peasant proprietorship 'you would make the peasants more conservative than the Conservatives. I am a Land Leaguer myself, and I would not be a Land Leaguer if it had anything behind it like Revolutions. I would fight against it'.[112] Daly commented favourably on Harris's letter and he accused Davitt of 'recently playing a rather shif-ting comedy' and of possessing a 'vacillating policy'.[113] The *Connaught Telegraph* later printed an editorial entitled 'Michael Davitt on the Rampage':

> To interpret the proper meaning of this new theory, it is simply this: to get the people of Ireland to abandon all future claims at ever attempting the establishment of a free and regenerated Ireland; to allow themselves be handed over, neck and crop, bag and baggage, to the mercy of an alien Government, which, at best, has little in store for the amelioration of the condition of the Irish race. They are bound to listen to the wild and

impracticable theories of Michael Davitt: they must sell their birthright and their Nationality to an alien and hostile Government . . . What next? Communism, pure and simple, will be the next step.[114]

This was a well-aimed broadside which weakened Davitt by querying his nationalism. John O'Connor-Power MP, an old adversary of Davitt's, also took the opportunity to attack him in replying to a speech Davitt made in Jersey city.[115]

Few Land League activists publicly came to Davitt's defence. Rev. Harold Rylett wrote a letter to the *Freeman's Journal* in favour of land nationalization and John Ferguson contributed a long letter in which he said that he found himself 'in perfect harmony upon the land question with Mr George'.[116] In defence of Davitt he claimed that he had suggested to Davitt that he avoid using either the term peasant proprietorship or land nationalization in his Liverpool speech and he rather implausibly argued that the 'nationalisation as advocated by Michael Davitt is precisely the same as the peasant proprietary of Charles Parnell'.[117] This claim was based on a rather clumsy piece of subterfuge engaged in by Davitt in his Liverpool lecture. Davitt had said:

> Mr Parnell advocates peasant proprietary. I am in favour of the land becoming the national property of Ireland. If peasant proprietary is conceded either by Lord Salisbury when he gets into power or by Mr Gladstone ere he gets out, I am perfectly satisfied that the purchase money that must be advanced by the State for carrying out such a scheme will become the title deed of the State to the land of Ireland, and the nationalisation of the land will be the consequence.[118]

It was this argument that Davitt used later when he claimed to be in harmony with Parnell on the land agitation. Peasant proprietorship would lead to land nationalization. After his release from prison in early June, Thomas Brennan, the ex-Fenian radical secretary of the Land League, unambiguously endorsed Davitt's policy. On 17 June the *Irish World* published an interview he had with Henry George the previous week. With regard to Davitt, he declared:

> I heartily endorse Davitt's actions and speeches since his release. It is necessary to base our fight on the true principles, and that is to nationalise the whole soil of Ireland — that of the town as well as that of the country — by taking what is now paid in rents for the common benefit of the people. When we win the social independence of the people we shall also win the political independence of the nation.[119]

This was not a new position for Thomas Brennan: indeed, he had hinted at this policy during a Land League national convention held on 21 April

1881. However, Brennan, like Davitt, also expressed his unwillingness to break with Parnell.

Matthew Harris attacked Davitt again on 12 July while admitting to 'a feeling of regret that Mr Davitt should have got into bad hands'.[120] By July 1882 Davitt was painfully aware of the intense opposition in both Ireland and America to his policy of land nationalization. On 7 June he had optimistically written in his diary that the press were 'no more hostile to Nationalisation of the Land than they were at the beginning of the Land League to Peasant Proprietary. The world advances'.[121] However, the press were not the problem; the Land League was. The opposition to his new policy had been ferocious and Davitt was particularly worried by the imputation that he was attempting to divide the Land League. In an interview for the *Freeman's Journal* given at Antwerp on his way back from New York he sought to reassure his detractors:

> If the scheme of nationalisation were advocated under the existing political relations between England and Ireland, I admit that probably the majority of our people in America would be opposed to the adoption of such a scheme, as I have admitted that peasant proprietary will, in all probability, be the system that will be substituted for landlordism and, as I over and over declared, I can afford to wait for the adoption of my views by an Irish people that will be ruled over by an Irish Parliament . . . I will not fight the question of Nationalisation against peasant proprietary if there is the slightest chance of creating dissension in the Land League.[122]

On his return to Ireland he declined to mount a campaign to promote his alternative agrarian policy. In fact, from 1882 Davitt increasingly exercised his social radicalism in Britain rather than in Ireland. In 1902, he pessimistically commented that, though still a believer in land nationalization, 'there are some faiths which cannot move Irish mountains, and I have to confess that mine has proved to be one of them'.[123]

While Davitt was in the United States Henry George had written to Ford urging him to advise Davitt to stand his ground: 'He is first and Parnell is nowhere, if he will only stand firm and not get scared.'[124] However, when Davitt returned to Ireland at the end of July George knew that the attempt to radicalize the Irish agitation was lost. He noticed a distinct change in Davitt and adduced that he was worried by the accusation that he had become a tool of his. This was an unfounded charge, wrote George to Ford, because 'no one could have made him my "trumpet"'. He continued:

> For in public and in private I have been engaged in pushing him to the front as the 'great leader'. But his enemies . . . charged him with being captured by Henry George and the *Irish World* — they saw that annoyed and affected him, and then they pushed it. All he had to do was simply to go forward and not mind them. But even their talk affected him so much

that he was oft afraid to be seen with me or to have me go where he went.
And so they made him morbidly afraid of the *Irish World*. It seems to me
pitiable weakness when a man's enemies can thus make him afraid of and
unjust to his friends.[125]

George retained much respect for Davitt but he realized that he could no
longer rely on him in public.

The confrontation between Michael Davitt and the Land League stymied
George's plans for Ireland. More and more he turned to Britain where his
ideas had found a sympathetic audience among advanced Radicals. Between
February and May 1882 George had spent most of his time in Britain and
his lectures had extended his influence and brought him closer to the British
land nationalization movement. Shortly after his arrival in Britain he had
attended and spoken at the annual conference of the Land Nationalization
Society in London.[126] In April an acquaintance, Walter Wren, had brought
him to dinner at the Reform Club where they dined with the Radical MPs,
John Bright and Joseph Chamberlain. George found Chamberlain, a member
of the Cabinet, to be 'an extremely bright man' and Chamberlain did develop
an interest in George's theories.[127] Bright, George decided, 'has got to the
end of his tether and will never get past where he is now'.[128] In fact, Bright
later admitted that he could not make 'head nor tail' of George's theories
and condemned *Progress and Poverty* for suggesting that 'any class may be
robbed if the nation or the poor require relief'.[129] After his return to Ireland
in May George continued to make occasional trips to Britain to spread his
message.

In Ireland he maintained his connection with the Land League movement,
such as it was, and in August attended the conference of the Irish Labour
League which, in part, operated as a legal substitute for the suppressed Land
League.[130] Also in August George had travelled west with James Leith
Joynes, an Eton master and later a leading British socialist, and after visiting
Matthew Harris in Ballinasloe they drove across country to Loughrea. They
were arrested almost as soon as they arrived in the town. After being searched,
questioned and detained for three hours they were brought before a resident magistrate who promptly released them.[131] Following a night's sleep
George and Joynes carried on to Athenry where George was once again
arrested as he was about to board a train. This time he was detained for
some ten hours. 'The reason given to the magistrate for my arrest', he later
claimed in a letter to *The Times*, 'was that I had consorted with suspicious
characters, in proof of which two constables swore that I had been seen
visiting the ruins of the old abbey with the Catholic curate, and going into
the shops of three suspects! The irony of the thing is that these three suspects
were sent to gaol some eight months ago, and are there still.'[132] George was
released apparently after the Chief Secretary for Ireland, G.O. Trevelyan,
sent telegrams to local officials in Athenry.[133] Joseph Cowen, the English

Radical MP, brought the matter up in the House of Commons on two consecutive days and it made international news.[134] Moreover, Joynes had come to Ireland with an agreement to provide reports for the conservative newspaper, *The Times*. On 4 September the paper published a lengthy submission detailing the arrests but in a leader gave its own attitude to the events, claiming that Joynes 'has himself chiefly to thank for the unexpected turn of his adventure'.

> Our readers will probably be of opinion that they got off very easily from a trouble of their own creating. One of them may not unfairly be described as a suspicious character. The other had taken great pains to make himself resemble one. The police, we think, did no more than their duty both in arresting them and in letting them go when the *prima facie* suspicion they had excited was not so confirmed as to justify their further detention.[135]

Later in the year Joynes published his account of his visit to Ireland and the arrests in a short book entitled *The Adventures of a Tourist in Ireland*. For his troubles he lost his job at Eton.[136] August also saw a futile effort by H.M. Hyndman and Peter O'Leary, a supporter of the Irish rural labourers' movement, to change the objective of the still-legal Land League of Great Britain from one of peasant proprietorship to one of land nationalization. None of the Irish MPs present at the annual convention spoke on the issue and, when put to a vote, O'Leary's motion was defeated by a large majority.[137]

George left Ireland for the United States on 4 October 1882.[138] On 1 October he was given a farewell dinner at the Gresham Hotel in Dublin. Davitt, John Ferguson, T.D. Sullivan and Dr Joseph Kenny were among the guests.[139] It was a quiet departure that excited no great interest in the national newspapers. On 3 October he travelled to Cork where he stayed overnight in the Victoria Hotel before departing from Queenstown on the following day. While in the Victoria Hotel he was visited by D.J. Galvin, the Mayor, and John O'Connor who had been a prominent member of the Cork Land League. The *Cork Examiner* also conducted an extensive interview with George where he explained his interest in land nationalization and criticized Parnell's policy of peasant proprietorship.[140] George had undoubtedly made an impact in Ireland but he had failed dismally in his attempt to win over the agrarian movement to a policy of land nationalization. His presence in Ireland had, however, given him access to Britain where his ideas received a more favourable reception. He had, at the very least, made people aware of his critique of the existing social formation.

THE RECEPTION OF HENRY GEORGE IN 1884

When Henry George returned to Ireland for a week in April 1884 his reception was tangibly different from that he had received in 1881. His earlier visit had coincided with the suppression of the Land League and the attitude had been very much one of all hands on deck. George's assistance at a difficult time had been both welcome and appreciated. By 1884 the climate had changed and Irish nationalism was less open towards foreign radicals. Moreover, while George's criticism of the Land League and peasant proprietorship had caused annoyance in 1882 it had not provoked a fissure between him and the Land League. In 1884 George's goodwill was of little interest to the Irish parliamentary party and his criticism of peasant proprietorship was seen as an attack on the nationalist platform.

Michael Davitt was aware of this altered atmosphere and he wrote warning George before his arrival in Dublin: 'We shall have to count upon the opposition of the Parliamentary influence as well as of the National League in Dublin.'[141] This indeed turned out to be the case. Even before George arrived R.J. Donnelly, of the Henry George reception committee, felt obliged at a meeting in Bray of the Parnellite nationalist organization, the National League, to point out that George was 'coming here, not to teach them Irish politics or nationality, but to instruct them in land reform'.[142] Speaking at the same meeting Davitt declared:

> With regard to Henry George's visit, he was invited here not to oust Mr Parnell from the leadership of the Irish people, not to supersede Mr O'Brien in the editorship of *United Ireland*, not to replace Alderman Meagher as Lord Mayor of Dublin, and not to interfere with anybody in Ireland except the landlords.[143]

Davitt went on to remind his audience that he 'and others advocated national proprietary against class proprietary, or the land for the people against peasant proprietary', because they had no confidence in class ownership. Also in April Davitt wrote an article for the British socialist monthly *Today*, which was edited by J.L. Joynes and Ernest Belfort Bax who were both members of the Democratic Federation. 'Peasant proprietary', he wrote, 'will not destroy, it will only extend the absolute ownership of land: *an ownership which will always be in the market for purchase and reconsolidation into larger estates.*'[144] The article restated his argument for land nationalization as a way of dealing with the Irish social problem.

Henry George lectured in Dublin and Belfast in April 1884. His Dublin meeting on 9 April was a resounding success that overshadowed the rest of his short visit, and the audience contained many of his friends from 1881–82 including Davitt, Donnelly, Amos Varian, Dr Joseph Kenny and J.B. Killen.[145] John Allingham, the Mayor of Waterford, presided and introduced George with a short speech in which he endorsed his views.[146] George unsurprisingly attacked peasant proprietorship by appealing to his urban Dublin audience: 'The land of the people meant the land for all the people, and this thing of peasant proprietary was not a leaning towards the land for the people, it was rather a leaning away from it. What would the men of Dublin gain from it? What would be gained for the whole people even if they were to make all the farmers of Ireland peasant proprietors?' From the audience somebody shouted: 'A new class of landlords!' 'Yes', replied George, 'and one that would be fully as hard and grasping.'[147] Unlike his earlier lectures George also took care to mark out the differences between his 'single tax' policy and the British idea of land nationalization. He did not mean 'making the land the property of the Government'. Rather, he meant 'making it the property of the people of the community'.[148] Both Donnelly and Davitt spoke afterwards in support of George and Donnelly declared that, although he was loyal to the National League, he believed that land nationalization should be added to the programme.

There was little chance of that happening. The week after his lecture *United Ireland*, the National League newspaper, mentioned that it had received a large number of communications commenting 'in more or less uncomplimentary terms' on George's visit.

> We can see no advantage in printing them. The incident is closed. His reception in Dublin must have made it clear to the dullest understanding that Mr George's attempts to discredit the Irish leaders and take the National platform to pieces were too ludicrous to be seriously resented, and the Irish people will have nothing to say to his plans for making the moon into green cheese.[149]

Later *United Ireland* accused George and Davitt of wishing to indulge in 'a chaotic socialist experiment'.[150] Worse still, Parnell launched a severe attack on George at a meeting in Drogheda on 15 April. The criticism was also intended for Michael Davitt. Parnell cautioned:

> It is necessary . . . to take advantage of this occasion to warn you against elements of future difficulty . . . and possibilities of grave disunion in our ranks, which may be obviated by my timely declaration. I refer to the project termed the nationalisation of land.[151]

Parnell went on to refute George's suggestion that the National League was being unfaithful to the motto of the Land League and he enunciated a strong defence of peasant proprietorship. Davitt later wrote to George: 'It is evident . . . that he meditates a direct attack on me soon.'[152] A direct confrontation between Parnell and Davitt did not materialize, however, until a number of years later and that was over quite a different matter. With George's departure for the United States the policy of land nationalization once again lost its immediacy in Ireland.

It is difficult to assess the depth of Henry George's influence in Ireland between 1881 and 1884. It is clear that the Irish parliamentary party stayed firmly with the objective of peasant proprietorship. Likewise, the tenant farmers who had much to gain from the official Land League policy were unlikely to evince much interest in nationalization of the land. Davitt and George's primary constituency was undoubtedly based on urban workers and agricultural labourers. When Matthew Harris spoke at a labourers' meeting in County Carlow in October 1882 he was followed by a speaker who declared 'the gospel preached by Michael Davitt and Henry George' to be 'the true solution of the question'.[153] Within the Land League several senior figures supported land nationalization although none of these could be said to be central among the national leadership except for Michael Davitt. However, John Ferguson, Thomas Brennan and Rev. Harold Rylett also accepted the policy.[154] Likewise, all George's lectures in Ireland contained a healthy contingent of former Central branch members on the platform. Dr Joseph Kenny, James Rourke, R.J. Donnelly, Amos Varian, Patrick A. Tyrrell, J.B. Killen and J.P. Quinn were the most consistent. Their presence does not, of course, prove their universal support for land nationalization, but it does indicate how seriously the Land Leaguers took George's policy of land reform. The influence of Davitt should not be overlooked here either.

Support for land nationalization was strong among Dublin radicals in the 1880s. Samuel Hayes, the Dublin socialist, claimed in 1885 to personally know at least thirty land nationalizers in the city.[155] Debates at the Saturday Club, where Dublin radical working men gathered to discuss social and political issues, were punctuated by references to land nationalization. Some participants conflated socialism and Georgite agrarian radicalism — one speaker, in December 1884, asserted that he was 'in favour of Socialism as advocated by Mr Henry George and Mr Michael Davitt'.[156] Shortly after its formation in late 1884 the Saturday Club held a debate on land nationalization. Such was the interest the discussion was adjourned to be carried on the following week. The *Freeman's Journal* reported the contributions of many of the participants and the overwhelming majority favoured nationalization.[157] In 1887 one of the first debates at the City of Dublin Workingmen's Club forum, which replaced the Saturday Club, was on land nationalization.[158] The strength of the policy can be roughly gauged from the fact that in 1891, when his political career was flailing, Parnell made the astonishing claim at a Dublin labour conference that he had 'always believed in the principle of nationalisation of the land'.[159] Parnell was, of course, being disingenuous. Nonetheless, it is important to note that he believed such sentiments would gain him support among Dublin's working classes.

Outside of Dublin it is more difficult to measure the success of George and Davitt's position. In Belfast there was certainly some support and Rev. J. Bruce Wallace, who invited George to lecture in 1885, assiduously promoted the policy into the 1890s. Indeed, in the final years of the 1880s and for the initial years of the next decade Wallace's newspapers, *Brotherhood* and the *Belfast Weekly Star*, made land nationalization their central principle.

George's influence was substantial within radical circles, such as they were in the 1880s, but his national influence was less important. Davitt could perhaps have compensated for this deficit but, out of fear of splitting the nationalist movement, he refrained from proselytizing. In 1890 *Brotherhood* commented: 'Mr Davitt, as everybody ought to know, is not an advocate of peasant-proprietary, but of making all land (apart from improvements) national property. Out of deference to Mr Parnell, and through fear of creating division among the Irish National Party, he has been for years somewhat silent on this topic.'[160] The important admission here is that not everybody in 1890 was aware that Davitt was a land nationalizer.

DUBLIN DEMOCRATIC ASSOCIATION

The Democratic Federation claimed no branch in Ireland between 1881 and 1885 despite the presence of some of its British members in the country shortly after its formation. Its members had been in Ireland to support the Land League and do not appear to have made any efforts to recruit. There were certainly foreign socialists in Dublin in the early 1880s and when *United Ireland* commented on an article by Hyndman in January 1884 it elicited a response from Irish supporters of socialism.[161] Admittedly, the most prolific defender of socialism, Patrick Webb, was resident in England but a letter also came from Limerick supporting the socialist movement. Both writers were acutely aware of the charge of 'cosmopolitism' that had injured Davitt and were quick to underline their nationalism. Webb wrote: 'And if I thought that by being a Socialist I was sacrificing one morsel of my principles as an Irish Nationalist, or that it would cause me to make one exertion the less for fatherland, I would never have become a Socialist.'[162] Likewise, the correspondent from Limerick defended the Democratic Federation while mentioning that he or she was of the opinion 'that one may be an Irish Nationalist and a Socialist, and I boast that I am both'.[163] Webb contributed a stream of letters advocating socialism.[164]

The attitude of the Democratic Federation (which became the Social Democratic Federation in August 1884) toward Ireland remained one of support for home rule and land reform. By 1884 it was less concerned with Ireland as attention was turned to recruitment and agitation in Britain, but in January the first issue of *Justice* restated its formal position: 'If there is one point on which we are more convinced than another it is that only by giving the completest self-government to Ireland can we prepare the ground for the growth of a good understanding between the democracies on both sides of St George's Channel.'[165] Later in the year J.L. Joynes wrote that while it was to be regretted that the class conflict in Ireland was 'complicated by the idea of nationality', socialists must recognize 'the entire right of the

Irish to settle their own difficulties, and to work out the solution of their own economical problem in their own way'.[166] The SDF had some sympathizers in Ireland during 1884 and *Justice* was available for sale in shops in Dublin and Derry by July.[167] For socialists and radicals the formation of the Saturday Club in Dublin in November was an important departure. The club, which met on Saturday evenings in the Rotunda, provided a debating forum which was independent of the nationalist movement. Social and political issues were discussed and the attendance was generally impressive with hundreds at some debates. Moreover, the *Freeman's Journal* carried extensive reports on the club meetings every Monday. As a result advanced ideas articulated during the debates often found their way into many Irish homes.

The Saturday Club also brought socialists and radicals into regular contact with each other. Its formation and the links it engendered probably encouraged those who attempted in December 1884 to form a branch of the SDF in Dublin. On 20 December *Justice* carried a letter signed by Samuel Hayes, Alexander Stewart and Richard Grace Russell informing Dublin readers of this endeavour to form a section. All three were involved with the Saturday Club. In early January 1885 *Justice* received another report from Dublin which indicated that an SDF branch had still not been founded although it asserted that 'the ground has been broken' and that they were putting forward their arguments at meetings of the National League.[168] 'Our attacks on the plunderers condemning profit-mongering in every shape are freely accepted and applauded.' At the Saturday Club, which was described as 'the only free public platform in Dublin', R.G. Russell had spoken in favour of land nationalization although he cautioned that it did not 'go far enough'. *Justice* also mentioned that another socialist, Robert Johnson, had spoken the same night. Johnson, according to the *Freeman's Journal*, claimed to be a follower of Henry George and Michael Davitt.[169] Likewise, Alexander Stewart argued for nationalization of the land and professed his admiration for George and Davitt. He was opposed to landlordism 'and the principle by which the working man was deprived of the fruits of his honest toil'.[170]

On 17 January *Justice* published a short notice inviting all 'the Dublin readers' to a meeting in the Oddfellows Hall in Upper Abbey Street the following day. Hayes, Stewart and Russell clearly intended to inaugurate a Dublin branch of the SDF at this meeting but the outcome was more complicated. The group had received a letter from the Socialist League which had seceded from the SDF in December and this introduced some confusion. It was decided, wrote Samuel Hayes eight months later, not to affiliate to either the SDF or the Socialist League 'because it would frighten away any who would be disposed to consider our principles, besides that all the influence of the Roman Catholic Church would be levelled against us, as also of the National League'.[171] The meeting decided to form 'a Democratic Association and advance our principles here without calling them by the name of Socialism'.[172] They adopted the name Dublin Democratic Association (DDA) which stated that its objective was 'to promote and defend the rights of labour, and to restore the land to the people'.[173] A committee was appointed at the 18 January meeting with a mandate to draw up rules and regulations for the association.[174] Alexander Stewart was appointed secretary and James Doyle was made treasurer.[175] Both Stewart and Doyle were officials in the Dublin branch of the Amalgamated Society of Engineers.[176]

Before its dissolution in May the Dublin Democratic Association had a membership of about sixty people.[177] It is possible to make an educated guess at the political composition if we accept that there were no great changes in Dublin between May and September. In September Hayes estimated that there were approximately fifteen socialists in the city and twice that many land nationalizers.[178] That would account for forty-five of the sixty members; the other fifteen or so were probably political radicals of various types. Land nationalizers certainly played leading roles in the DDA, and socialists such as Russell and Stewart displayed a pronounced interest in the policy. It is possible to positively identify only a handful of the membership: R.G. Russell, Samuel Hayes, Alexander Stewart, James Doyle, Amos Varian, Adam O'Toole, D. O'Malley, Thomas Fitzpatrick, Andrew Byrne, Patrick A. Tyrrell and Edward O'Connor.[179]

Two of these, Varian and Tyrrell, were former members of the Central branch of the Land League.[180] Varian, a Unitarian and originally from Cork, was undoubtedly the most widely known recruit and he had been through a variety of organizations since the suppression of the Land League. By occupation he was a merchant with a brush-manufacturing business in Talbot Street.[181] He had been vice-president of the Dublin Total Abstinence League and was a member of the short-lived Dublin Franchise and Industrial Association.[182] In 1882 he had been chairman of the important Political Prisoners Aid Society and he was also a member of the Irish Labour League.[183] The Labour League, or Irish Labour and Industrial Union, existed in 1882 ostensibly to promote the interests of agricultural labourers who felt entitled to a dividend for assisting the tenant farmers in the 'land war'. In the end it was dominated by Parnell and the parliamentary party and became not much more than a lightly veiled front for the Land League.[184] 'The principal officers of the Labour League', according to a police report, 'were at one time officers of the Land League.'[185] Varian and Tyrrell were both supporters of Michael Davitt and Varian was a radical home ruler who, while supporting an extension of the franchise, saw it as 'only patching new cloth upon an old garment'. What was required he argued were new institutions dedicated 'to liberty, equality and fraternity'. He had been president of the Davitt branch of the Land League and later was a leading member of the Davitt branch of the National League which included radicals like R.J. Donnelly, James Poole and, naturally, Michael Davitt (as honorary president).[186]

Adam O'Toole, another leading DDA member, was a former member of the Dublin branch of the First International.[187] He encapsulated the close relationship between socialism and land nationalization. While he spoke in favour of socialism in late 1887 it is clear that in 1885 he was a land nationalizer.[188] Indeed, O'Toole had been a supporter of *The Radical* and in June 1882 had written a long letter to that paper praising Davitt and suggesting that nothing 'will ever satisfy the Irish people but, to use Michael Davitt's words, "a return to the National System", i.e. Land Nationalisation'.[189] Although socialists and land nationalizers worked together in the Dublin Democratic Association it would be a mistake to conflate the two policies. At a socialist meeting in 1886 one Dublin radical declared that he 'would go in for nationalisation of the land. As to Anarchy, the Anarchist would be the first man to call for a policeman if a corner boy attacked him. Men could not suddenly become angels on earth, even under the Socialistic system'.[190] It is true that this speaker was attacking what would be seen as the wilder shores of socialism but his remarks exemplify the real division that existed between the two currents of social radicalism. Land nationalizers and socialists viewed the world from different perspectives, and the land reformers were inevitably of a less radical hue.

The DDA held its second meeting on 25 January and it was decided to hold a series of twelve public meetings 'for the advancement of democratic principles'.[191] The first public meeting was held on 5 February in the Oddfellows Hall with James Doyle in the chair. The subject under discussion was artisans' dwellings and Alexander Stewart moved a resolution demanding that Dublin Corporation build healthy homes for the working classes and let them 'at a rent to cover the interest of capital, taxes and cost of maintenance alone'.[192] This objective was reminiscent of some of the 'stepping stone' proposals advocated by the SDF which so irritated the group that had split to form the Socialist League. Indeed, the DDA was to be consistent in its promotion of social reforms and Alexander Stewart and Samuel Hayes helped to organize a debate on artisans' dwellings at the City of Dublin Workingmen's Club shortly after their own meeting.[193] Stewart lectured again on the housing problem on 9 and 13 April.[194] At the 5 February Democratic Association meeting discomfort with the National League was also voiced. A member by the name of Allen remarked that 'although he was as strong a Nationalist as anyone in the room he did not believe the interests of working men should be trampled underfoot in the interests of the tenant farmers'.[195] R.G. Russell also expressed his opinion that the housing issue was only one part of the social question and they 'should strike at the root of the whole social question by considering the question of private property in land'.[196]

Over the next few months the DDA continued to organize meetings which were advertised in the *Freeman's Journal*. Adam O'Toole spoke on 'Democracy Defined', Amos Varian on 'Franchise and Representation', Edward O'Connor on 'The Social Question', Alexander Stewart on 'Democratic Demands' and Andrew Byrne on 'The Social Revolution'.[197] Members of the DDA also used the Saturday club as a forum for political argument. A meeting of the club on 31 January saw a heated dispute on socialism. A foreign socialist, probably the German-Dane Fritz Schumann, called on workers to support trade unionism and 'to connect themselves with their toiling brethren in England and upon the Continent'.[198] Schumann, who was later a member of the Socialist League, was a Marxist. In 1881 he had written to a friend in London: 'You are aware that in Germany and in France, and Belgium, Holland, Denmark, Italy (England has not advanced to that point), the Socialists divided themselves in two camps: 1st, the Revolutionary party, and 2nd, the Reform party. We know (at least, we think so) that our last battle will be with the Reformers, they are really now our worst enemy.'[199] At the Saturday Club his argument was direct.

> He had heard them condemn the connection of working men with Monsieur Rochfort. He would say nothing of that; but would advise them to inscribe upon their banners such names as Dr Karl Marx, Engels, or Lassalle, men who . . . had spent their lives in the effort to raise and improve the condition of workingmen. Karl Marx was the great prophet of the labour movement, and his works upon nationalisation were the foundations upon which the theories of Henry George and other minor reformers were built.[200]

Michael Cusack, who had helped found the Gaelic Athletic Association, was outraged; he charged that Marx was the creator of an organization in which 'such destructive agents as petroleum oil had been employed', and he implored the audience to leave such 'international business' alone. After a rambling speech and a confrontation with Alexander Stewart, Cusack stalked out of the building.[201]

Cusack was not alone in his horror of socialism. At the end of March *Justice* reported that Alexander Stewart had been dismissed by his employers 'for his advocacy of Socialism as a remedy for the wrongs of labour'.[202] Stewart was born in Glasgow in 1854. At the age of twenty-one he had been elected to represent his trade, patternmakers, on Glasgow Trades Council and later still he had been chairman of the Glasgow Land League.[203] In Dublin he was an active trade unionist and president of the local branch of the Amalgamated Society of Engineers.[204] He would seem to have left Dublin during the summer of 1885 for England. In 1889 he was elected to the School

Board in Newcastle-on-Tyne as an independent Labour candidate.[205] In 1885 he had indicated his belief in the efficacy of parliamentary politics: 'If certain classes were to obtain the support of working men at the elections, they must be prepared in return to accept delegates from working men's unions or organisations, or devise some means by which representative workmen should be returned to Parliament.'[206] Stewart moved to Belfast in the early 1890s where he was a member of the Independent Labour Party, and in the 1920s he was still involved in labour politics in the city.[207]

At the beginning of April members of the Dublin Democratic Association participated in a debate at the Saturday Club on women's suffrage. In 1885 the Women's Suffrage Association highlighted the anti-democratic restriction of the parliamentary franchise with a series of meetings in Dublin. The organization was arguing for the limited measure of votes for 'all unmarried women who possess the qualifications which entitle men to vote'.[208] This demand, despite its exclusion of married women, was quite radical and progressive. The argumentation used by some supporters, however, was not always particularly advanced. Thus, Alfred Webb at a suffrage meeting proposed the official motion and said that he knew 'that women of the highest education and intelligence who were householders and taxpayers would not have a vote, while the very gatekeepers who attended to the entrance at their residences would be entitled to exercise the franchise'.[209] Andrew Byrne chaired the April debate at the Saturday Club and those present seemed evenly divided on the issue. Those against votes for women laced their arguments with a condescending sexism. One speaker referred to the Ladies' Land League and said that he was glad when their work ceased 'and they retired to the obscurity which was far more honourable to them than the field of politics'. Another asked if any gentleman would like 'to see his wife at the polling booth rubbing skirts with a fish woman from Pill-lane'.[210] That comment evoked shouts of protest from angry workers who saw it as a conservative argument. Amos Varian spoke strongly in favour of women's suffrage saying that there was 'nothing in the principle of government restricting it to men, for [the] mind was neither masculine nor feminine'. He held that the right to vote for women was a 'just and inalienable right'.[211] Adam O'Toole also spoke in support of women's rights and James A. Poole remarked that he could not see why married women were excluded from the demand. Poole, who was possibly a member of the DDA, has been identified by C.D. Greaves as an acquaintance of Friedrich Engels.[212] In the early 1880s, Poole, a Catholic who held an MA degree from Trinity College, ran an academy at 29 Harcourt Street where he held classes to prepare candidates for civil service, Royal Irish Constabulary, solicitors' apprentice and other examinations.[213]

The Dublin Democratic Association held a day-long conference in the Oddfellows Hall on 3 May.[214] It was intended as a first 'quarterly conference' but there were not to be any more. According to Samuel Hayes the DDA had by May become a financial failure and the membership had diminished. He partially blamed this on the National League 'who did all they could to crush it'.[215] It was decided to adjourn until October and attempt to resume then. That never happened. The Dublin Democratic Association, despite its short life, undoubtedly marks the beginning of modern socialism in Ireland. While not formally socialist the DDA was quite closely associated with the Social Democratic Federation, and *Justice* carried regular notices of its meetings in Dublin. Hayes later commented that if they had formed an open socialist society they would have affiliated with the SDF 'who supplied us with a great quantity of literature which we distributed broadcast throughout the city'.[216] In a sense, with its admixture of socialists and land reformers, the DDA almost mirrors the Democratic Federation in its early days.

NOTES AND REFERENCES

1   Irish historians have made occasional glancing references to Henry George but, by and large, only with reference to his connection with Michael Davitt. His visits to Ireland receive a constrained treatment in a number of studies on his influence in Britain. See also the Irish sections in the biographical studies. C.A. Barker, *Henry George* (New York, 1955), pp. 341–77; Peter d'Alroy Jones, 'Henry George and British socialism, 1879–1931', MA thesis, Victoria University of Manchester, 1953, pp. 81–5, 96–112; E.P. Lawrence, *Henry George in the British Isles* (Michigan, 1957), pp. 13–28.

2   John W. Boyle, *The Irish Labor Movement in the Nineteenth Century* (Washington, 1988); Emmet O'Connor, *A Labour History of Ireland, 1824–1960* (Dublin, 1992). Henry George is nowhere mentioned in O'Connor's work while Boyle only mentions him in passing and ignores his first, and longest, visit to Ireland.

3   When I say that the agrarian movement was at its height I am referring generally to the 'first phase' of the agitation (1879–82) which is commonly known as the 'land war'.

4   J.A. Hobson, 'The influence of Henry George in England', *The Fortnightly Review*, 1 Dec. 1897, p. 844.

5   E.P. Lawrence, op. cit.; John Saville, 'Henry George and the British labour movement', *Science and Society*, vol. xxiv, Fall 1960; John Plowright, 'Political economy and Christian polity: the influence of Henry George in England reassessed', *Victorian Studies*, vol. xxx, no. 2, Winter 1987. Saville accepts George's importance although he rejects the alleged primacy of Henry George in the emergence of the British 'socialist revival'.

6   Henry Pelling, *America and the British Left: From Bright to Bevan* (London, 1956), p. 56.

7   W.T. Stead, 'The Labour Party and the books that helped to make it', *Review of Reviews*, pt xxxiii, 1906, p. 571.

8 Andreas Scheu to Reeves, 21 Sept. 1884, Andreas Scheu Papers, IISH.

9 Karl Marx to F.A. Sorge, 20 June 1881, in Karl Marx and Friedrich Engels, *Selected Correspondence* (Moscow, 1965), p. 343. Hereafter cited as *Sel. Corr.*

10 John Rae, *Contemporary Socialism* (London, 1884), p. vi.

11 E.P. Lawrence, 'Henry George's British mission', *American Quarterly*, vol. 51, no. 3, 1951, p. 233.

12 Henry George, *Progress and Poverty: An Inquiry into the Cause of Industrial Depressions, and of Increase of Want with Increase of Wealth. The Remedy* (London, 1889), p. 233.

13 ibid., p. 239.

14 James J. Shaw, 'The nationalisation of the land', *Journal of the Statistical and Social Inquiry Society of Ireland*, pt lxii, July 1884, p. 504. Shaw was perfectly correct in his reference to Marx's adverse attitude to the content of George's theories. Marx had written privately: 'The whole thing is . . . simply a socialistically decked-out attempt to *save capitalist rule* and actually *re-establish* it on *an even wider basis* than its present one. This cloven hoof . . . peeps out unmistakably from the declamations of Henry George'. (Marx to F.A. Sorge, 20 June 1881, *Sel. Corr.*, p. 343.) Shaw went on to suggest that George himself was likely to be driven to socialism because 'how can he answer Karl Marx, who says that it is also just to attack the vaster and more baleful monopoly of capital?' (James J. Shaw, op. cit., p. 506.)

15 During his 1881–82 visit George was absent from Ireland, while he visited Britain, for most of February to May 1882.

16 Henry George, op. cit., pp. 86–9.

17 ibid., pp. 89–90.

18 Henry George, *The Irish Land Question: What it Involves and how alone it can be Settled. An Appeal to the Land Leagues* (London, 1881), p. 1.

19 ibid., pp. 1–2.

20 ibid., pp. 6–10.

21 ibid., p. 6.

22 He argued vehemently against compensating landlords and declared that it was wrong to suggest that 'the Creator . . . intended a few to roll in luxury, while their fellows toiled and starved for them'. (ibid., p. 22.)

23 ibid., p. 33.

24 ibid., p. 35.

25 ibid., p. 35.

26 ibid., p. 36.

27 A.R. Wallace, 'How to nationalise the land: a radical solution of the Irish land problem', *Contemporary Review*, Nov. 1880; R. Harrison, 'The Land and Labour League (some new light on working class politics in the eighteen seventies)', *Bulletin of the International Institute for Social History, Amsterdam*, no. 3, 1953.

28 Henry George to Patrick Ford, 10 Nov. 1881, Henry George Papers, NYPL.

29 C.A. Barker, op. cit., p. 346.

30 Michael Davitt, *The Fall of Feudalism in Ireland* (London, 1904), p. 716.

31 N.D. Palmer, *The Irish Land League Crisis* (New Haven, 1940), pp. 124–5.

32 Paul Bew, *Land and the National Question in Ireland, 1858–82* (Dublin, 1978), p. 137.

33   Henry George to Patrick Ford, 10 Nov. 1881, Henry George Papers, NYPL.
34   ibid.
35   ibid.
36   Henry George to Patrick Ford, 22 Nov. 1881, Henry George Papers, NYPL.
37   *Irish Times*, 26 Nov. 1881; *Freeman's Journal*, 26 Nov. 1881, 13 Mar. 1882.
38   On the Ladies' Land League, see Margaret Ward, *Unmanageable Revolutionaries: Women and Irish Nationalism* (Dingle, 1983), pp. 4–39. Ward, however, is mistaken in her assertion that the Ladies' Land League in Ireland arose from a letter written to a Dublin newspaper by Fanny Parnell and published on 1 January 1881. In fact, branches of the Ladies' Land League had already been formed in Cork by December 1880. The Cork women adopted the following pledge:

> We'll never wed the Land League foes,
> Nor court those land-grabbing paupers
> These are the pledges, one and all,
> Of old Ireland's patriot daughters.
>
> (*Cork Examiner*, 23 Dec. 1880.)

39   *Freeman's Journal*, 12 June 1882.
40   Margaret Ward, op. cit., pp. 31–5.
41   Henry George to Patrick Ford, 10 Nov. 1881, Henry George Papers, NYPL.
42   ibid.
43   Henry George to Thomas Briggs, 27 Oct. 1881, published in *The Radical*, 5 Nov. 1881.
44   *Freeman's Journal*, 10, 12 Nov. 1881.
45   *Freeman's Journal*, 15 Nov. 1881.
46   ibid.
47   ibid.
48   ibid.
49   Henry George to Patrick Ford, 28 Feb. 1882, Henry George Papers, NYPL.
50   *Freeman's Journal*, 15 Nov. 1881.
51   Henry George to Patrick Ford, 15 Nov. 1881, Henry George Papers, NYPL.
52   Henry George to Helen Taylor, 20 Nov. 1881, Henry George Papers, NYPL.
53   *Belfast Morning News*, interview republished in *The Radical*, 26 Nov. 1881.
54   Henry George to Patrick Ford, 8 Dec. 1881, Henry George Papers, NYPL.
55   *Irish World*, 3 Dec. 1881.
56   Henry George to Patrick Ford, 28 Dec. 1881, Henry George Papers, NYPL.
57   ibid.
58   ibid.
59   George had always seen an alliance with the 'English democracy' as essential if the Irish agitation was to have any lasting impact. Before he sailed for Ireland he wrote to the English advanced Radical, William Webster: 'I have long regarded England as the real centre of the great fight, not only because of the conditions which bring, or ought to bring, the evils of the land monopoly into peculiar clearness, but because it is still to a large extent the intellectual centre of the English-speaking peoples.' (*The Radical*, 3 Sept. 1881.) He wanted the Irish agrarian agitation to spill over into Britain.
60   *Irish World*, 21 Jan. 1882.

61 *Irish World*, 28 Jan. 1882. In March 1882 Ford was claiming the following outlets in Ireland — Dublin: Mrs Keogh, 141 Upper Dorset Street; M. Cleary, 7 Great Brunswick Street; C. Walsh, 39 Upper Stephen Street; Longford: Mr B.L. McHugh, Richmond Street; Belfast: Mr D. O'Hara, 70 Hercules Street; T.P. McCormack, 43 Davis Street; Fermanagh: Patrick Cox, Rosslea; Monaghan: James Rice, Coach Factory; Limerick: Mr T. O'Connor, 3 Military Road; Mayo: Mrs Connolly, Castlebar; John O'Kane, The Square, Claremorris; Galway: Patrick Lyons, Shop Street, Tuam; Cork: S. Tracy, 13 Great Georges Street; D. O'Herlihy, 10 Great Georges Street West. (*Irish World*, 25 Mar. 1882.)

62 *Cork Examiner*, 20 Jan. 1882.

63 Henry George to Patrick Ford, 7 Jan. 1882, Henry George Papers, NYPL.

64 ibid.

65 *Irish World*, 4 Mar. 1882.

66 Henry George to Patrick Ford, 14 Jan. 1882, Henry George Papers, NYPL.

67 Henry George to Patrick Ford, 4 Feb. 1882, Henry George Papers, NYPL.

68 *Ulster Examiner*, 4 Feb. 1882; *Irish World*, 25 Mar. 1882.

69 *Freeman's Journal*, 28 Feb., 1882.

70 Henry George to Patrick Ford, 21 Jan. 1882, Henry George Papers, NYPL.

71 Henry George to Patrick Ford, 28 Feb. 1882, Henry George Papers, NYPL.

72 Henry George to Patrick Ford, n.d. but late Feb. 1882, Henry George Papers, NYPL.

73 Henry George to Patrick Ford, 10 Nov. 1881, Henry George Papers, NYPL.

74 *Freeman's Journal*, 18 Nov. 1881.

75 Henry George to Patrick Ford, 22 Nov. 1881, Henry George Papers, NYPL.

76 ibid.

77 Henry George to Patrick Ford, 8 Dec. 1881, Henry George Papers, NYPL.

78 Henry George to Patrick Ford, 28 Dec. 1881, Henry George Papers, NYPL.

79 Henry George to Patrick Ford, 8 Dec. 1881, Henry George Papers, NYPL.

80 Wilfred Scawen Blunt, *The Land War in Ireland: Being a Personal Narrative of Events* (London, 1912), p. 62. Blunt mistakenly claimed that George was 'violently atheistical' in this book (p. 317). The opposite, in fact, was true and George's polemics are infused with references to God.

81 Henry George to Patrick Ford, 22 Nov. 1881, Henry George Papers, NYPL.

82 H.M. Hyndman, *Further Reminiscences* (London, 1912), p. 43.

83 T.W. Moody, 'Michael Davitt and the British labour movement, 1882–1906', *Transactions of the Royal Historical Society*, vol. ii, 1953.

84 Francis Sheehy-Skeffington, *Michael Davitt* (London, 1967), pp. 191–2, 218.

85 Henry George, 'Letter in defence of Michael Davitt and the Irish Land League' (1882), Henry George Papers, NYPL.

86 F.S.L. Lyons, *Charles Stewart Parnell* (London, 1977), pp. 230–1.

87 *The Nation*, 1 July 1882.

88 *The Nation*, 8 July 1882.

89 *Irish World*, 3 June 1882.

90 ibid.

91 Diary 1882, Michael Davitt Papers, TCD.

92 *Irish World*, 20 May 1882.

100 *THE ORIGINS OF MODERN IRISH SOCIALISM*

93 Quoted in Malcolm Brown, *The Politics of Irish Literature: From Thomas Davis to W.B. Yeats* (Washington, 1972), p. 291. John O'Leary went further in a letter to John Devoy where he claimed to have met Davitt who had allegedly told him that he had become 'a convinced Socialist, whatever that may exactly mean'. See John O'Leary to John Devoy, 14 June 1882, in William O'Brien and Desmond Ryan (eds.), *Devoy's Postbag, 1880–1928* (Dublin, 1979), p. 125.

94 *Connaught Telegraph*, 15 July 1882.

95 F.S.L. Lyons, op. cit., p. 233.

96 *Manchester Examiner and Times*, 22 May 1882.

97 ibid.

98 *Freeman's Journal*, 11 July 1882.

99 *Freeman's Journal*, 7 June 1882.

100 ibid.

101 *Freeman's Journal*, 9 June 1882.

102 ibid.

103 *Freeman's Journal*, 12 June 1882.

104 ibid.

105 ibid.

106 *Freeman's Journal*, 19 June 1882.

107 F.S.L. Lyons, op. cit., p. 233.

108 *Freeman's Journal*, 17 June 1882.

109 *Freeman's Journal*, 21 June 1882.

110 ibid.

111 ibid. Harris was not alone in his scepticism of British advanced Radicalism. The Land Leaguer and Invincible, Patrick J.P. Tynan, commented in later years: 'Some Irish nationalists at this time formed the acquaintance of many of the leading English republicans, a small body of liberty-loving intelligent men. They tried to ignore, however, the national difference of the two peoples; and disregarded the fact, that extreme as they were on all social issues, on the question of Ireland they were as intolerant as the most bigoted Tory . . . On this subject their ideas of union were that Irishmen should become Englishmen. In their ranks were many amiable and liberty-loving ladies. Miss Helen Taylor and Miss Jessie Craigen were prominent among these.' (P.J.P. Tynan, *The Irish National Invincibles and their Times* [London, 1894], p. 238.)

112 Joseph Lee, *The Modernisation of Irish Society, 1848–1918* (Dublin, 1973), p. 69.

113 *Connaught Telegraph*, 24 June 1882.

114 *Connaught Telegraph*, 1 July 1882.

115 *Freeman's Journal*, 10 July 1882; *Connaught Telegraph*, 15 July 1882.

116 *Freeman's Journal*, 26 June, 5 July 1882.

117 *Freeman's Journal*, 5 July 1882.

118 *Freeman's Journal*, 7 June 1882.

119 *Irish World*, 17 June 1882. Social radicalism was an important component of Thomas Brennan's political thought and had been throughout the Land League agitation. Like Michael Davitt, he argued that the Land League should view the British working class in a more favourable light. At a land demonstration in Carlow in March 1881 he argued: 'I think there is fast growing up a feeling among workingmen of all countries that they should join in a grand movement

for the redemption of labour from the coercion of moneyed power. We have no fight with the English workingmen; they have been betrayed, as you have often been betrayed, by men who are anxious only for their own interests . . . We need to commence by uniting the workingmen in Ireland, no matter how they work or at what altar they kneel.' (*Freeman's Journal*, 21 Mar. 1881.)

120 *Freeman's Journal*, 12 July 1882.
121 Diary 1882, Michael Davitt Papers, TCD.
122 *Freeman's Journal*, 29 July 1882.
123 T.W. Moody, op. cit., *passim*. William O'Brien and Desmond Ryan (eds.), op. cit., p. 120fn.
124 Henry George to Patrick Ford, 20 June 1882, Henry George Papers, NYPL.
125 Henry George to Patrick Ford, 4 Aug. 1882, Henry George Papers, NYPL.
126 *Freeman's Journal*, 1 Feb. 1882. Among those present were Helen Taylor, Alfred Wallace and Dr G.B. Clarke.
127 Henry George to Patrick Ford, 22 Apr. 1882, Henry George Papers, NYPL.
128 ibid.
129 Letter from John Bright (1882), published in the *Daily Telegraph*, 12 Oct. 1909.
130 *Freeman's Journal*, 22 Aug. 1882.
131 J.L. Joynes, *The Adventures of a Tourist in Ireland* (London, 1882), pp. 19–23.
132 *Times*, 6 Sept. 1882.
133 C.A. Barker, op. cit., p. 371.
134 *Freeman's Journal*, 12 Aug. 1882; C.A. Barker, op. cit., pp. 371–2.
135 *Times*, 4 Sept. 1882.
136 J.L. Joynes to Henry George, 7 Dec. 1882, Henry George Papers, NYPL.
137 *Cork Examiner*, 14 Aug. 1882.
138 C.A. Barker, op. cit., p. 377.
139 *Freeman's Journal*, 2 Oct. 1882.
140 *Cork Examiner*, 4 Oct. 1882.
141 Michael Davitt to Henry George, 19 Mar. 1884, Henry George Papers, NYPL.
142 *United Ireland*, 12 Apr. 1884.
143 ibid.
144 Michael Davitt, 'The Irish social problem', *Today*, no. 4, Apr. 1884, p. 254.
145 *Freeman's Journal*, 10 Apr. 1884; *Irish Times*, 10 Apr. 1884.
146 *Freeman's Journal*, 10 Apr. 1884.
147 *Irish Times*, 10 Apr. 1884.
148 *Freeman's Journal*, 10 Apr. 1884.
149 *United Ireland*, 19 Apr. 1884.
150 *United Ireland*, 2 Aug. 1884.
151 *Freeman's Journal*, 16 Apr. 1884.
152 Michael Davitt to Henry George, 8 Aug. 1884, Henry George Papers, NYPL.
153 *Cork Examiner*, 9 Oct. 1882.
154 *Freeman's Journal*, 5 July 1882; T.W. Moody, *Davitt and Irish Revolution, 1846–1882* (Oxford, 1982), p. 523; *Freeman's Journal*, 26 June 1882.
155 Samuel Hayes to H.H. Sparling, 12 Sept. 1885, Socialist League Papers, IISH.
156 *Freeman's Journal*, 22 Dec. 1884.
157 *Freeman's Journal*, 22, 29 Dec. 1884.
158 *Freeman's Journal*, 21 Mar. 1887.

159   *Freeman's Journal*, 16 Mar. 1891.
160   *Brotherhood*, 11 Jan. 1890.
161   *The Radical*, 28 May 1881; *United Ireland*, 5 Jan. 1884.
162   *United Ireland*, 12 Jan. 1884.
163   *United Ireland*, 19 Jan. 1884.
164   *United Ireland*, 12 Jan., 2, 9, 16 Feb. 1884.
165   *Justice*, 19 Jan. 1884.
166   *Justice*, 4 Oct. 1884.
167   *Justice*, 26 July 1884.
168   *Justice*, 3 Jan. 1885.
169   *Freeman's Journal*, 22 Dec. 1884.
170   ibid.
171   Samuel Hayes to H.H. Sparling, 12 Sept. 1885, Socialist League Papers, IISH.
172   ibid.
173   *Justice*, 14 Feb. 1885.
174   *Justice*, 24 Jan. 1885.
175   *Freeman's Journal*, 26 Mar. 1885; *Justice*, 21 Mar. 1885.
176   James Doyle to *The Commonweal*, 7 Mar. 1886, Socialist League Papers, IISH.
      Doyle had displayed an interest in socialism as far back as 1881 when, as
      secretary of the Dublin Amalgamated Society of Engineers, he had attended
      a lecture, chaired by T.D. Sullivan, on 'Economic Socialism'. (*Freeman's Jour-
      nal*, 21 Oct. 1881.) Doyle inclined very much toward Irish nationalism and
      in one letter, to William Morris, he wrote: 'In speaking of Ireland I do not
      mean a foreign colony settled about Belfast, I mean the natives (aborigines).'
      (James Doyle to William Morris, 18 July 1886, Socialist League Papers, IISH.)
      However, in another letter, criticizing the distribution in Ireland of leaflets ad-
      dressed to English workers, he spoke of the necessity of persuading Irish
      workers to 'accept the gospel of Socialism as far more preferable to the very
      doubtful but hard won "advantages" of national independence'. (James Doyle
      to *The Commonweal*, 8 Oct. 1886, Socialist League Papers, IISH.)
177   Samuel Hayes to H.H. Sparling, 12 Sept. 1885, Socialist League Papers, IISH.
178   ibid.
179   *Justice*, 14 Feb., 21 Mar. 1885; *Freeman's Journal*, 16 Apr. 1885. I have in-
      cluded Thomas Fitzpatrick in the list of Dublin Democratic Association
      members even though *Justice* refers to a 'P. Fitzpatrick'. Errors with initials
      were common in reports and Thomas Fitzpatrick, who joined the Socialist
      League later in 1885, is almost certainly the person referred to. See *Justice*,
      14 Feb. 1885.
180   T.W. Moody, *Davitt and Irish Revolution*, p. 576.
181   His business address was 92 Talbot Street. See *Thom's Official Directory of the
      United Kingdom of Great Britain and Ireland, 1882* (Dublin, 1882), pp. 1470,
      1767.
182   *Freeman's Journal*, 24 Oct., 14 Nov. 1881, 1 Aug. 1882. Varian strongly believed
      that the franchise should be extended. In February 1881, he asserted that British
      legislation in Ireland had been 'a failure' and that the country would remain
      'on the brink of revolution until such government is altered' and 'until the fran-
      chise is granted to the working classes'. (*Freeman's Journal*, 22 Feb. 1881.)

183 *Freeman's Journal*, 10 July, 11 Sept. 1882.

184 *Freeman's Journal*, 22 Aug. 1882.

185 DMP Files, 1882: Report from E.G. Jenkinson (Superintendent's Office, G. Division, 12 Aug. 1882), National Archives.

186 *Freeman's Journal*, 13 Apr. 1885, 21 Nov. 1883. Amos Varian (1823–1904) was influenced in his political thought by his Young Irelander brother, Isaac (1812–68), who had been jailed in Cork in 1848 along with his cousin, Ralph, following the Young Ireland rising at Ballingarry, Co. Tipperary. Isaac, who established the brush manufacturers which Amos later ran, had been centrally involved with the Desmond Club and wrote for *The Nation*. His best-known article, 'The Crisis', was published on 2 January 1847 and dealt with the Famine disaster. It was probably this article that Amos read to applause at a Land League meeting in July 1881 (see *Freeman's Journal*, 22 July 1881). Isaac's article argued that the experience of the Famine ought to encourage the Irish people to struggle for legislative independence; presumably Amos held that this point was similarly valid during the crisis of 1881.

187 *Justice*, 7 Jan. 1888.

188 ibid.; *Freeman's Journal*, 22 Dec. 1884.

189 *The Radical*, 3 June 1882.

190 *Freeman's Journal*, 15 Jan. 1886.

191 *Justice*, 31 Jan. 1885.

192 *Justice*, 14 Feb. 1885.

193 *Justice*, 7 Feb. 1885.

194 *Freeman's Journal*, 7, 13 Apr. 1885.

195 *Justice*, 14 Feb. 1885.

196 ibid.

197 *Justice*, 21 Mar., 4 Apr. 1885; *Freeman's Journal*, 28, 31 Mar., 14 Apr. 1885.

198 *Freeman's Journal*, 2 Feb. 1885.

199 Letter published in *The Radical*, 28 Mar. 1881.

200 *Freeman's Journal*, 2 Feb. 1885.

201 ibid.

202 *Justice*, 28 Mar. 1885.

203 Bob McClung, 'Alex Stewart, Belfast', *Labour Opposition*, July 1925.

204 *Freeman's Journal*, 13 Apr. 1885.

205 Bob McClung, op. cit.

206 *Freeman's Journal*, 5 Jan. 1885.

207 Bob McClung, op. cit. When the Northern Ireland Labour Party was founded in 1924 Alexander Stewart became its first president. Arthur Mitchell, *Labour in Irish Politics, 1890–1930* (Dublin, 1974), p. 221.

208 *Freeman's Journal*, 6, 7 Feb. 1885.

209 *Freeman's Journal*, 7 Feb. 1885.

210 *Freeman's Journal*, 6 Apr. 1885.

211 ibid.

212 C.D. Greaves, *The Irish Transport and General Workers' Union: The Formative Years, 1909–23* (Dublin, 1982), p. 4. Unfortunately, Greaves failed to cite his source for this information and his assertion that Poole was a 'friend' of Engels

is almost certainly an overstatement. Poole did display an interest in land nationalization and in April 1884 attended a lecture by Henry George in Dublin.

213 *Freeman's Journal*, 19 Sept., 1 Oct. 1881.
214 *Justice*, 18 Apr. 1885.
215 Samuel Hayes to H.H. Sparling, 12 Sept. 1885, Socialist League Papers, IISH.
216 ibid.

4.

The Socialist League in Dublin, 1885-87

The rebirth of the Democratic Federation as a thorough-going socialist organization in 1883 meant changes in the leadership. Gone, by late 1883, were most of those who had founded the federation in 1881 with H.M. Hyndman as a focus for advanced Radicalism. In their place the organization had attracted a steady trickle of workers and intellectuals who were ready to commit themselves wholeheartedly to socialism and who eschewed Radicalism as at best misguided and at worst capable, in the words of William Morris, of playing 'the part of reactionists in the first step towards the new order of things'.[1] This influx of eager and articulate converts, however, inevitably led to a challenge to Hyndman's rather presidential manner of running the federation, and ultimately to a damaging fissure within the leadership.

Although the publication of *Socialism Made Plain* marked the effective victory of socialism within the Democratic Federation, it was the annual conference of August 1884 that confirmed the trajectory. The conference, not unexpectedly, accepted the obvious and adopted the name Social Democratic Federation for the organization. More importantly, the Federation finally induced the Labour Emancipation League to affiliate by adopting five of the six points of the programme of the league. Joseph Lane, who distrusted Hyndman, was subsequently elected to the SDF Executive.[2] Moreover, Eleanor Marx and Dr Edward Aveling, neither admirers of Hyndman, also secured election to the executive. The conference decided to abolish the position of permanent president in the federation and, in the interests of greater democracy, allow the executive elect its chairperson at each meeting.[3] Hyndman was, in all but word, deposed and he no longer exercised an overwhelming influence on the leadership. He felt this deficit keenly and his pique was a significant factor in the ensuing split. 'Hyndman', wrote Morris to J.L. Joynes after the split, 'can accept only one position in such a body as the SDF — that of master; some may think that position on his part desirable; I don't and I cannot stand it.'[4] Initially the new executive felt unsure on the question of the rotating chairperson. Fortunately, Hyndman was unable to attend a meeting immediately after the conference and Morris was elected to the chair. Again at the subsequent meeting on 12 August Hyndman arrived late and found that Morris had once more replaced him as chairperson.[5] Writing confidentially to Andreas Scheu, Morris informed him of an attempt at this meeting to set aside the conference decision on the chairmanship: 'I spoke to them . . . pointing out to them that if they so much as discussed the question of the Chairmanship they were striking a blow at the roots of the Federation; that we (the Council) were the creation of the Conference, and that in attacking its authority we were attacking our own; and I finished by saying that I could not as chairman put any resolution for setting aside the decision of the Conference.'[6]

The divisions in the SDF, however, ran deeper than a dispute over Hyndman's presumptuousness. Andreas Scheu, the Austrian anti-parliamentary Marxist, had never got on with Hyndman, partly because of Hyndman's shoddy attitude towards foreigners in the British socialist movement but also because of Scheu's aversion to 'palliatives'.[7] Scheu believed that Hyndman's real objective was to create a parliamentary 'third force' that was capable 'of bringing down the Government . . . and forcing it by threats to carry out his wishes'.[8] Scheu was a believer in participatory revolution where the mass of people would move to overthrow the state — he did not believe in the existence of a 'parliamentary road to socialism'. Moreover, in common with other leading members, he disliked and objected to Hyndman's apparently cynical view of workers' political and industrial self-activity. For Hyndman, to use E.P. Thompson's phrase, social reforms 'were the carrot for the donkey: and the donkey was the people'.[9] W.J. Clarke, a member of the executive, had his own views on Hyndman's motives and his allegation of 'self-seeking' made to Hyndman supporters on the executive became one of the immediate causes of the split. An attempt was made to expel Clarke from the federation because of his remarks but this move was vigorously opposed by most of the executive. Morris wrote:

> Now it may be admitted that Mr Clarke had been injudicious in his remarks, but surely expulsion was much too heavy a penalty to inflict on a useful and energetic member of the Federation for the crime of a little incautious talk to *members of the Council*. Moreover, others had notably been guilty of the crime such as it was, probably we all had, more or less: certainly Messrs Frost, Champion and Hyndman had. In short the attack on Clarke

was made because he, like others of us, had objected to Mr Hyndman's tendencies and had the courage to let it be known: while his injudicious way of doing this gave a handle against him.[10]

The dispute greatly raised the temperature within the SDF executive.

Hyndman had also irritated members of the executive in a wrangle over control of *Justice*, the party newspaper, which had operated under his complete control. When it was suggested that the paper be brought under the collective control of the executive, Hyndman winced. It was, he argued, 'impossible to recognise any right on the part of the present Executive to claim control over a journal which has been made what it is by the extraordinary efforts of a few persons'.[11] More pointedly he assured Morris that 'the best council possible cannot manage a journal such as *Justice* . . . Without a spark of personal feeling in the matter, I cannot consent to sacrifice my own work and that of others . . . to what is a wholly unworkable and hopeless arrangement, suggested by people who have never done the paper any good whatever'.[12] Eleanor Marx, furthermore, had run foul of Hyndman who saw both her and Aveling as representatives of the Engels coterie which he heartily mistrusted.[13] Marx for her part considered Hyndman to be jingoistic and in a letter to Wilhelm Liebknecht she accused him of being opposed to developing a united international socialist movement.[14] Hyndman exercised his prejudices and personal dislikes by intriguing with his supporters to outflank those he viewed as his enemies.

His attempt to 'outflank' Andreas Scheu provided the straw that broke the proverbial camel's back. Scheu had left London for Edinburgh in July 1884 and, with John L. Mahon, an Irishman, he organized an effective socialist group in the city. In Scotland, Henry George's theories had found a receptive audience and a strong land reform movement was in progress. The Georgite Scottish Land Restoration League was particularly successful and in the 1885 general election it put forward five candidates and one, Dr G.B. Clarke, no longer a member of the federation, was elected.[15] Under the circumstances Scheu accepted Mahon's advice that the SDF would have little chance of success and instead they established the Scottish Land and Labour League. In truth this probably suited Scheu as it provided some autonomy for what was essentially a branch of the SDF. The objectives of the league were essentially those of the SDF, and Scheu and Mahon undoubtedly intended it as the Scottish section of the federation. Hyndman had other ideas. While the SDF accepted the affiliation of the Scottish organization, Hyndman set about promoting a small branch of the federation in Glasgow. Scheu had travelled to Glasgow and the west of Scotland and made some recruits for his league but a visit by Hyndman in October ended any chance of a *rapprochement* between Scheu's organization and the Glasgow SDF branch. After Hyndman returned to London the league formally approached the Glasgow branch and suggested a collaboration. Glasgow in turn wrote to Hyndman for his advice and he wrote back accusing Scheu of being an anarchist, an organization wrecker and a friend of Johann Most, the Austrian revolutionary anarchist.[16] Morris was in Scotland lecturing when Scheu was attacked in this 'treacherous manner' and he returned to London enraged.[17] 'These charges', he wrote to a correspondent, 'I knew to be untrue and I saw, therefore, that it was no longer any use trying to smother the smouldering discontent in the Federation.'[18]

The SDF split on 27 December 1884 at a heated meeting of the executive. A majority of its members voted against Hyndman but then, led by William Morris, they withdrew from the SDF rather than spend months infighting with the Hyndmanite faction which was still a powerful force. Morris was joined by Dr Aveling, Joseph Lane, Robert Banner, Eleanor Marx, Ernest Belfort Bax, W.J. Clarke, J. Cooper, Sam Mainwaring and John L. Mahon. Scheu, in Edinburgh, also declared his support. With the split the political differences between the group that formed around Morris and Scheu and Hyndman's SDF emerged in a clearer light. 'The Socialist League formed apart from the SDF', wrote Mahon in early January 1885, 'because its members are not *State* socialists, and do not care to uphold jingoism.'[19] Indeed, Mahon was eager to underline Hyndman's imperialist predilections and within days of the split he wrote to the secretary of the SDF asking if he would 'kindly state if Mr H.M. Hyndman in his address to the Electors of Marylebone declared distinctly in favour of "a spirited foreign policy" and objected to disendowment of the State Church . . . Please answer at once as we wish to know before writing to foreign papers'.[20] The Socialist League, which was inaugurated in London on 30 December, was undoubtedly to the left of the SDF. It contained libertarian Marxists like Morris and Scheu, and others, such as Joseph Lane, who were influenced by the theories of anarchism. Morris immediately sought Engels's advice on the new departure and in a letter to Scheu he wrote: 'I saw Engels who said that we were weak in *political* knowledge and journalistic skill, and that we should find it very difficult to carry on a weekly paper really well . . . I must confess that though I don't intend to give way to Engels, his advice is valuable.'[21] In the event the Socialist League established a monthly paper, *The Commonweal*, and Engels contributed an article to its first edition in February 1885.

Morris was appointed editor. The Socialist League and Morris were for a time synonymous, and his libertarian vision presented a serious alternative to the 'British Marxism' marketed by Hyndman and the SDF. Morris himself was innately modest, in sharp contrast to the egotism of Hyndman, and he never saw himself as a major intellectual figure. 'I feel myself very weak', he wrote to Scheu, 'as to the science of socialism on many points; I wish

I knew German, as I see I must certainly learn it: Confound you chaps! What do you mean by being foreigners? . . . You see I am but a poet and artist, good for nothing but sentiment.'[22] In truth Morris proved an effective propagandist and an original socialist thinker. Anti-parliamentarianism, which was a keystone of his politics, became a main plank of the League's platform as did a greater emphasis on the objective of a socialist society — rather than the 'stepping stones' that later became an end in themselves for many British socialists. Morris also laid great emphasis on education:

> I do not care for a mechanical revolution. I want an educated movement. Discontent is not enough, though it is natural and inevitable. The discontented must know what they are aiming at when they overthrow the old order of things. My belief is that the old order can only be overthrown by force; and for that reason it is all the more necessary that the revolution . . . should not be an ignorant but an intelligent revolution . . . [Socialism is] not a change for the sake of change, but a change involving a high and noble, the very noblest, ideal of human life and duty: a life in which every human being should find unrestricted scope for his best powers and faculties.[23]

The manifesto of the Socialist League argued the case for classical Marxism and denied that reforms could provide an equitable solution for the working class: 'No number of merely administrative changes, until the workers are in possession of all political power, would make any real approach to Socialism.'[24] It argued strongly for internationalism and the politics of class struggle.

THE SOCIALIST LEAGUE AND IRELAND

Among those who signed the manifesto of the Socialist League were Thomas Maguire and John L. Mahon, both of Irish extraction, but the league began life with no members in Ireland. Interestingly E.T. Craig, once the organizer of the Owenite Ralahine community, was an early member and, although an old man, he spoke at a number of Socialist League propaganda meetings. The league, like the SDF, was an advocate of home rule for Ireland. 'We are internationalists not nationalists', Morris wrote in March 1885, 'yet we sympathise with the Irish revolt against English tyranny.'[25] Morris had visited Ireland in 1877 on business and had noted its poverty: 'The villages we passed were very poor-looking, the cottiers' houses in outside appearance the very poorest habitations of man I have yet seen, Iceland by no means excepted' and 'a dirty and slatternly city is Dublin . . . Guinness seems the only thing of importance there.'[26] And five years before he became a convinced socialist he spoke of passing the Curragh 'where our army of occupation sits' and he related how he had heard stories of the savagery of government yeomanry during the time of the 1798 rebellion.[27] His instincts were naturally on the side of the Irish, although he never held a naïve view of the home rule or Fenian movements. Morris, as a member of the Democratic Federation, had also experienced lecturing to Irish audiences in Britain:

> I duly gave my lecture on Sunday, at the Irish National League rooms in Blackfriars Rd: all or most Irish there; and Parnellites to the backbone; but dear me! such quiet respectable people! I was able to please them by assuring them of my sympathy for their views, and also by telling them I had read and much admired translations of their ancient literature: one man whom I spoke with afterwards knew all about the old stories and could speak Irish well.[28]

Morris was first and foremost an internationalist and support for the Irish struggle happily involved an indictment of British government policy. By 1885, however, British socialists were more concerned with establishing a base among British workers than they were with the Irish question. The SDF, particularly, scaled down its work in support of the Irish agitation and while the organization continued to play a role in anti-coercion demonstrations, it no longer sought a leading position in the movement. James Doyle, a Dublin socialist, noticed this in 1886 and in a letter to the Socialist League he accused *Justice*, the SDF paper, of labelling the Irish 'reactionary'.[29] What Doyle had in fact recognized was a suspicion of Irish nationalism among British socialists who considered themselves internationalists. This relative withdrawal is probably best exemplified by a letter sent by the SDF to the Socialist League in January 1887. The Socialist League had sent a circular letter to a number of clubs and organizations including the SDF proposing to hold a public demonstration 'for the purpose of advancing the cause of the Irish people' at which motions on behalf of the citizens of London would express 'warmest sympathy with the Irish people in their struggle to free themselves from Foreign Rule and from Landlord plunderers' and demand the right of 'the Irish nation . . . to settle with the Landlords without any restriction whatever from the English Parliament'.[30] H.W. Lee, secretary of the SDF, tartly replied:

> Your letter was duly laid before the Council at the last meeting, and I was instructed in reply to say that they think that the present time . . . inappropriate for such action as you propose, and are also of the opinion that the best help that we can give to the Irish in their struggles is to occupy as much as possible the Government with an agitation on behalf of the workers of Great Britain.[31]

This, of course, was a rather circuitous way of expressing solidarity.

Ernest Belfort Bax outlined the theoretical basis to the Socialist League's anti-imperialism in the first issue of *The Commonweal*:

> The establishment of socialism . . . on any national or race basis is out of the question. Tall talk about the 'Anglo-Saxon race' or 'the great democracies of English-speaking peoples, in union with the more ancient democracy of England' . . . can but disgust the socialist who is at once logical and honest. No, the foreign policy of the great internationalist socialist party must be to break up these hideous race monopolies called empires, beginning in each case at home. Hence everything which makes for the disruption and disintegration of the empire to which he belongs must be welcomed by the socialist as an ally.[32]

It was presumably for these reasons that in April 1885 the league's paper published a section entitled 'Irish Notes' by the novelist E. Owens Blackburne. Blackburne, from Howth in County Dublin, had taken out a subscription to *The Commonweal* in March and the 'notes' were a thoroughly nationalist list of misrule in Ireland from 1607 to 1798.[33] The 'notes' were a once off, however, and were not continued as a regular feature. Blackburne (whose real name was Elizabeth Casey) never went beyond the subscription to membership of the Socialist League.

ESTABLISHING THE DUBLIN BRANCH

John L. Mahon, as secretary of the Socialist League, made serious efforts to establish contacts in Ireland. From the beginning, the Socialist League knew of the existence of the Dublin Democratic Association and had sent it copies of '*To Socialists*', the open letter explaining the break with the SDF. Indeed Samuel Hayes of the DDA cited this letter as one of the reasons they stopped short of forming an SDF branch in Dublin.[34] The DDA, however, existed until May 1885 and seemingly had no further communication with the Socialist League, probably because the league viewed it as a covert SDF branch.[35] Elsewhere the league made meagre progress. P.F. Hayden of Graiguenamanagh in County Kilkenny wrote in mid-February to tell Mahon that he had received a letter from him as well as copies of the Socialist League manifesto. He distributed the manifesto although he claimed not to entirely concur in all the views expressed, and he mused that he did not expect a socialist state could ever really exist. More hopefully he promised to encourage the local shop to stock *The Commonweal* and he said he would sell a few copies himself every month.[36] Such a paper would undoubtedly have nonplussed many in Kilkenny in 1885. Further up the country Pakenham

Thomas Beatty, of Mount Pleasant in County Louth, wrote about the same time enclosing three guineas for the propaganda fund and asking for membership of the league: 'Mr George Shaw will, no doubt, be my socialist godfather, and make the necessary promises in my name.'[37] It appears, however, that Pakenham Beatty spent much of his time in England and, even if he did not, he was clearly no coal-porter and did not represent any inroad into the Irish working class.[38] Beatty was a friend of George Bernard Shaw who had involved himself with the socialist movement in London and was friendly with William Morris and the Socialist League at this time.

Over the next few months there were only faint glimmers of hope from Ireland. At the beginning of April, J.P. O'Carroll, who gave an address in Trinity College in Dublin, wrote requesting copies of socialist books including a book by Lassalle, and William Morris provided the material some weeks later.[39] A day after the letter from O'Carroll, Mahon received a note from D.C. Campbell of Derry. Mahon had evidently written to Campbell's father but was assured by his son that he 'is very far from being a socialist, although a Radical'.[40] Campbell, however, took out a twelve-month subscription to The Commonweal and in a later letter informed Mahon that 'people here look upon anything like socialism as awful . . . The only real socialist in Derry beside ourselves is a Mr Dorman'.[41] This was probably Robert Dorman who was later to become a prominent socialist in Dublin. Campbell also mentioned the Rev. J. Bruce Wallace, the Belfast Christian socialist, as 'an enthusiastic socialist'.[42] In truth Wallace's 'socialism' was Georgite land nationalization with a more pronounced social conscience.

In July the Irish situation improved significantly. An English member of the Socialist League, Michael Gabriel, had moved to Bayview Avenue in the North Strand area of Dublin and in June he wrote to the league requesting a dozen copies of The Commonweal and some leaflets. 'I intend doing what I can', he wrote, 'but the ground is not of the best.'[43] But, the following month, the League received two important letters. The first came in the form of a short note from the nationalist intellectual T.W. Rolleston, then editor of the Dublin University Review.[44] Rolleston requested for review 'all the numbers of The Commonweal containing press by Mr W. Morris'.[45] This letter was the beginning of an interest that socialism enjoyed from the Dublin University Review that lasted through 1885 and 1886. The owner of the journal, the Protestant nationalist Charles Hubert Oldham, took out a subscription to The Commonweal in August while mentioning that 'Mr Michael Davitt has been speaking to me about it'.[46] Rolleston, himself, took out a twelve-month subscription in January 1886.[47] C.H. Oldham, as well as founding the important Dublin University Review, was also a prime mover in forming the Contemporary Club in Dublin in 1885. This club, which gathered in a first-floor room at the corner of College Green and Grafton Street, was composed of a remarkable collection of intellectuals including Rolleston, John O'Leary, John F. Taylor, William Stockley, Douglas Hyde, James Walker, W.B. Yeats and John Butler Yeats. William Morris was to visit the club in April 1886.[48] Taylor and Walker were both prominent in the Saturday Club and Taylor, a barrister and an eloquent public speaker, was particularly popular with its members. The outcome of the material sent for review in July 1885 was a lengthy article entitled 'The Socialist League and its poet' in the August edition of the *Dublin University Review*. The article, written by 'H. Rowlandson', probably T.W. Rolleston himself, began:

> The present century was ushered in by a vast revolution, in which the system of government by caste was eradicated by fire and sword in such fashion that the problem for statesmen since has been, not to plant anew the old institutions, but to make any wholesome growth whatever strike root in the scorched soil. In the meantime the privilege of caste has been supplanted by that of Capital — a weed which requires hardly any precedent conditions of high or beautiful human qualities for growth, except a certain stability and order . . . For several decades the capitalists, who are the real rulers and leaders of men in these days, have held almost undisputed sway, and the state of things which has resulted is so monstrous and horrible that there seems every likelihood that the century, as it opened with one revolution, may close with another, aiming at even more radical changes in the face of European society.[49]

This was a heady assault on capitalism, and Rowlandson went on to give a brief history of the Socialist League and some quotations from its manifesto. 'One is led to think', he continued, 'that Mr Morris's artistic sense . . . has had at least as powerful an effect as his humanity or his reason in inducing him to throw himself into the Socialist movement of today.'[50] Lengthy extracts from *The Commonweal* were reprinted and commended, and the article asked rhetorically of Morris:

> Does Mr Morris, it may be asked, actually believe in armed revolution, with battle and blood-shedding, as a legitimate inauguration of the new age of the organisation of industry? However shocking it may seem, or be, it must be replied that he is, without doubt, sternly prepared to face even that necessity, if it should prove to be one. That it will so prove few Socialists appear to doubt. And indeed it does seem as if universal suffrage and the most democratic institutions possible to conceive, would be unable to secure the peaceful passing of the required legislation; so strong will be the influence and interests of capital engaged in its life-and-death struggle with labour.[51]

All this was splendid propaganda for the Socialist League and would have provided an appetizing introduction to William Morris and the league for

Dublin's intellectual circles. At the end of the article, however, the author used the emergence of the Socialist League as an indictment of 'commercial' capitalism and suggested that socialism had, as yet, made little progress in Ireland because the country had not gone down the road of industrialization. If that happened, he warned, 'so surely will the doctrines of the Socialist League take root in our soil, and in due time bear, in our streets also, that crop of the dragon's teeth'.[52]

The second letter received from Ireland by the Socialist League in July 1885 came from George King of Phibsboro Road in Dublin. King, who was to become a leading activist in the Dublin branch, enquired after the August issue of the league's paper and asked if there was a branch in Dublin. He declared an interest in land nationalization and wrote that he had been a reader of *Justice* but was unsure of the connection between the Socialist League and the SDF.[53] King, unlike others who were to join the league, was a strong supporter of the movement for home rule:

> There is more faith in the value of political power amongst the mass of the Irish people at the present moment than perhaps ever was before, even the extreme physical force men have appeared to give politics one chance more, in a word Mr Parnell is Ireland as far as the great bulk of the people is concerned.
>
> More can see that it is almost impossible to get anyone to give any attention to the socialist movement, not that there are not socialists in Ireland and Dublin too. I hope to live to see a strong socialist party in our own . . . parliament — but first catch your hare — we want first of all to get that parliament.[54]

King's attitude to parliament was in contradiction to Morris who in *The Commonweal* in September wrote that 'by entering Parliament, which is pledged by its very nature to go no further than palliation, the Socialists would be . . . helping Parliament to fulfil its functions, and this would oppose revolution and not further it'.[55] Whether King was, at this stage, entirely aware of the Socialist League's attitude to parliament is unclear. Nonetheless he offers an insight into the thinking of some Dublin socialists at that time. On the nationalist–unionist conflict he wrote:

> There are for all practical purposes only two parties in Ireland. One wants an independent Irish democratic parliament, some of the best men here [do] not agree with the Irish parliamentary party in all that they have done or what they propose to do but they have agreed to sink all differences and go rabid for a native legislature. The other party I need only say is true blue Tory — socialist means either a robber or a madman.[56]

King's letter prompted *The Commonweal* to insert the statement that 'Michael Gabriel is at work for the cause in Dublin' in its August edition.[57] The following month the paper urged 'all sympathisers with our movement' in Dublin to contact the secretary, now H.H. Sparling, at the league's head office in London.[58] The league was clearly making a determined effort to build a branch in the Irish capital.

Samuel Hayes, of the now-defunct Dublin Democratic Association, made contact after seeing this notice. In a lengthy letter he wrote that he presumed that they were considering establishing a Dublin branch and, for their information, he outlined the development and demise of the DDA which had 'adjourned' (or, in truth, collapsed) four months before: 'There are I suppose about 15 socialists in Dublin and twice that many land nationalizers.'[59] Unlike Gabriel, Hayes was an established socialist activist in Dublin and was able to offer a list of contacts. After warning of the enervation of socialism in Dublin he wrote:

> If, however, you decide to form a branch here I shall be pleased to join it and will give you the names and addresses of the Socialists who belonged to the Dublin Democratic Association but many of them will be afraid to join an Association of so pronounced a character as yours for fear of losing their employment.[60]

As Alexander Stewart of the DDA had apparently lost his job on account of his membership the previous year, this was not an idle fear for Dublin socialists. Hayes's attitude to the home rule movement was also coloured by the treatment received by the DDA and was a sharp contrast to the views of George King.

> [The DDA] met with great opposition by the National League who did all they could to crush it — for you must remember that the nationalists are not even Democrats, but in reality are Conservatives of the most intolerant and bigoted type who allow no opinions to be listened to if they can keep it but their own. They are 'nationalists' certainly but, as *Justice* said the other week, so also is Prince Bismarck and the Prince of Wales. Nationalism, no matter of what type, I consider objectionable as socialists must of necessity be *Internationalists*.[61]

This was the type of argument that irritated some Dublin socialists like James Doyle and it was also, it has to be said, a very linear understanding of internationalism. It contained little of the subtlety of Ernest Belfort Bax's perspective on imperialism. Hayes also informed Sparling that he intended to soon begin publication of a monthly journal to be called *The Monthly Review* which would be devoted to the discussion of subjects of political, social and general interest. This plan ultimately came to nothing.

Sparling quickly replied to Hayes and requested the list of names and addresses offered which he then forwarded to Gabriel.[62] Hayes, however, struck a note of pessimism: 'Most of the persons mentioned are rather disheartened as far [as] the propagation of socialism is concerned in this country owing to the failure of the Dublin Democratic Association and the strong opposition it met with. It is impossible to get the people in this country to think for themselves — they believe everything they hear both from their political leaders and clergy.'[63] He also mentioned how when *The Commonweal* had first been issued in February he had distributed handbills to advertise it and had brought it to the attention of a number of newsagents. Despite his gloom he had trudged on and he was still interested in assisting in the formation of a Socialist League branch. Michael Gabriel, in October, reported that he had 'not at present sufficient reason for saying we can form a branch here soon' but he remained optimistic.[64]

Also in October, William Morris wrote an article on Ireland for *The Commonweal*. He suggested that Parnell, in all probability, would succeed in achieving his objective and that the next parliament could be the last in which Irish representatives would sit at Westminster. He continued:

> Well, this is revolutionary, and we revolutionists rejoice in it on those grounds, and in the blow which it will deal at the great Bourgeois Power — the British Empire: also it may well be that Ireland must become national before she can be international. Yet we must ask ourselves what is to come next; will Ireland ruling herself be progressive, revolutionary that is, or reactionary? Will Socialists find their work easier in the Parnellite Ireland than now? Will Michael Davitt be as dangerous a rebel as he is now? There is no doubt as to the answer to those questions if we are to go no further than Mr Parnell would have us; the fullest realisation of his programme would bring Ireland to pretty much the state of things which Liberal reformers want to realise in England as a bar to the march of Socialism . . . An improved landlordism founded on a wider basis and therefore consolidated; that would lead, it seems to me, to founding a nation fanatically attached to the rights of private property (so-called), narrow-minded, retrogressive, contentious and — unhappy.[65]

Morris supported the demand for home rule but he held no illusions about the type of society that would evolve in a bourgeois independent Ireland. Pointing to the example of Italy he insisted that, despite national freedom, poverty still existed because the class system still stood. Only an international socialist revolution, he argued, could bring real freedom for the working classes in Ireland. If only the Irish, he wrote, would learn this lesson 'and make up their minds that even if they have to wait for it their revolution shall be part of the great international movement; they will then be rid of all the foreigners that they want to be rid of'.[66] This position taken by Morris, however, while abstractly correct in socialist terms, was not centred on a real examination of the objective conditions for international social revolution at that time. It reflected a feeling among many British socialists that the 'revolution' was imminent if not tomorrow then in a matter of years. Morris followed Marx in his concluding exhortation:

> To the Irish, therefore, as to all other nations, whatever their name and race, we Socialists say, Your revolutionary struggles will be abortive or lead to mere disappointment unless you accept as your watchword, WAGE-WORKERS OF ALL COUNTRIES UNITE![67]

This article was a useful corrective for those socialists who dreamt of a progressive Irish state under Parnell. What Morris said proved true: class divisions would continue in a bourgeois independent Ireland and the country took many years before partially confronting a domineering rural-based conservatism. On the other hand his suggestion that the Irish people await an international revolution represented a 'purism' that would gain few adherents in Ireland. Morris, overall however, did consider the Irish struggle a positive agitation in terms of its beneficial consequences. In early 1888 he wrote:

> Democratic ideas tending towards Socialism have been evolved from the Irish struggle, and men's minds have been familiarised thereby with resistance to authority; the precariousness of livelihood under the capitalist has been brought home more and more among the workers, and the preaching of Socialism has inspired them with hope to change all that.[68]

Those who joined the Socialist League in Dublin therefore received a clear delineation of the organization's policy on Ireland shortly before the branch was inaugurated. Home rule was supported because it weakened the British Empire not because of any innate progressive qualities it held. It was a timely article. Gabriel had made real progress and he wrote in early November that he had 'made the acquaintance of a few men who seem to go the whole way with us. The Democratic Association which is now extinct supplies about four up to date'.[69] Gabriel remained cautious, perhaps on the advice of Hayes and others, and he wrote to London:

> If we succeed in forming a branch of the Socialist League our policy will be one of quiet endeavour to undermine such associations as are within our reach, rather than to start meetings on our own account for the present. Any open assertion of ourselves as a Socialist body would be resented here by almost all classes, which would prevent us from getting audiences. Moreover, we expect to do better work by eating into such meetings as the Saturday Club.[70]

Indeed Gabriel quickly made his presence felt at the Saturday Club where on 14 November he argued against returning working men to parliament. 'What would be the use of sending labour candidates to Parliament? It would be no use whatever to send them to talk to capitalists and landlords, whose interests were different from theirs. As working men they would never get anything by using a vote.'[71] This was raw anti-parliamentarianism from Gabriel who belonged to the anarchist wing of the Socialist League.[72] Rather strangely he argued a month later that home rule would be 'of very little benefit to Ireland if working classes were not represented in the local parliament'.[73]

On 22 November Gabriel wrote again to London to inform them that he now had a group of about seven men 'who are first-rate material for the cause' and they had taken the decision to form a branch.[74] The branch was formally established at a meeting on 13 December 1885 with Samuel Hayes appointed as secretary and John A. Ryan of Great Brunswick Street given the position of treasurer.[75] Ryan, who was a regular contributor at the Saturday Club, had been a member of the short-lived Dublin branch of the First International.[76] Other founding members included John O'Gorman, Auguste Coulon, Fritz Schumann, Thomas Fitzpatrick, George King and Arthur Kavanagh. O'Gorman and King, like Ryan, were former members of the Dublin branch of the International. The branch selected the Odd-fellows Hall at 10 Upper Abbey Street as the venue for its weekly meetings which were held every Thursday evening.[77] The monthly membership report gave membership at the end of December as ten.[78]

ARGUING FOR SOCIALISM

The Socialist League in Dublin followed the example of the Dublin Democratic Association and utilized the Saturday Club to argue the politics of socialism. A debate on Bradlaugh on 5 December provided Fritz Schumann with an example of one of the central difficulties faced by socialists in Ireland. Charles Bradlaugh MP had been refused admission to the House of Commons because as an avowed atheist he could not take the requisite oath: the subject before the Saturday Club was 'Ought Bradlaugh now be admitted to the House of Commons?'. Most of the speakers railed against Bradlaugh as an atheist who would, as was argued by one speaker, 'turn their most sacred shrines into cow-sheds'.[79] Andrew Byrne and John A. Ryan argued Bradlaugh's case but Schumann ran into trouble when he raised the religious aspect of the question. 'The chairman', claimed Schumann, 'has allowed atheism to be assailed with not a word in support of it (groans).' The chairman's response was swift: 'This gentleman has said now that he will defend atheism, and I say I won't hear it (applause).'[80] That was the end of discussion on atheism. Religious sensibilities in Ireland provided an enormous impediment for socialist organizers during the late nineteenth and early twentieth centuries. George King counselled Sparling on this difficulty:

You may rely on it that the priests will oppose to the death any attempt to establish a socialist propaganda in this country and, if you know Ireland anyway well at all, I need not tell you what power they have. They will oppose socialists simply because they are good Catholics. Dr Aveling or Charles Bradlaugh, it is all the same, they are enemies of the faith no matter though they may be good friends of Ireland . . . The one fact that the average Dublin working man knows about the [Paris] commune is that during the struggle the Archbishop of Paris was shot.[81]

James Doyle, who joined the branch in 1886, admitted he was glad that the Socialist League discouraged attacks on religion and he declared that he could not 'see what socialism has to do with religion'.[82] This fear felt by Irish socialists like Doyle of being seen as irreligious was one shared by socialists in Scotland which had its own religious tensions. Indeed the Scottish Land and Labour League, which had affiliated to the Socialist League, was of the opinion that 'in Scotland it would be most damaging to the cause to bring in religious controversy'.[83] In Ireland the subject was best avoided.

Other debates at the Saturday Club proved more successful and former members of the Dublin Democratic Association also spoke in support of socialist ideas. A debate on 19 December on the 'Social Condition of the Working Man', chaired by Adam O'Toole, saw Andrew Byrne, another former DDA member, claim that all the ills of the working man arose 'from the relations between capital and labour, and the day was rapidly coming when the cause of labour would have to meet capital with something different to speech-making or public meetings'.[84] Michael Gabriel would seem to have settled into the Club rather quickly and he was selected to preside at a debate entitled 'Next Irish Parliament' which was held on 2 January 1886.[85] This was an important advance as it indicated that Gabriel was not viewed as a marginal outsider by Dublin's radical circles. At the debate John A. Ryan spoke against the notion that republican states were necessarily favourable toward social change:

They might have in a Republic a very grinding aristocracy and a very impoverished proletariat. It would be wiser for a class who favoured a Republic to go in for social reforms rather than political changes (applause). In a Republic like America there was less chance for alternate success in a social movement intended to raise the working class such as Michael Davitt (loud cheers) had in view, than there was in a Monarchy like England.[86]

Ryan concluded by advocating nationalization of the land which was loudly cheered, and it is possible that he was an 'old-stager' who was a member of the league primarily because of his previous membership of the International. Over the following year he took a very limited role in the branch and was excused by King because 'he was sick most of the time'.[87] In fact

Ryan died in early 1887 after a five-month illness.[88]

Renewed interest in socialism was evinced by the *Dublin University Review* in December 1885 when it published an article by William F. Bailey under the title 'The coming socialism', a concerted attack using the traditional shibboleths. The danger, intoned Bailey, 'is a real one, and is to be feared chiefly because it derives its force from principles almost altogether selfish'.[89] He continued:

> Are we to extirpate those who have acquired wealth either by means of their personal gifts or the personal gifts of their ancestors, merely to set up a kind of democratic plutocracy whose wealth shall be the creation of revolution rather than of personal skill or merit? Far better would it be never to have disturbed the old system, hard as its yoke might have pressed, than to have effected merely this.[90]

Bailey's attack is interesting if only to illustrate the fears aroused by the growth of socialism across Europe. For him the socialists were trying to overturn 'the inborn promptings of human nature': greed.[91] For the socialists such attributes were not seen as innate and the struggle was for, in the words of William Morris, 'that true society which means well-being and well-doing for one and all'.[92] Bailey saw such communitarianism as impossible: 'Give the penniless money, give the landless an estate, and each will inevitably become as ardent and selfish in defending what he regards as his rights as ever was capitalist or landlord.'[93]

Socialism was continuing, however, to secure its toehold in Dublin. Over the early months of 1886 the Socialist League continued to gain recruits. In January the branch reported fourteen members, in March it was sixteen and by April the branch had seventeen members.[94] It was a minuscule organization but seventeen organized revolutionary socialists were enough to raise the spectre of socialism in Dublin. The branch's first public meeting was held in the Oddfellows Hall on 7 January with the suggestive title of 'Problems of Socialism'. Fritz Schumann was chosen to chair the meeting. A burly looking Danish artisan, he was one of the most active members of the Socialist League in Dublin.[95] He may have been from the German-speaking region close to the border between Denmark and Germany and he appears to have been a well-read and intelligent socialist advocate with a fondness for Shakespeare.[96] Schumann was a leading member of the Danish Social Democratic Workers' Party and lived in London in the late 1870s as a political refugee. In September 1878 he had attended the International Socialist Congress in Paris as a delegate for the Danish socialists and for the International Labour Union. In November that year he visited Karl Marx but Marx considered him an intriguer and distrusted him.[97] The chosen speaker at the Dublin Socialist League meeting was a new member, Roman Ivanovitch Lipmann, a Russian of Jewish extraction who was a follower of the Paris-based Jewish Marxist Pyotr Lavrov, a close friend to the Marx family.[98] Lipmann was an intellectual who seemed more at home in Trinity College than among the working class and his speeches appeared unnecessarily abstruse. The league had advertised the meeting in the *Freeman's Journal* which possibly prompted it to send the journalist that turned up.[99] The attendance, according to the newspaper, numbered about thirty 'apparently respectable citizens and clerks' but Samuel Hayes estimated 'a crowded attendance' of over sixty.[100] 'Of course', wrote Hayes, 'the papers do all they can to make us look absurd' but it was nonetheless excellent coverage for the league.[101] *The Commonweal* was distributed before the meeting and Schumann sat beneath a sign bearing the motto 'Friendship, Love and Truth'. Lipmann's address involved a review of the progress of socialism in different European countries and he concluded with the assurance that the working class would find socialism an advantageous social system. However, according to the journalist from the *Freeman's Journal*, 'owing to his accent and the highfalutin language in which the paper was written, it was impossible almost to grasp its very nature, or to understand any ideas it was intended to convey'.[102] Lipmann was never to prove a particularly successful propagandist.

An interesting discussion followed the reading of Lipmann's paper in which a number of members of the branch participated. A speaker from the Loyal National Repeal Association argued that socialism had no place in Ireland and that 'the one great object of every Irishman was to gain national independence for his country'.[103] Thomas Fitzpatrick, a young member of the league who was later to become a prolific socialist speaker, replied with the Morris position on Ireland.

> It was right that every country should govern itself, but he denied that everything depended on the form of Government in a country. France and America had the republican form of Government, but the working man in these countries was as badly off as he was in any other country (hear, hear), and he considered that it was wrong for any man to say that nationalism would cure all the evils of a country. The tendency of the age was towards internationalism not nationalism. It was absurd to think that the separation of Ireland from England would alone benefit the working men of Ireland (hear, hear).[104]

Gabriel and a number of others also spoke in support of socialism and the *Freeman's Journal* published a long, if somewhat hostile, report of the meeting. It was a modestly successful beginning for the Socialist League in Dublin.

Gabriel was in action again at the Saturday Club on 9 January where he made a speech calling for working-class organization and arguing against 'palliatives'. 'Whatever item of expenditure was reduced', he said, 'wages would sink by a proportionate amount.'[105] Moreover, he asserted that the 'idea of looking to any Parliament, whether Irish or English, to do anything for them was a mistake', and that 'everything depended on the organisation and co-operation amongst the working classes'. Gabriel's anarchism included a distaste for piecemeal reforms and even extended to the dubious assertion that 'agitation about rack-renting would not do them any good at all'.[106] Such sentiments were hardly encouraging for the many victims of rack-renting in Dublin at the time. In terms of the Saturday Club, nonetheless, the Socialist League was doing well and Gabriel reported to Sparling in late January that they had six members on the Saturday Club committee and 'supplied about half the speakers'.[107] The latter assertion was an exaggeration, but both league and former DDA members constituted a substantial proportion of speakers at the weekly debates.

The decision by the Socialist League to announce its presence in Dublin with a public meeting was not one welcomed by all the citizens of the city. The board of management at the Oddfellows Hall, where branch meetings were held, was outraged at the publicity given to the socialist meeting, and when the league attempted to organize another public meeting the following week it moved to expel them from the premises. Initially the Oddfellows insisted that the problem was that 'public meetings of any description' were not permitted on their premises, but the Socialist League responded to this by placing an advertisement in the *Freeman's Journal* stating that only members and the press were invited — although membership was advertised at the suspiciously low price of one penny a week.[108] When the branch members arrived at the hall on 14 January, however, they found a notice posted on the door which read: 'Socialists — No Socialistic meetings will be permitted to be held in this hall. By Order.'[109] The board of management had also sent the league a letter explaining that its objection was to socialism and that 'at any risk' they would prevent the advertised meeting from going ahead.[110] Moreover, the officers of the Oddfellows Society and a small force of policemen were present to ensure that no meeting took place. A crowd gathered but the Oddfellows were adamant and the branch eventually directed those interested to a room over a public house at the corner of Fownes Street on Wellington Quay. Schumann chaired and the meeting began with a motion against smoking in the overcrowded room which Michael Gabriel seconded. The motion fell and Gabriel lit his pipe. More seriously, Schumann protested against their exclusion from the Oddfellows Hall and remarked that 'already socialists are being persecuted in Dublin'.[111] A discussion then began on the paper presented by Lipmann the previous week and a general exposition of socialism was requested. Gabriel gave what Schumann described as 'the left-wing of Socialism or Anarchism'.

Socialism, he said, was capable of a good many interpretations. His ideas on the Social question were that all their evils were caused by class government. He was opposed to a million of men ruling one man, or one man ruling a million. The power of one man to govern another should be swept away under the Socialist system.[112]

Gabriel also mentioned that he believed that 'the present system of marriage should be modified'. That anarchism exerted a real influence on the Dublin Socialist League was again indicated the following week when Schumann concluded a paper he delivered to the Saturday Club on technical education by saying that 'with the great living philosopher, the apostle of anarchy, or liberty — which is the same thing — with Herbert Spencer, he would say education is closely associated with change, in fitting men for higher things and unfitting them for things as they are'.[113] This does not of course prove Schumann to be an anarchist — anarchism and anti-parliamentarian Marxism enjoyed a very close relationship at times during the early years of the British 'socialist revival'. Morris, while not an anarchist, was very close to anarchism on many points.[114]

Despite an orderly meeting the landlord of the public house at the corner of Fownes Street refused to allow the league to hold any more meetings. Gabriel reported to Sparling that this was because the landlord had been approached and 'advised' by the police.[115] This was not the only occasion that the Socialist League came to the attention of the police in Dublin. During the bottlemakers' dispute in April 1886 a police report indicated that they were aware that the Dublin socialists 'have taken the matter up' and that they were expected to raise it at a meeting of the Saturday Club.[116] Likewise, when Morris visited Dublin in the same month plain-clothes policemen were sent to observe his address at the Saturday Club 'to note any particular incident and to be able to give evidence of any strong language if such be used'.[117] In November, while spying on a meeting of the Young Ireland Society, the Dublin Metropolitan Police noted the presence of Fritz Schumann and R.I. Lipmann.[118] They were there to hear James Poole read a paper on the 'Education of Young Nationalists'. Later in the month the Socialist League was listed in a police document on 'National Associations in Ireland' which 'are instituted to create and sustain a feeling in favour of separation from England'. The document assessed the branch membership to be twenty-one and cited its object to be the desire to 'improve the condition of the working classes generally and to bring about equality as much as possible'. The members, claimed the report, 'are mostly foreigners and intermixed with low Fenians'.[119] It is interesting that the police worries largely revolved around the socialists' links with separatism.

The Socialist League, now finding it impossible to book a meeting room, was forced to rely on Auguste Coulon to provide them with an upstairs room in his place of business at 50 Dawson Street. Coulon, a Frenchman, operated as a 'Professor of Languages' in Dublin to make his living.[120] However, after a public meeting on 9 February his address was reported in the *Freeman's Journal* and his business suffered. 'We thought', wrote Gabriel, 'we were not justified in allowing one man to ruin himself even though he were willing.'[121] The league continued to have difficulties in obtaining a regular meeting place. The 9 February meeting occurred at a time when socialism in Britain was gaining a certain notoriety. The SDF in London had the day before organized a march of the unemployed to Trafalgar Square. Tens of thousands attended and militant speeches were made by Hyndman, John Burns, H.H. Champion and John E. Williams as well as by Sparling from the Socialist League. The demonstration ended in a riot when some of the participants attacked the upper-class clubs that lay on their route out. The rioting allegedly began when a poorly dressed man threw a war medal through the window of the Carlton Club shouting: 'We were not the scum of the country when we were fighting for bondholders in Egypt, you dogs!'[122] It was an explosion of working-class discontent and the establishment was shocked. Sparling was quoted in the *Freeman's Journal* as saying that 'although they did not approve of the riotous proceedings . . . they were not sorry for what had occurred, because it was good that the upper class should realise the fact that society does not rest upon such secure bases as they imagined'.[123]

Fear of social revolution was in the air and Radical MP Joseph Chamberlain hurried to insist that 'the only possible excuse for a revolution was that there was no constitutional method of obtaining redress for grievances, but in this country constitutional means of redress were brought between all'.[124] The report of the Dublin public meeting was printed in the *Freeman's Journal* alongside horrified reports on the London rioting. The league meeting, strangely, focussed on a paper on Lassalle by Lipmann rather than on a discussion of the previous day's events. Indeed it was business as usual and the rioting was apparently not even mentioned during the discussion afterwards.[125] Thomas Fitzpatrick chaired the meeting in the course of which a man named Cashman pointed out that in his opinion 'people here would have nothing to do with Deism or Atheism' but would probably agree to the abolition of the class system and a redistribution of wealth.[126] Home rule was raised as an issue by John O'Regan, a member of the league who had 'been some time on the Continent'.[127] O'Regan claimed that 'there would be more scope for a socialist movement under an Irish government here than under Imperial government'.[128] It is clear that there was no unanimity within the branch on the question of home rule. In a general sense, commented George King in a letter to London, they 'would never make much headway here until the Home Rule question is settled'.[129]

SCHUMANN AND THE BOTTLEMAKERS' DISPUTE

The Socialist League's most successful venture in Dublin was, through Fritz Schumann, its involvement in support of Dublin bottlemakers locked out by their employers. Schumann's role made him a figure of approbation among the city's trade unionists and the league got the opportunity to practise its internationalism in a very real and positive sense. The dispute began on 20 February 1886 with the lockout of nearly three hundred finishers, blowers and gatherers from Dublin's three bottle factories. The issue was an attempt to enforce a wage reduction which the bottlemakers were unwilling to accept. Since 1875 there had been a steady erosion of the wages of bottlemakers in Dublin. In 1877 the employers insisted on making a deduction off the amount of work completed by not paying for two dozen of what were called 'refused' bottles. In 1878 and 1879 there were further wage cuts but the situation seemed to improve in 1883 when the employers granted an increase in regular wages and overtime.[130] In 1884, however, there was a reduction of wages in the Scottish bottlemaking industry and Dublin employers moved to lower their labour costs. The Dublin bottlemakers in April 1884 consented to give up their wages and be paid by the piece in future. This, according to the workers, involved a wage decrease of 22 per cent.[131] Wages in Dublin were roughly equal to those in the English bottlemaking industry with wages in Scotland significantly lower than both regions. The Dublin factories, nonetheless, were making substantial profits despite the stiff competition from Scotland.[132] In February 1886 the employers demanded another wage reduction, this time a reduction in the payment for each gross of bottles of six pence.[133] The workers refused and requested their employers to meet a deputation to discuss the dispute. The outcome was an attempt by the three factories to enforce the new wage level and the workers were effectively locked out.

Within a few days of the lockout the employers met with the workers and offered to decrease the proposed reduction to four-and-a-half pence per gross and then at a meeting on 26 February they suggested submitting the dispute to arbitration. The workers accepted this proposal on the basis that they be reinstated prior to arbitration on the original wage rate.[134] Consequently the workers at the Ringsend Bottle Company and at Messrs Campbell on the North Lotts resumed work but Messrs King on Charlotte Quay remained closed. Messrs King refused to take back four of the bottlemakers and they refused to dismiss the five men who had accepted the wage reduction and continued to work during the lockout.[135] Hostility towards those who had worked was intense; indeed the two bottleworkers who had accepted the employers' rate at the Ringsend Bottle Company had been assaulted during the dispute and were placed under police protection.[136] Messrs King, however, held firm and the manager was dispatched to Sweden to recruit an alternative workforce. The Swedes, twenty-five bottleworkers with forty-seven dependants, arrived in March to the Charlotte Quay factory to discover that they had been recruited as strikebreakers.[137] Fritz Schumann, as a fellow Scandinavian, was requested by the bottlemakers to approach the Swedes and inform them of the dispute. The Swedes were horrified to hear that a lockout was in progress and told Schumann that they had been deceived by the manager who had assured them that there was no dispute. The manager, said Schumann, had told them that 'the reason was because he could not get men elsewhere; that there were a few bottlemakers in Dublin out of work, but that there were only the drunken loafers hanging about the public houses'.[138]

The Swedes stopped work and contacted the Swedish consul about the situation. They also appointed Schumann as their representative and approached a solicitor to discuss their legal position.[139] The living conditions of the Swedes at Charlotte Quay were precarious and they only survived with the assistance of Schumann and the recently created Dublin Trades Council. Schumann was the Swedish bottlemakers' delegate to the trades council and it was his responsibility to look after what he referred to as 'the Scandinavian Colony at Charlotte Quay'.[140] When T.J. O'Reilly of the trades council declared colourfully that the Swedes had to suffer 'hardships and privations that would shock a Fiji islander', he was highlighting genuine distress.[141] Schumann requested a doctor to visit the Swedes and in a letter to the *Freeman's Journal* he publicized the doctor's findings.[142] A woman and a girl had bronchitis, four women had feverish colds, four infants had serious coughs and a girl was suffering from a skin disease. In a letter to Schumann the doctor claimed that 'the atmosphere . . . is most unwholesome, and if they are allowed to remain in it typhus fever . . . will probably break out among them'.[143] On 11 April a public meeting about the dispute was held at Irishtown with Schumann and William Graham of the bottlemakers as the main speakers. Five trades bands and a considerable crowd attended and heard Schumann explain the position of the Swedes and comment that the situation 'showed the necessity for internationalism'.[144]

In the event Messrs King were forced to back down and to compensate the Swedes for having brought them to Ireland under false pretences. On 26 April they returned via Copenhagen with £450 which their solicitor had elicited from Messrs King and, through Fritz Schumann, they expressed their pleasure 'at being removed from the disagreeable position in which they were placed'.[145] The *Freeman's Journal* commented that they 'certainly displayed a most uncompromising fealty to the principles of Trades Unionism' and had kept their promises to the Dublin bottlemakers 'in the most straightforward fashion'.[146] At a meeting of the Dublin Trades Council on 25 April a special vote of thanks was passed commending Schumann for 'his untiring exertions' in the interests of the bottlemakers and Dublin trade unionism.[147] In accepting the vote of thanks Schumann mentioned that he was preparing a paper on the matter which he would forward to the *Social Democrat* for publication. Writing to Sparling in July Schumann explained that the dispute had convinced the Dublin bottlemakers of the concrete advantages of international solidarity:

> The necessity for international communication and action between the workers in the Glassbottle trade was strongly felt during their late strike here, and I was asked to draw up Rules etc. for an International Society of that trade. This I did and they have met a hearty approval in Berkshire, Lancashire and Dublin and now are to be laid before the Congress to meet in London in September. The Societies in Germany, Denmark, Sweden and Norway have resolved to send delegates.[148]

Schumann went on to suggest that the Socialist League 'would do useful work and gain ground among the workers' by backing the new union practically by allowing the league's hall in London to be used for the congress.[149] He also asked Sparling to send notices to socialist papers in France, Spain and Italy inviting bottlemakers in those countries to send delegates. The league did make its hall available and the inaugural congress of the International Union of Glass Bottlemakers was held there between 16 and 19 October with delegates from England, Scotland, Ireland, Germany, Austria and Denmark.[150] The conference was a success and the union was firmly established. Schumann had played a pivotal role in concretizing the type of internationalism that was more often talked about than practised.

WILLIAM MORRIS IN DUBLIN

By March 1886 Michael Gabriel was expressing satisfaction with the pace of progress in Dublin and was confident of the hegemony of the Socialist League among socialist circles in the city: 'I am of [the] opinion that if a branch of the Federation started here we could get along faster, we have postponed receiving several applications as we want to feel some of our man before admitting him.'[151] To increase its profile the branch attempted to bring in a prominent British socialist to address meetings in Dublin. Schumann had made some efforts to induce Dr Edward Aveling to travel to the city but they were to no avail.[152] In February a group of people known to R.I. Lipmann decided to invite William Morris, perhaps encouraged by the article on him in the *Dublin University Review* the previous August. The prime mover was undoubtedly James Walker of the Contemporary Club.[153] Lipmann, who was secretary of the branch at this stage, wrote to London on the notepaper of the Philosophical Society of Trinity College enthusing that 'Morris's visit to Dublin I expect will do us unmeasureable of good. I know so many ladies of "big College guns" who are so anxious to hear him'.[154] There was clearly some confusion here as the socialists believed Morris was coming to Dublin for their benefit. Whatever occurred Michael Gabriel wrote to London in February informing Sparling that they had removed Lipmann as secretary as he had 'been acting in such a way as to entirely prevent us from carrying on our meetings'.[155] Gabriel replaced him as branch secretary. It is likely that Lipmann had attempted to arrange the Morris meeting as a university event behind the back of his own branch. On the same day that Lipmann wrote bragging about 'big College guns', Michael Gabriel was writing: 'I hear in the form of rumour that Mr Morris intends coming here next month on the invitation of gentlemen not connected with the Socialist League, amongst whom is one of our members (Lipmann, Sec). If this is the case, if comrade Morris could by using his influence manage to get the meetings he addressed advertised as under the auspices of the Socialist League it would be giving us a good "leg up"'.[156] Such was not Lipmann's agenda and in a letter, this time on the notepaper of the *Dublin University Review*, he expressed his opinion that it 'would be most injurious to the cause' if the meetings were held under the name of the Socialist League.[157] Lipmann, nonetheless, was reinstated as secretary in April.[158]

Morris's series of Dublin meetings was well advertised in advance in the *Freeman's Journal* and in the *Dublin University Review*.[159] The April issue of the *Dublin University Review* also published a ten-page article by Lipmann entitled 'The progress of socialism', which he introduced as taken 'from the writings of P. Lavrov and Karl Marx'.[160] His article was an interesting, if somewhat awkwardly and abstrusely written, survey of European socialism, in particular of social revolutionaries in his home country of Russia. Lipmann, in passing, remarked on the Irish question:

> When Ireland raises her ancient flag of Nationalism in the form of peaceful agitation, or in the form of threatening disturbance, or in the form of agrarian and political assassinations . . . there underlies the one idea of the struggle of labour against capital, however expressed, in the forms of struggling, warring and protesting groups against the reigning power that protects that capital, and aids its exploitation of labour and its concentration. It is only voluntary blindness that will prevent our seeing that underlying element of the contemporary social crisis.[161]

Lipmann also argued that socialism was about more than the conflict between labour and capital: it had a moral dimension. 'Socialism appears', he wrote, 'as claiming the best, the most just, and most moral social intercourse; its objects are to extirpate competition that severs people into hostile classes and to establish a solidarity of peoples on the only possible firm foundation.'[162] Lipmann's abstruseness, however, provoked an attack from a supporter of the SDF, Allen Upward, who in a subsequent issue retorted: 'Are your readers to think that the contemptible academic kind of Socialism treated of by Mr Lipmann really represents that mighty movement? No Sir.'[163] The April edition of the *Dublin University Review* also published a review of the socialist Edward Carpenter's book of poetry *Towards Democracy*.[164]

William Morris arrived in Dublin on the morning of 9 April. At 7 a.m. six or seven members of the branch met him 'with much (too sleepy to spell) fidelity' at the quayside in Kingstown*.[165] It was a time of great political excitement as Gladstone's first Home Rule Bill had been introduced in the House of Commons the previous day. The 'people here', he wrote to Jenny, his eldest daughter, 'are in great excitement about the Home Rule business: when we got to Kingston [sic] we found that the news was there before us, Gladstone's speech all in full in the Irish papers. It was as I supposed it would be — a piece of constitution making of the most ingenious kind'.[166] On the evening of his arrival Morris gave a lecture on the 'Aims of Art' at the Molesworth Hall for the people that had initiated the visit. This meeting had to be held before properly advertising Morris as a socialist because 'the majority', claimed Gabriel, 'of those who will pay his expenses are against Socialism'.[167] The audience, according to Morris, was made up primarily of 'ladies and gentlemen' with 'a few workmen scattered among the audience, and our comrades of the Dublin branch put in an appearance'.[168] The 'ladies and gentlemen', and presumably the ladies of the 'big College guns', were not pleased by Morris's lecture as he argued strongly for socialism 'as a necessity for the new birth of art'.[169] Writing to Sparling, Morris claimed that many of the 'respectables' left the room at an early stage of the proceedings.[170]

The following evening Morris spoke at the Saturday Club on the topic 'What is Socialism?' The audience, mostly of working-class men, numbered about six hundred and Morris was well listened to during his forty-five-minute speech.[171] He made the blunder of referring to Dublin's main street as Sackville Street 'which is popularly known as O'Connell Street, a name which the authorities refuse to accept' but 'on a hint from the chairman, I corrected with all good will, and so was allowed to go on, with cheers'.[172] His speech cogently argued the socialist case:

> Workers everywhere must first of all learn to combine. Trades unions had done a great deal since the time when he was a boy, but they should now look upon the matter from a different point of view. Trades unions claimed for the masters some share of the wealth which was produced, but they should now say — 'We will have masters no longer, because we don't need

---

*Kingstown is now known as Dún Laoghaire.

them. What we claim is that men shall have all the produce of their labour'. (Applause and hisses.) Socialists looked forward to a society in which all wealth should be held collectively. The greatest happiness of all was a higher ideal than the greatest happiness of the greatest number. The maxim of Socialism was 'from each what he can do, and to each what he needs.'[173]

A poor debate followed but when the chairman closed the meeting and asked Morris to sum up, the audience decided that it was too early to finish the discussion. General tumult ensued for about fifteen minutes and all six hundred joined in singing 'God Save Ireland'.[174] Morris, regardless, left with the impression that 'a large part of the audience [was] sympathetic'.[175]

Fritz Schumann's rooms at 19 William Street were the venue the next evening, 11 April, for a private meeting between William Morris and the members of the Dublin branch. He found the Dublin socialists 'energetic and enthusiastic' and spent what he termed 'a very satisfactory evening' in their company.[176] It was also, no doubt, an evening for reflection on the difficulties faced by socialists in Ireland. Writing in *The Commonweal*, after his return to Britain, Morris outlined them thus:

> It is clear that at present the religious matter is the difficulty; but I cannot help thinking that when Home Rule is established the Catholic clergy will begin to set after their kind, and try after more and more power, till the Irish gorge rises and rejects them. The Protestant religious feeling being dogmatic, and not political, is hopeless to deal with. Meanwhile, open-air meetings are not possible for us in Dublin — at least till we are stronger in numbers . . . Of course, though I saw many people in Dublin (and many of them, by the way, not far from Socialists), my short stay in one place in the country could not add much to my power of judging of our chances of success there. It is a matter of course that until the Irish get Home Rule they will listen to nothing else, and equally so that as soon as they get Home Rule they must deal at once with the land question. On the whole, I fear it seems likely that they will have to go through the dismal road of peasant-proprietorship before they get to anything like Socialism; and that road in a country so isolated and so peculiar as Ireland, may be a long one.[177]

The last engagement for Morris was to be two nights later so he had the opportunity to renew his acquaintance with Dublin which, several years before, he had described as 'dirty and slatternly' although 'not altogether an ugly town'.[178] Now, he admitted, he found his opinion slightly modified: 'Dublin on the whole I rather like: there is a sort of cosy shabbiness about it which, joined to the clear air, is pleasant.'[179] Morris visited the Contemporary Club while in the city where he probably met C.H. Oldham, T.W. Rolleston and other Dublin writers and intellectuals. The young W.B. Yeats, who was a member of the club, may first have come across Morris at this time. He was certainly moving in these circles and had his first poems and articles published in the *Dublin University Review* between April 1885 and November 1886. Yeats admired Morris; when he moved to London in 1887 he regularly attended Socialist League lectures in the hall attached to Kelmscott House, Morris's home in Hammersmith, and was soon a regular supper guest in the house itself. Moreover, he became acquainted with H.H. Sparling and George Bernard Shaw through Kelmscott House and he join-ed a French class begun by a group of socialists who intended to visit Paris. Yeats found, however, that he did not like working-class socialists and he liked them even less after a Socialist League meeting during which he was harshly criticized for preferring Parnell to Davitt. Later, following another disputatious meeting, he ceased attending socialist lectures although he re-tained a high regard for Morris. This continued respect may not have been unrelated to Morris's praise for *The Wanderings of Oisín* (1889), which Yeats had presented to May Morris in the expectation that her father would see it. 'You write my sort of poetry', Morris told him during an accidental meeting, and he promised to mention the book in *The Commonweal*. However, Yeats's fleeting interest in socialism faded despite his liking for Morris.[180]

On Tuesday, 13 April 1886, the day of his final meeting in Dublin, William Morris took a trip to the Wicklow mountains which struck him as being 'very beautiful'.[181] That evening he delivered a lecture on the 'Political Outlook' for the Dublin Socialist League at 30 Great Brunswick Street. The meeting was almost entirely composed of working-class men; Morris after-wards commented that they 'seemed for the most part heartily with me' and he deemed the discussion a success.[182] The visit, in general terms, pro-vided the Socialist League in Dublin with good propaganda and increased the profile of socialism in the city. However, it did not in truth provide the branch with the 'leg up' that Michael Gabriel had expected. In fact, April marked the zenith for the league in Ireland and its decline began as sum-mer approached.

THE DECLINE OF THE DUBLIN SOCIALIST LEAGUE

Summer was a quiet time for Dublin radicals: the Saturday Club, which provided such a focus for the league, adjourned, as it did every year, for the duration of the summer. In 1886 the political climate was particularly unfavourable to its work and it is no coincidence that interest in the Dublin Socialist League waned from April onwards.

On 8 April Prime Minister William Gladstone introduced the Govern-ment of Ireland Bill to the House of Commons. Parnell, in a speech that afternoon, outlined his reservations about aspects of the bill but stated that the Irish MPs would accept it as an adequate settlement of the home rule question if certain amendments were made. Nationalists in Ireland greeted Gladstone's bill with euphoria and the entire country followed the debates on the bill with great enthusiasm. Most people were convinced that home rule was imminent. However, by the end of May it was clear that divisions in the Liberal Party meant that Gladstone stood little chance of getting the measure passed. On 8 June, the Home Rule Bill was rejected by 343 votes to 313. Joseph Chamberlain split the Liberal Party and, with another ninety-three MPs, formed the Liberal Unionists. The subsequent general election was dominated by the issue of Irish home rule and throughout the remainder of the year most Irish people were riveted by the issue. In May Fritz Schumann, in a letter to Sparling, admitted to the problems created for the Socialist League branch: 'It is extremely difficult just now to get people to think of anything but Home Rule. All which we will be able to do in the way of lecturing is to prepare for the Winter session.'[183] At the end of June, George King wrote to the league in London: 'We have given up our weekly meetings. No one would attend. Dublin men do not believe in meetings during the summer.'[184]

The branch may have adjourned its weekly meetings but its members were sufficiently in touch with each other to have an argument which required the attention of Sparling. What the differences were can only be guessed at but Sparling travelled to Dublin in August to try to pull the branch together.[185] 'I am happy to be able to inform you', wrote John O'Gorman in early August, 'that Comrade Sparling has succeeded in settling most of the differences that existed between members of the branch and there is now a fair prospect that the branch will be on a firm basis.'[186] The branch could ill-afford such internal strife. In June it had advanced its own analysis of the wider problems for socialists in Ireland:

> Anyone having even a superficial knowledge of the ideals of the Irish people, both on political and religious subjects, will readily admit that it's no easy matter for Socialists to hold their own amongst them . . . The majority of the people will not tolerate any movement that appears to them to be out of harmony with the national sentiment; they believe that the mere attainment of a Parliament on College Green will be a cure for all the ills they are afflicted with; reason and logic are powerless in the face of appeals to race-hatreds and past wrongs. The great difficulty is the religious one; the priests have the people so well in hand, that anything they set their faces against has more than ordinary difficulties to overcome. Their influence at the present time is most powerful on account of the change of front on the part of the hierarchy in their attitude to the national movement. Ireland being so much isolated, and the attention of the people being so much devoted to one particular subject, it is scarcely to be wondered that they are less advanced on subjects of more importance to their welfare. All things considered the wonder is not that we have done so little, but

that we have been able to keep the flag flying so long in the face of all the difficulties we have had to contend against.[187]

This certainly pinpointed the central problems for Irish socialists but the form and tone were arguably condescending and whinging. One wonders whether this article in *The Commonweal* precipitated the division that Sparling was obliged to heal. This would not be surprising as there were clear differences between Socialist League members on the issue of home rule. As regards 'race-hatreds', Morris had written more sympathetically:

> For my part I do not believe in the race-hatred of the Irish against the English: they hate their English *masters*, and well they may . . . But when Irish people have got rid of their masters, Irish and English both, there will . . . be no foreigners to hate in Ireland, and she will look back at the present struggle for mere nationality as a nightmare of the charmed sleep in which Landlordism and Capitalism have held her so long, as they have other nations.[188]

Whatever the reason, the summer recess or internal division, the branch began to wilt despite John O'Gorman's optimism. By the end of the summer the Dublin Socialist League seemed lethargic if not moribund. Joseph Karpel, a Russian member of the branch, wrote to the league in London in early September to inform it of a number of hands being laid off at Clery & Co. on O'Connell Street but this was simply a report for *The Commonweal* rather than an indication that the Dublin socialists had an involvement.[189] On 11 September *The Commonweal* published an article on the *Freeman's Journal* by J.E. McCarthy, a Dublin factory worker who joined the local branch ten days later.[190] Whatever the local organizational difficulties, McCarthy made plain his faith in socialism: 'Socialism will continue to advance like a prairie-fire. The tyranny, cruelty, greed and inhumanity of commercialism has lighted it. When the revolution has passed, there will rise out of the ashes of the old order a grander, nobler and happier society, in which men will be helping brothers not bloated masters and starving slaves as we find them today.'[191] This expectant vision of a happier and noble world characterized many of those who participated in the early years of the 'socialist revival'. It was a time of hope and energy when socialist activists felt that the ineluctable tide of history was on their side. McCarthy contributed another article, this time on 'Technical Education in Ireland', during October. Reporting on a lecture on this topic at the City of Dublin Workingmen's Club, he wrote:

> Now, every Socialist is in favour of universal technical education, but most decidedly *not under capitalism*. Schumann, a Danish Socialist, fully proved some time ago to Dublin working men the wretched condition of the workers in continental countries where this education is established. All

workers may rest assured that any benefits arising from greater or more skilful production will not be reaped by them, but by the exploiting classes alone, as long as Capitalism is King.[192]

Meanwhile the Socialist League in London was beginning to develop some problems. May Morris, a daughter of William Morris, wrote to Andreas Scheu in late September complaining of 'constant bickering among a few of the London members' of the league: 'I am sick of the contentions — those who are not on either side (fancy *sides* in our small body) talk of nothing else, even while admitting that the whole thing is nonsensical.'[193] The council of the league had on 17 May expelled Karl Reuss as a spy for the German police. Reuss, and some supporters, countercharged Victor Dave, another league member, with being a spy and this accusation was backed by a Reuss-biased 'commission' which exonerated Reuss himself. Both Reuss and Dave were anarchists, although from contending factions.[194] Anarchism in Britain at the time was a rather diffuse and murky affair. It later emerged that Reuss actually was the spy after he betrayed Johann Neve, an anarchist wanted in Germany, but in October 1886 *The Anarchist*, which was Britain's only native anarchist paper, devoted almost the whole of its front page to an article attacking the Socialist League and supporting Reuss.[195] The dispute in London was noted in Dublin where members of the branch received copies of *The Anarchist*. On 17 October, John O'Gorman, now apparently secretary of the Dublin branch, wrote to Sparling informing him that 'some of our people are desirous of seeing what the Council has to say to the charges made by *The Anarchist*'.[196] Sparling replied dismissing the charges but this failed to satisfy Dublin members. Writing again on 24 October, O'Gorman said that the letter was badly received and that on the motion of Michael Gabriel, and seconded by a member named O'Connor, a resolution was unanimously adopted stating:

> That we consider as most unsatisfactory the letter from the Central office purporting to be from the secretary, but unsigned by any person; that we do not look upon the statement in *The Anarchist* as as much beneath notice as stated in that letter; that we cannot endorse the action of the Council in expelling Reuss, or sheltering Dave, until we shall have satisfactory proofs of the innocence of the one and of the guilt of the other.[197]

This was essentially a vote of no confidence in the executive of the Socialist League. That they should have taken the word of *The Anarchist* over that of their own council also indicates the influence and strength of anarchism in the Dublin branch. 'If the matter', wrote O'Gorman, 'be capable of explanation, it had better be cleared up once and for all. If a mistake has been made it ought to be acknowledged even if a little hurtful to personal pride.'[198] The council of the league, reeling from the attack by *The Anarchist*, must have found this stance by one of its branches rather disconcerting. O'Gorman later distanced himself from the position taken by the branch; he told Sparling that he himself did not see the Reuss–Dave squabble as particularly important and that 'what some of our members (and I regret to say the most energetic of them) principally find fault with is the apparent want of impartiality shown by the Council'.[199] On 9 November the Dublin branch convened a special meeting to consider the affair. After a long 'desultory' discussion it was decided to let the matter drop and O'Gorman let Sparling know that his 'letters and assurances considerably lessened the hostility to the Council (practical Anarchists, we) that was displayed at other meetings'.[200] Complaints from Dublin, however, did not entirely end here as George King wrote to London in mid-November alleging that *The Commonweal* had become the organ of the council rather than a medium for the branches.[201]

Otherwise, the Dublin Socialist League remained largely inactive through October and November although Gabriel delivered an address on 'The Temperance Question from a Socialist Stand-point' on 11 November. His argument, common in the socialist movement, was 'that while the adoption of temperance might benefit only a section of the workers, it would make them more thoughtful, more discontented, and thus pave the way for the Social Revolution'.[202] This championing of sobriety fed into a wider movement for temperance in Ireland which, while well meaning in its intentions, was often highly moralizing and patronizing in its implications. Almost invariably, the working classes (and labourers rather than tradesmen) were seen as the element to be redeemed and rescued from the evils of drink. This did not go entirely unnoticed, and when, for example, rural labourers' leaders in 1881 called on their followers to abstain from alcohol they were angrily replied to by a Listowel labourer who resented the imputation that the labouring class was peculiarly intemperate in its drinking habits. Dismissing this 'wholesome advice' as 'a gratuitous insult' he wrote: 'I say the labourer is as much entitled to legitimate refreshment in the shape of a pint or two of porter as the farmer is to his Jameson, or the landlord to his Saumur or Medoc.'[203] Nonetheless, support for the redemptive aims of the temperance movement was particularly strong among socialists in the late nineteenth century and many activists saw cultural change as an important part of the socialist project.[204]

In late November 1886, O'Gorman wrote to London to say that the Dublin branch was on the brink of collapse.[205] By now the council of the league was further at war with itself on the issue of parliamentary action. A section of the council, gathered around Dr Aveling, Mahon, Bax and Eleanor Marx, had come out strongly in opposition to the policy of anti-parliamentarianism. It was a dispute that would drag on for some time until the dissidents opted out of the Socialist League altogether. While it had no direct bearing on the desolation in Dublin, it hardly encouraged the members to maintain the branch. O'Gorman wrote to Sparling: 'You may fancy that the Dave affair may be the cause of this but I say positively it is not, we would have died of inanimation three weeks ago were it not for the row over that business. One or two may use that as an excuse for resignation but they would have invented some other excuse if it had never existed.'[206] It is clear that demoralization had set in because of the league's lack of success, which was partly the result of the dominance of the home rule issue in 1886. On 11 December George King contacted the league in London to say that he, J.E. McCarthy, John O'Gorman, Joseph Karpel, Samuel Hayes, Thomas Fitzpatrick and O'Connor had all decided the Dublin branch was finished and 'you may therefore consider the Dublin branch of the Socialist League dissolved'.[207] Clearly there was some problem with this process, however, as O'Gorman made two efforts in December to convene a branch meeting to discuss the distribution of a leaflet that London was preparing.[208] Then in late December Auguste Coulon sent out notices to all the members to meet in his place and nearly all attended as well as one who had resigned and two who had not been members. It was decided to agree nothing on the future of the branch until after the Christmas holiday.[209]

The festive season, however, failed to regenerate the spirit of the branch and it limped its way out of existence within two or three months. Ironically one of the last acts of the branch was to attend a funeral. On 27 January 1887 John A. Ryan, the founding treasurer of the branch, died after a long illness and most of the members came together at his funeral at Glasnevin a few days later.[210] Members did, however, continue to take advantage of available platforms and on 24 January Thomas Fitzpatrick joined a debate at the Coffee Palace in Townsend Street, attacking a lecturer who recommended thrift, temperance and technical education for the working class. He told an audience of some three hundred labourers that 'however good temperance and its kindred virtues may be in themselves, or might benefit isolated individuals, their general adoption under the present system of Society would not materially improve the position of the workers'.[211] Gabriel and Fitzpatrick patently differed on the virtues of temperance. Fitzpatrick went on to agree with J.E. McCarthy, contending that 'technical education would only make the worker a more skilful tool in the hands of the capitalist'.

The last communication between what remained of the Dublin branch and the London office of the Socialist League occurred on 24 March 1887 when O'Gorman wrote to say that a meeting arranged for the previous Sunday had not taken place because 'the speakers turned up but there was no audience'.[212] The Socialist League was finished in Dublin as an organized force but its members, by and large, remained active over the next few years.

NOTES AND REFERENCES

1   *Justice*, 11 Oct. 1884.
2   For Lane's view of Hyndman, see John Quail, *The Slow Burning Fuse: The Lost History of the British Anarchists* (London, 1978), pp. 24–6, 33–5.
3   E.P. Thompson, *William Morris: Romantic to Revolutionary* (New York, 1976), pp. 344–5.
4   William Morris to J.L. Joynes, 25 Dec. 1884, William Morris Papers, BL.
5   William Morris to Andreas Scheu, 13 Aug. 1884; William Morris to Andreas Scheu, 20 Aug. 1884, published in Phillip Henderson (ed.), *The Letters of William Morris* (London, 1950), pp. 210–12. Hereafter cited as *Letters*.
6   William Morris to Andreas Scheu, 13 Aug. 1884, *Letters*, p. 210.
7   'On every possible occasion', Andreas Scheu later wrote, 'Hyndman . . . related how . . . Gladstone mocked at the appeal of the . . . Federation because it contained the name of a foreigner [Scheu], which proved that the basic ideas of the social democratic propaganda could not be wholly home-grown.' See E.P. Thompson, op. cit., pp. 342–3.
8   ibid., p. 341.
9   ibid., p. 341.
10 William Morris to Robert Thompson, 1 Jan. 1885, *Letters*, pp. 226–7.
11 H.M. Hyndman to William Morris, 27 Nov. 1884, William Morris Papers, BL.
12 H.M. Hyndman to William Morris, 8 Dec. 1884, William Morris Papers, BL.
13 Yvonne Kapp, *Eleanor Marx: Volume II: The Crowded Years, 1884–1898* (London, 1976), p. 58; H.M. Hyndman, *Further Reminiscences* (London, 1912), p. 138.
14 Yvonne Kapp, op. cit., p. 59.
15 E.P. Thompson, op. cit., pp. 351–2.
16 ibid., pp. 353–4. On Johann Most's activities while in Britain, see John Quail, op. cit., pp. 11–13 and *passim*.
17 William Morris to Robert Thompson, 1 Jan. 1885, *Letters*, p. 227.
18 ibid., p. 227.
19 J.L. Mahon to Derbyshire, 3 Jan. 1885, Socialist League Papers, IISH.
20 J.L. Mahon to Sec. SDF, 31 Dec. 1884, Socialist League Papers, IISH.
21 William Morris to Andreas Scheu, 28 Dec. 1884, Andreas Scheu Papers, IISH.
22 William Morris to Andreas Scheu, 20 Aug. 1884, Andreas Scheu Papers, IISH.
23 *Daily News*, 8 Jan. 1885.
24 *The Commonweal*, Feb. 1885.
25 William Morris to James Mavor, 27 Mar. 1885, Andreas Scheu Papers, IISH.
26 William Morris to Mrs Burne-Jones, Oct. n.d. 1877, *Letters*, p. 95.
27 ibid., pp. 95–6.
28 William Morris to Jane Alice Morris, 7 May 1883, *Letters*, p. 171.
29 James Doyle to William Morris, 18 July 1886, Socialist League Papers, IISH.
30 Socialist League to Sec. SDF, 7 Jan. 1887, Socialist League Papers, IISH.
31 H.W. Lee to Socialist League, 11 Jan. 1887, Socialist League Papers, IISH.
32 *The Commonweal*, Feb. 1885.
33 E. Owens Blackburne to Socialist League, n.d. but Mar. 1885, Socialist League Papers, IISH.

34　Samuel Hayes to H.H. Sparling, 12 Sept. 1885, Socialist League Papers, IISH.

35　Hayes (ibid.) gives the distinct impression that no communication was conducted with the Socialist League after the 'open letter' on the split was received. On the other hand he claims the DDA had strong links to the SDF.

36　P. Hayden to J.L. Mahon, 16 Feb. 1885, Socialist League Papers, IISH.

37　Pakenham Beatty to Sec. Socialist League, 12 Feb. 1885, Socialist League Papers, IISH.

38　See the letter from Pakenham Beatty to Sec. Socialist League, 27 May 1885, Socialist League Papers, IISH, where he gives his address as Mill Hill Park, Acton, Middlesex.

39　J.P. O'Carroll to Socialist League, 3 Apr. 1885, Socialist League Papers, IISH. Also see note attached.

40　D.C. Campbell to Sec. Socialist League, 4 Apr. 1885, Socialist League Papers, IISH.

41　D.C. Campbell to Sec. Socialist League, 16 Apr. 1885, Socialist League Papers, IISH.

42　ibid.

43　Michael Gabriel to J.L. Mahon, June n.d. 1885, Socialist League Papers, IISH.

44　T.W. Rolleston was a member of the Young Ireland Society which he joined in November 1884. He favoured home rule as a stepping stone to complete independence. See Leon Ó Broin, *Revolutionary Underground: The Story of the Irish Republican Brotherhood, 1858–1924* (Dublin, 1976), p. 37.

45　T.W. Rolleston to Socialist League, 17 July 1885, Socialist League Papers, IISH.

46　C.H. Oldham to Manager, *The Commonweal*, 30 Aug. 1885, Socialist League Papers, IISH. Another prominent figure to purchase material from the Socialist League was Edward Dowden who requested copies of Morris's *Chants for Socialists* in early 1887. Edward Dowden to *The Commonweal*, 10 Mar. 1887, Socialist League Papers, IISH.

47　T.W. Rolleston to Socialist League, 1 Jan. 1886, Socialist League Papers, IISH.

48　Marcus Bourke, *John O'Leary: A Study in Irish Separatism* (Tralee, 1967), p. 181.

49　H. Rowlandson, 'The Socialist League and its poet', *Dublin University Review*, Aug. 1885, p. 45.

50　ibid., p. 49.

51　ibid., p. 54.

52　ibid., p. 55.

53　George King to Socialist League, 28 July 1885, Socialist League Papers, IISH.

54　George King to H.H. Sparling, 26 Sept. 1885, Socialist League Papers, IISH.

55　*The Commonweal*, Sept. 1885.

56　George King to H.H. Sparling, 26 Sept. 1885, Socialist League Papers, IISH.

57　*The Commonweal*, Aug. 1885.

58　*The Commonweal*, Sept. 1885.

59　Samuel Hayes to H.H. Sparling, 12 Sept. 1885, Socialist League Papers, IISH.

60　ibid.

61　ibid.

62　Michael Gabriel to H.H. Sparling, n.d. but late Sept. 1885, Socialist League Papers, IISH.

63　Samuel Hayes to H.H. Sparling, 16 Sept. 1885, Socialist League Papers, IISH.

64 Michael Gabriel to H.H. Sparling, 20 Oct. 1885, Socialist League Papers, IISH.
65 *The Commonweal*, Oct. 1885.
66 ibid.
67 ibid.
68 *The Commonweal*, 7 Jan. 1888.
69 Michael Gabriel to Socialist League, 11 Nov. 1885, Socialist League Papers, IISH.
70 ibid.
71 *Freeman's Journal*, 16 Nov. 1885.
72 For Gabriel's acknowledged anarchism see the report of the Socialist League meeting in *Freeman's Journal*, 15 Jan. 1886.
73 *Freeman's Journal*, 14 Dec. 1885.
74 Michael Gabriel to Socialist League, 22 Nov. 1885, Socialist League Papers, IISH.
75 Samuel Hayes to H.H. Sparling, 14 Dec. 1885, Socialist League Papers, IISH.
76 *The Commonweal*, 5 Feb. 1887.
77 Samuel Hayes to H.H. Sparling, 14 Dec. 1885, Socialist League Papers, IISH. Hayes lived at 28 Georges Place (north) while Ryan resided at 145 Great Brunswick Street.
78 Monthly Membership Report, Dublin branch, Dec. 1885, Socialist League Papers, IISH.
79 *Freeman's Journal*, 7 Dec. 1885.
80 ibid.
81 George King to H.H. Sparling, 26 Sept. 1885, Socialist League Papers, IISH.
82 James Doyle to Socialist League, 7 Mar. 1886, Socialist League Papers, IISH.
83 Alexander R. Donald to J.L. Mahon, 1 Feb. 1885, Socialist League Papers, IISH.
84 *Freeman's Journal*, 21 Dec. 1885.
85 *Freeman's Journal*, 4 Jan. 1886.
86 ibid.
87 George King to H.H. Sparling, 11 Dec. 1886, Socialist League Papers, IISH.
88 *The Commonweal*, 5 Feb. 1887.
89 William F. Bailey, 'The coming socialism', *Dublin University Review*, Dec. 1885, p. 341.
90 ibid., p. 341.
91 ibid., p. 350.
92 William Morris, 'True and false society', *Collected Works, Volume 23* (London, 1915), p. 237.
93 William F. Bailey, op. cit., p. 350.
94 Monthly Membership Reports, Dublin branch, Jan., Mar., Apr. 1885, Socialist League Papers, IISH.
95 *Freeman's Journal*, 8 Jan. 1886, describes Schumann as a burly artisan. His nationality is confirmed in *The Commonweal*, 23 Aug 1888.
96 *The Radical*, 28 Mar. 1881.
97 Karl Marx to Alfred Talandier, 10 Nov. 1878, in Karl Marx and Friedrich Engels, *Collected Works*, Volume 45 (London, 1991), pp. 336–42, 551.
98 On Lavrov see Yvonne Kapp, op. cit., *passim*.

99 *Freeman's Journal*, 5 Jan. 1886.
100 *Freeman's Journal*, 8 Jan. 1886; Samuel Hayes to H.H. Sparling, 9 Jan. 1886, Socialist League Papers, IISH.
101 Samuel Hayes to H.H. Sparling, 9 Jan, 1886, Socialist League Papers, IISH.
102 *Freeman's Journal*, 8 Jan. 1886.
103 ibid.
104 ibid.
105 *Freeman's Journal*, 11 Jan. 1886.
106 ibid.
107 Michael Gabriel to H.H. Sparling, 20 Jan. 1886, Socialist League Papers, IISH.
108 *Freeman's Journal*, 14 Jan. 1886.
109 *Freeman's Journal*, 15 Jan. 1886.
110 Samuel Hayes to H.H. Sparling, 18 Jan. 1886, Socialist League Papers, IISH.
111 ibid.
112 ibid.
113 *Freeman's Journal*, 25 Jan. 1886.
114 On Morris and anarchism see L.T. Sargent, 'William Morris and the anarchist tradition', in Florence Boos and C.G. Silver (eds.), *Socialism and the Literary Artistry of William Morris* (Missouri, 1990), pp. 61–73. I do not agree, however, with the author's conclusion that Morris was ultimately an anarchist in his political thought.
115 Michael Gabriel to H.H. Sparling, 20 Jan. 1886, Socialist League Papers, IISH.
116 'Report on bottlemakers' strike, Irishtown meeting of April 11, 1886', CSORP (1886) 7469, National Archives.
117 ibid.
118 DMP Files, 1886: Superintendent's Office, G. Division, 15 Nov. 1886, National Archives.
119 DMP Files, 1886: Superintendent's Office, G. Division, 19 Nov. 1886, National Archives.
120 *Thom's Irish Almanac and Official Directory, 1886* (Dublin, 1887), p. 1665.
121 Michael Gabriel to H.H. Sparling, 21 Feb. 1886, Socialist League Papers, IISH.
122 John Quail, op. cit., pp. 43–4.
123 *Freeman's Journal*, 10 Feb. 1886.
124 *Freeman's Journal*, 24 Feb. 1886.
125 *Freeman's Journal*, 10 Feb. 1886.
126 ibid.
127 Samuel Hayes to H.H. Sparling, 2 Jan. 1886, Socialist League Papers, IISH.
128 *Freeman's Journal*, 10 Feb. 1886.
129 George King to Socialist League, 30 June 1886, Socialist League Papers, IISH.
130 *Freeman's Journal*, 26 Feb. 1886.
131 *Freeman's Journal*, 19 Feb. 1886.
132 *Freeman's Journal*, 26 Feb. 1886.
133 *Freeman's Journal*, 19 Feb. 1886.
134 *United Ireland*, 27 Feb. 1886.
135 *Freeman's Journal*, 2 Mar. 1886.
136 *Freeman's Journal*, 26 Feb. 1886.
137 *Freeman's Journal*, 26 Apr. 1886.

138 *Irish Times*, 12 Apr. 1886.
139 ibid.; *Freeman's Journal*, 26 Apr. 1886.
140 *Freeman's Journal*, 15 Apr. 1886.
141 *Freeman's Journal*, 26 Apr. 1886.
142 *Freeman's Journal*, 15 Apr. 1886.
143 Dr F.J.B. Quinlan to Fritz Schumann, 14 Apr. 1886, published in ibid.
144 *Irish Times*, 12 Apr. 1886.
145 *Freeman's Journal*, 27 Apr. 1886.
146 ibid.
147 *Freeman's Journal*, 26 Apr. 1886.
148 Fritz Schumann to H.H. Sparling, 20 July 1886, Socialist League Papers, IISH.
149 ibid.
150 *The Commonweal*, 6 Nov. 1886.
151 Michael Gabriel to H.H. Sparling, Mar. n.d. 1886, Socialist League Papers, IISH.
152 Samuel Hayes to H.H. Sparling, 14 Dec. 1885, Socialist League Papers, IISH; *Freeman's Journal*, 15 Jan. 1886.
153 Michael Gabriel to H.H. Sparling, 7 Mar. 1886, Socialist League Papers, IISH. Walker was also involved with the Saturday Club.
154 R.I. Lipmann to Socialist League, 21 Feb. 1886, Socialist League Papers, IISH.
155 Michael Gabriel to H.H. Sparling, Feb. n.d. 1886, Socialist League Papers, IISH.
156 Michael Gabriel to H.H. Sparling, 21 Feb. 1886, Socialist League Papers, IISH.
157 R.I. Lipmann to Socialist League, 2 Mar. 1886, Socialist League Papers, IISH.
158 Monthly Membership Report, Dublin branch, Apr. 1886, Socialist League Papers, IISH.
159 *Freeman's Journal*, 8 Apr. 1886; *Dublin University Review*, Apr. 1886, p. 359.
160 R.I. Lipmann, 'The progress of socialism', *Dublin University Review*, Apr. 1886, p. 303.
161 ibid., p. 310.
162 ibid., p. 311.
163 A.U., 'The socialist candidate', *Dublin University Review*, June 1886, p. 494.
164 H. Rowlandson, 'Towards democracy', *Dublin University Review*, Apr. 1886, pp. 319–28.
165 William Morris to Jane Alice Morris, 9 Apr. 1886, *Letters*, p. 253.
166 ibid., p. 252.
167 Michael Gabriel to H.H. Sparling, 7 Mar. 1886, Socialist League Papers, IISH. Gabriel had expressed his disgruntlement with Walker and his friends in an earlier letter to London: 'The mass of us are of [the] opinion that the gentlemen who have . . . guaranteed Mr Morris's expenses would have been doing a great deal better for the cause had they given us the money to carry on a steady series of public meetings which . . . we are, at present, unable to do.' (Michael Gabriel to H.H. Sparling, 21 Feb. 1886, Socialist League Papers, IISH.)
168 *The Commonweal*, 8 May 1886.
169 ibid.
170 William Morris to H.H. Sparling, Apr. n.d. 1886, Socialist League Papers, IISH.

171 *The Commonweal*, 8 May 1886.
172 ibid.
173 *Irish Times*, 12 Apr. 1886.
174 *The Commonweal*, 8 May 1886.
175 William Morris to H.H. Sparling, Apr. n.d. 1886, Socialist League Papers.
176 ibid.; *The Commonweal*, 8 May 1886.
177 *The Commonweal*, 8 May 1886.
178 William Morris to Mrs Burne-Jones, Oct. n.d. 1877, *Letters*, p. 95.
179 William Morris to Mrs William Morris, 15 Apr. 1886, *Letters*, p. 253.
180 Marcus Bourke, op. cit., p. 181; E.P. Thompson, op. cit., pp. 554–5; A.N. Jeffares, *W.B. Yeats: Man and Poet* (Dublin, 1996), pp. 40–2, 45.
181 William Morris to Mrs William Morris, 15 Apr. 1886, *Letters*, p. 253.
182 *The Commonweal*, 8 May 1886.
183 Fritz Schumann to H.H. Sparling, 12 May 1886, Socialist League Papers, IISH.
184 George King to Socialist League, 30 June 1886, Socialist League Papers, IISH.
185 Fritz Schumann to Socialist League, 2 Sept. 1886, Socialist League Papers, IISH; John O'Gorman to Socialist League, 3 Aug. 1886, Socialist League Papers, IISH.
186 John O'Gorman to Socialist League, 3 Aug. 1886, Socialist League Papers, IISH.
187 *The Commonweal*, 5 June 1886.
188 *The Commonweal*, Oct. 1885.
189 Joseph Karpel to Socialist League, 13 Sept. 1886, Socialist League Papers, IISH.
190 *The Commonweal*, 11 Sept. 1886; John O'Gorman to H.H. Sparling, 21 Sept. 1886, Socialist League Papers, IISH.
191 *The Commonweal*, 11 Sept. 1886.
192 *The Commonweal*, 16 Oct. 1886.
193 May Morris to Andreas Scheu, 27 Sept. 1886, Socialist League Papers, IISH.
194 John Quail, op. cit., p. 55.
195 ibid., pp. 55–6.
196 John O'Gorman to H.H. Sparling, 17 Oct. 1886, Socialist League Papers, IISH.
197 John O'Gorman to Socialist League, 24 Oct. 1886, Socialist League Papers, IISH.
198 ibid.
199 John O'Gorman to H.H. Sparling, 7 Nov. 1886, Socialist League Papers, IISH.
200 John O'Gorman to H.H. Sparling, 9 Nov. 1886, Socialist League Papers, IISH.
201 George King to H.H. Sparling, 15 Nov., 1886, Socialist League Papers, IISH.
202 *The Commonweal*, 20 Nov. 1886.
203 *Cork Examiner*, 21 Oct. 1881.
204 For British socialists and temperance, see Chris Waters, *British Socialists and the Politics of Popular Culture, 1884–1914* (Manchester, 1990), pp. 32–5, 135, 137–8, 140.
205 John O'Gorman to H.H. Sparling, 23 Nov. 1886, Socialist League Papers, IISH.
206 ibid.
207 George King to H.H. Sparling, 11 Dec. 1886, Socialist League Papers, IISH.

208 John O'Gorman to H.H. Sparling, 14 Dec. 1886, Socialist League Papers, IISH.
209 John O'Gorman to Socialist League, 21 Dec. 1886, Socialist League Papers, IISH.
210 *The Commonweal*, 5 Feb. 1887.
211 *The Commonweal*, 29 Jan. 1887.
212 John O'Gorman to Socialist League, 24 Mar. 1887, Socialist League Papers, IISH.

5.

Socialism and Labour
Politics, 1887-92

The experience of the Socialist League taught Dublin socialists that public opinion had altered significantly since 1872. Just fourteen years before, the Dublin branch of the International Working Men's Association had faced the fists and clubs of an anti-socialist mob. In 1886 socialists held unmolested public meetings and enjoyed some measure of tolerance in the city. Moreover, some former Internationalists re-entered socialist political life. The Socialist League had encountered little organized opposition despite its difficulty in finding halls for its public meetings. In March 1886, a man named Magennis had lectured in the Rotunda on socialist 'snakes in the grass'. The meeting, chaired by a Fr Murphy of Glasgow, sought to warn Dubliners of 'socialistic and atheistic inroads, and their anti-national and anti-Catholic tendencies'.[1] However, the Socialist League felt confident enough to rebuff this attack with a public meeting on 'snakes in the grass' to which Magennis was specifically invited.[2] On the other hand, the issue of home rule had utterly dominated Irish politics throughout 1886 and this had made it rather difficult to carry on an effective socialist propaganda. In 1887, an unemployment crisis was to help the socialists to partly overcome this problem.

The collapse of the Dublin Socialist League and the preoccupation with home rule did not mean the end of socialism in Ireland. Joseph Karpel, the Russian member, continued to distribute *The Commonweal* although he complained to London in early 1887 that the average sale was scarcely a dozen a week.[3] Auguste Coulon advised the league in February to discontinue sending the paper as he alleged that Karpel and John O'Gorman had collected money for papers sold 'but don't seem to be paying it'.[4] Whatever view London took, *The Commonweal* continued to circulate in Ireland.[5] Likewise, the Socialist League maintained its position on Ireland and in March declared that in its opinion 'the Irish question will help to sow the seed of revolution throughout the British islands'.[6] Despite its continued interest, however, the Socialist League never regained its foothold in Dublin although it did undoubtedly retain some members.

The Social Democratic Federation was quick to take advantage of the demise of the Socialist League branch and in late November 1886 *Justice* requested all sympathizers in Dublin 'willing to assist in the formation of a branch' to write to H.W. Lee at the SDF head office in London.[7] A branch was not formed as a result of this plea and the request was repeated in April 1887 when those interested were asked to communicate with J.E. McCarthy, the erstwhile member of the Socialist League, at 44 Dawson Street in Dublin.[8] Apart from McCarthy, it would appear that some individual recruits were made although a branch was never to be formed. Two lawyers, James Bryce Killen and the Englishman, Allen Upward, seem to have been members during 1887.[9] Killen, a Presbyterian from Belfast, was a former leading Land Leaguer who in November 1879 had been charged with seditious libel along with Michael Davitt and James Daly after a meeting in Gurteen, County Sligo.[10] Later, in November 1881, he was interned as a 'suspect' under the Coercion Act.[11] Upward, then aged twenty-four, later became known in Britain as a writer and poet. (He was, from 1913, an influence on, and an acquaintance of, the poet Ezra Pound.[12]) Aside from Killen and Upward, another Dublin socialist, J.S. Hall, seems to have been a member of the SDF, advocating the platform of the SDF at a meeting in August 1887.[13]

In September 1886, as the Socialist League was declining, Auguste Coulon established an International Club in the city with the intention of uniting the various nationalities in Dublin and ensuring 'the establishment of socialism on a firmer basis'.[14] It was open to all those who held radical opinions even if not socialists. The address given was Coulon's business premises at 50 Dawson Street. Coulon wrote to the Socialist League in London for literature and for foreign newspapers to read at meetings while asking them to write a private note to Michael Gabriel who 'is very lazy now'.[15] John O'Gorman reported in December that Coulon had covered the club-room walls with foreign socialist newspapers.[16] The only significant action by the International Club appears to have been its hosting of a Paris Commune celebration in March 1887. The gathering in Dawson Street on 17 March heard an address by Fritz Schumann on the principles and aims of the Commune while Coulon wound up the social evening with a rendition of the 'Marseillaise'.[17] It was reported in *The Commonweal* that English, Welsh, Scot, Irish, French, Danish, Russian and American radicals were present.[18] McCarthy provided the decorations and banners and

Thomas Fitzpatrick was scheduled to deliver a talk on 'Archbishop Croke's No-tax Manifesto' although it is not certain that this went ahead.[19] The Commune celebration was an annual feature in Dublin's socialist calendar for at least the next decade. In 1885 the Dublin Democratic Association had held a night of song and recitations on 5 March and, even though the reason was not given, it was most probably a commemoration of the Commune.[20] The Dublin Socialist League in March 1886 similarly organized a social evening but, according to Michael Gabriel, it was 'a small private meeting' because they were afraid of it 'being broken up' if openly advertised.[21] By 1887 such fears had largely evaporated.

Within Ireland, socialism remained a largely Dublin affair until the early 1890s. In Belfast, however, there did exist a group around Rev. Bruce Wallace who were seen as Christian socialists but were primarily land nationalizers. Through the short-lived Irish Land Restoration Society they brought Henry George to Belfast for a lecture in January 1885.[22] George, at the time, was concluding a tour of Britain. Wallace may also have been instrumental in arranging a visit by Samuel Hayes in early 1887. Hayes spoke on socialism at the Abercorn Hall in Victoria Street on 20 March.[23] *Justice* reported the attendance as large and claimed that Hayes's address was 'very well received'.[24] The meeting failed, however, to encourage the emergence of a distinct socialist group in Belfast.

THE NATIONAL LABOUR LEAGUE (1887)

When John O'Gorman wrote in March 1887 to inform the Socialist League in London of a failed meeting he also mentioned that Fritz Schumann and some others were attempting to organize 'a large one'. 'They have started', he continued, 'what they call a "Labour League", a nondescript sort of body, their reason for doing this being the fear that the name Socialist would frighten away those whom they want to reach. How far they will succeed remains to be seen.'[25] In fact the National Labour League was, in the short term, to prove exceptionally successful for a socialist-led organization. The name, of course, was of little import — both the Scottish Land and Labour League and the London-based Labour Emancipation League were thoroughly socialist. O'Gorman's qualm was ultimately one of doctrine. He, and many members of the Socialist League, looked askance at any initiative that smacked of reformism or a dilution of 'pure' socialism.

The objection to 'palliatives' was deep-rooted in the Socialist League and it was a central line of delineation between it and the Social Democratic Federation. William Morris, at his most unbending, in April 1885 commented to a correspondent:

> We the revolutionists hold that it is impossible to patch the present society so-called and that any attempt to do so by putting forward a cry for the amelioration of the condition of the workers under the present system will tend to retard the movement which has begun for the destruction of that system.[26]

In his political activity, Morris, of course, was involved in occasional struggles for reforms and in 1890 he admitted that 'every gain won by the combination of labour hastens the day when the odious distinctions of class will be abolished'.[27] His overriding belief, nonetheless, was that reforms would only be conceded by parliament 'with the intention of . . . being either a nullity or a bait to quiet possible revolution'.[28] It was with such views in mind that John O'Gorman and others would have looked at the proposed Labour League. It must be said, however, that Morris met some opposition in the Socialist League to his narrow position on reformist campaigns. Thomas Binning, a long-time trade unionist and an opponent of anti-parliamentarianism, wrote a lapidary criticism of Morris for *The Commonweal* in early 1888:

> It is all very well for people in comfortable circumstances to go in for the 'whole hog', to deprecate the vulgar comfort of the middle classes and to make light of ameliorative changes in the conditions of the workers. But those whose daily life is brightened and made happier and more hopeful by these little changes so slightingly spoken of are not likely to be favourably influenced by the abstract notions of doctrinaires . . . The workers have been told by those whose function it is to administer spiritual consolation, that their privations in this life will be compensated in heaven; and it seems to me to be pretty much the same thing to ask them to forego an advantage within their grasp for the promise of a beatific state of society in the indefinite future.[29]

What the objection to 'palliatives' entailed for most Socialist League activists was an isolation from the real struggles of working-class people. Housing, unemployment, suffrage and so on were all issues that struck a chord in working-class Dublin. The Socialist League, in contrast, had held propagandist meetings which primarily concentrated on issues of socialist theory. The most stark example of this must surely be the meeting held to discuss Lassalle while London, metaphorically speaking, burned.[30]

The National Labour League, which existed between March and November 1887, owed more to the SDF influence than to that of the Socialist League.[31] In Britain the SDF in the early part of the year organized many marches and meetings of the unemployed. It was a period of high unemployment and acute social tensions which exploded into violence on a few occasions. Socialist League members, by and large, did not participate in the unemployed agitation in the earlier months of 1887 as the league saw the protests 'as intended to be advertisements for the SDF'.[32] The unemployment situation in Ireland was similarly bad and emigration increased sharply through March and April. Emigration in 1887 reached 82,923 which was the highest figure since 1883. April and May, traditionally the worst months, accounted for 33,836 of the year's total.[33] On 21 February a group of unemployed Dublin workers assembled at Beresford Place and walked to the City Hall where they met T.D. Sullivan, the Lord Mayor, and requested that he consider their grievances. In a petition a few days later, James Keane, Christopher Mahon and John O'Neill called on Sullivan to convene a meeting of the unemployed of the city. Sullivan refused and claimed that until he had received the delegation he had heard 'nothing of an unusual distress in the city'. He also pointed out that it was the government which had responsibility for unemployment: 'There will be no prosperity in Ireland until Irishmen in an Irish Parliament have the power of making laws for the Irish people.'[34]

On 6 March a mass meeting of the unemployed was held on Harold's Cross Green with J.B. Killen presiding. Killen told a crowd of 3,000 that the land and all the instruments of production should belong to the community and that the worker was 'justified in using any means whatever in order to get rid of the idle class that fattened upon his misery'.[35] He also made it clear, however, that he saw T.D. Sullivan, whom he knew personally from Land League days, as 'an honest, a patriotic and a generous gentleman' who 'if he could have done anything for them, would have done so'. Killen similarly claimed that the demonstration was not in opposition to the National League, the mainstream nationalist organization, but was simply anxious that something should be done 'for the people of the city as well as for the tenant farmers of Ireland'.[36] Other speakers were less kind to Sullivan and the National League. James Keane, an unemployed worker, attacked the Lord Mayor and accused Dublin Corporation of squandering £100,000 which it had received from the government. At the very least, he protested, 'the Corporation could get a loan from the Government and make a bit of a line of railway and could give employment to the 4,300 men who are walking about the city of Dublin at the present time'.[37] A man called Brown went further: 'The attention of the National League had been engrossed to the wants of a certain class to the detriment of the people of Dublin. No landlord had ever treated his tenants as badly as the farmers had treated their labourers.'[38] James Keegan, an American sailor, proposed a direction for the unemployed agitation in the foundation of an organization 'whose object would be to find out that the present social system was all wrong'.[39] He argued that there could be no improvement in working-class conditions until capitalism was abolished. Allen Upward, another socialist, complemented this argument:

Parliamentary agitation had been getting Land Act after Land Act, but where was the act to help the workingmen of the city? The workingmen should form a Labour League, and teach the world that the working classes were the vast majority and had a right to power (applause). The world had been long enough governed by kings and lords, and later still by the middle class, but the power had now come into the hands of the working classes, and the Government of the country ought to be in the hands of the people who had the power (applause).[40]

The Harold's Cross Green meeting was as much a socialist rally as it was a demonstration of the unemployed. And, despite Killen's protestations, the prevalent tone was clearly one of irritation with the National League and its fascination with agrarian politics. While 1886 had seen Dublin socialists hold their first successful indoor public meetings, 1887 saw socialism preached openly in the streets of the city. Socialists also participated in debates at the City of Dublin Workingmen's Club on Wellington Quay. This club organized a series of debates, begun on 5 March, to replace the forum provided by the temporarily defunct Saturday Club.[41] The first discussion which dealt with the issue of economic protectionism saw P.A. Tyrrell, formerly of the Dublin Democratic Association, argue for the promotion of Irish manufacturing industry.[42] Tyrrell was at that stage secretary of the Irish Industrial League which believed working-class prosperity lay in the development of indigenous industry.[43] The debate was adjourned and carried on again on 12 March when James Keegan pointed out that neither free trade nor protectionism would bring any relief to the workers whose salvation could only be found in 'the overthrow of the present system of society'.[44]

A week after the Harold's Cross meeting, on 13 March, another demonstration was held in Dublin. This time, it was a Sunday evening march from the Custom House at Beresford Place to the Wellington Monument in the Phoenix Park. The day before, the city had been extensively postered and leaflets advertising the event had been widely distributed.[45] About 1,500 people assembled for the march with many more joining in along the route.[46] In the Phoenix Park, speeches were delivered by Killen, Keane, Keegan, Hall and Toomey. Large quantities of socialist leaflets were distributed and *The Commonweal* later carried a report that 'the Socialist propaganda is being favourably received by the workers' in Dublin.[47] This was not entirely correct as J.T. Toomey, a former Socialist League member, suffered hisses and shouts of 'no socialism' when he suggested that both 'religion and law kept the people down' and advised those present not to allow themselves 'be put down by ill-disposed aristocrats or ill-disposed clergy'.[48] Toomey's sin, however, was undoubtedly his adverse comments on religion, and the other speakers received a much better hearing. James Keane informed the crowd that the march organizers were intent on founding a labour union in the city. James Keegan made the same point and said that the movement had nothing to do with the home rule question but believed that 'some change would have to be effected in society in order to improve the condition of the workingmen'.[49] Shortly after this mass meeting the National Labour League was founded. According to *Justice*, which first mentioned the league on 2 April, socialists were well represented on the committee.[50] Two weeks later the paper published an optimistic report from Dublin which accentuated a certain antagonism to rural interests: 'Social Democracy is slowly but surely taking root here. At the workingmen's clubs, at labour meetings and at the Trades Council, farmers have been denounced as a "useless worthless class" and accused of tyrannising over the labourers who fought their battles for them. Social Democrats are now cheered whereas they were not tolerated a year ago.'[51]

In the second half of March, Dublin socialists took part in two more debates at the City of Dublin Workingmen's Club. On 19 March, Adam O'Toole, J.T. Toomey and Allen Upward spoke in favour of land nationalization with Upward proposing that they 'should strengthen the hands of Michael Davitt, and his supporters, in his efforts for land nationalisation'. Toomey provoked a mixture of laughter and applause when he advocated 'nationalization of the land with triennial parliaments, manhood suffrage and woman suffrage too'.[52] The following week Toomey and James Keegan contributed to a discussion on the working-class standard of living in which they both argued that this had not improved over the previous fifty years.[53] On 3 April the National Labour League held its first mass outdoor meeting in the Phoenix Park. A crowd of about 5,000 listened to speeches in favour of the 'stepping stones' of the SDF programme although, through some misunderstanding, a telegram of support from the SDF in London was not read to the meeting.[54] This success was followed on 17 April with another mass meeting on Harold's Cross Green where 3,000 gathered and heard speeches from Labour League members.[55]

The Labour League took rooms at 2 Bachelor's Walk and began advertising its weekly meeting in the *Freeman's Journal*. Two more outdoor meetings were held in the early weeks of May 1887. On 1 May a large rally was organized on The Bull in Clontarf with J. Bagnell Evans, a barrister who practised on the South Wales circuit, presiding. Carlisle Hickey, who represented bakers on Dublin Trades Council, spoke, as did Upward and Toomey, and a motion highlighting the antipathy toward Dublin Corporation was moved that included the observation that 'when we look at the scanty wages of the labourers who do the hardest municipal work of the Corporation, we consider that the remuneration of the higher and ornamental officials in the Corporation is excessive and might be reduced'.[56] Again, this was an oblique attack on the National League which dominated city politics. Not long after this meeting another demonstration was held on Dollymount

Strand which attracted a crowd of about 1,200.[57] Despite its obvious success the Labour League received very little publicity in the national newspapers. One member, Michael Hickie, claimed that the labour organization was 'studiously and persistently boycotted by both the public and the Press . . . The Tory, Liberal and home ruler agreed in one thing at least — viz., to run down the National Labour League'.[58] Unfortunately for the league it was activated at a time when nationalist Ireland was mobilizing in opposition to a new coercion bill. Moreover, unlike the Industrial League, the Labour League was wholly uninterested in accommodating itself within the nationalist movement.

On 22 and 29 May the Labour League held meetings at the Custom House steps in Beresford Place. Hundreds attended and speeches were delivered by J.S. Hall, John Cantwell, James Keegan and others. Twenty policemen who turned up at the first meeting were presented with copies of the Socialist League leaflet 'Ireland a Nation'.[59] John O'Gorman had ordered 2,000 copies at the end of March for distribution at Labour League events.[60] Police attention was also evident at an unemployed march in the last week of May. The procession was rather dramatically headed by a black flag on a pikestaff on which was impaled a loaf of bread. The police seized the flag, broke up the march and refused to allow speeches.[61] The Labour League also took up the issue of housing in Dublin and on 26 May Thomas Fitzpatrick gave a lecture on this subject at the rooms in Bachelor's Walk. A proposal to establish a 'house league' was discussed.[62] At the same meeting a new seven-member committee was elected, of which five were socialists: Fitzpatrick, Karpel, McCarthy, Olgoman and Swords.[63] It was also decided to extend the socialist agitation outside Dublin city. On 5 June a meeting was held in Howth, a fishing village about nine miles north of Dublin. The league ran a special excursion steamer for those attending and the principles of the organization were expounded by Hall, Cantwell, Brown, Fitzpatrick and others. According to *The Commonweal* more than fifty names, mostly fishermen, were handed in to form a branch in the town.[64] A fortnight later another outdoor meeting was organized in Kingstown but that would appear to have been the extent of the Labour League's incursion into the rest of Ireland.[65] In fact, after June it would seem that the league reverted to indoor meetings at its new room in Carpenter's Hall at 75 Aungier Street. This may have been the result of a financial crisis as the league decided on 9 June to appeal to the Knights of Labor in America for funds 'to carry on the labour agitation in Ireland'.[66] Michael Hickie also complained in October that the organization suffered from a lack of 'means'.[67]

At the weekly meeting of the league on 21 July, J.E. McCarthy, a member of the SDF, was elected secretary.[68] The rest of the committee was composed, in the main, of socialists of one type or another. The National Labour League included members of the SDF and the Socialist League and even members of the Irish Industrial League. Nonetheless, the attitude of the league to the Industrial League was one of hostility. F.J. O'Hagan, a Labour League member, explained:

> They are two bodies working on totally different lines. The Industrial League merely seeks to plaster the sores of the present commercial system, while the Labour League goes to the root, and demands the abolition of that system.[69]

Moreover, the Labour League consciously distanced itself from the 'political question' of legislative independence where the Industrial League was quick to organize a meeting, 'What effect will Coercion have on our industries?', when government repression was threatened.[70] In a sense the Labour League adopted an ostrich-like stance on national politics, avoiding a potentially divisive debate in the interests of unity on labour issues. One member, in a letter to the loyalist newspaper *The Union*, wrote in June 1887:

> The League is non-sectarian and non-political, having members of every class and creed and all shades of thought and opinion . . . Parliament is being blocked by passing exceptional laws, fiercely contested by rival parties, while the working men go without employment unless they accept in many cases starvation wages. Lord Randolph Churchill points out how some millions are wasted yearly on naval and military matters, while nothing is done to adjust the relations between employers and employed in Dublin and provinces.[71]

While the Industrial League embraced nationalism, the Labour League attempted to stand above it. However, the proclamation of the National League on 19 August was an event that inevitably outraged most Irish people. The National League had been founded by Parnell in October 1882 in part to replace the banned Land League, and its suppression found Dublin's socialists with their hands hanging. Or more precisely, they ignored the crisis and continued with their regular meetings.

The last attempt at an outdoor socialist meeting in 1887 was an independent venture by James Keegan and Auguste Coulon. Keegan had promised in March that he would lecture in the Phoenix Park on socialism under the auspices of the recently founded National Amalgamated Sailors' and Firemen's Union.[72] On 7 August, he and Coulon took advantage of a large crowd at a band promenade and started a meeting. Keegan explained 'the aims and principles of International Socialism'.[73] It went well until the end when there was 'a good deal of horse-play' by 'some well-dressed rowdies' in the crowd.[74] At a Labour League meeting on 25 August political divisions within the organization became clear when J.S. Hall delivered a lecture advocating the platform of the SDF. J.B. Killen and Joseph Karpel spoke in support while Michael Gabriel, James Keegan and Thomas

Fitzpatrick opposed.[75] Gabriel and Fitzpatrick were both anarchists and probably still members of the Socialist League. Apart from its weekly meetings the Labour League appeared to have been largely inactive during September. At a meeting on 13 October a new manifesto was read by J.E. McCarthy and then discussed by, among others, George King, Gabriel, Fitzpatrick and Coulon.[76] The *Manifesto of the National Labour League to the Working Men of Ireland* was a revolutionary declaration:

> The time has arrived when it behoves you, fellow workers, to organise and combine for a just participation in the wealth produced by you, but which is filched from you by the action of the landlord and capitalist class . . . All over the civilised world the people are rising against their tyrants, the capitalist class. Shall you, men of Ireland, remain behind in the great struggle that labour is making for its emancipation? Too long the people have been kept apart by false issues raised by their rulers. The interest of labour is the same all the world over, and it is only by a friendly understanding with the workers of every country that we will be able to secure for labour its just rights. The Labour League will agitate for the breaking of the last link in the chain that binds the white slave to the chariot wheels of his capitalist lord.[77]

A week later the Labour League held a meeting to protest against the impending execution of the 'Chicago Anarchists'.[78] The men, four in all, were hanged on 11 November for allegedly throwing a bomb at police in the Haymarket in Chicago the previous year. The evidence against them had been quite weak and none of the men could be directly connected to the bomb.[79]

J.E. McCarthy sent a report of this 20 October public meeting to the conservative *Irish Times* along with a copy of the National Labour League manifesto. According to this report the chairman at the lecture had described the condemned men as 'martyrs whose names will be honoured in every land when labour's cause is won and freedom reigns supreme'.[80] *The Irish Times* was perturbed by this 'curious report of a meeting held last night in Dublin' and devoted a long editorial to an attack on the Labour League. A few days later two letters were published in the paper relating to this meeting. The first was from a pseudonymous writer who had attended the meeting; the attendance, he claimed, numbered between thirty and forty ('mostly of the clerk and artisan class') and the most advanced views were expressed by a young man wearing a red muffler.[81] This was probably Thomas Fitzpatrick who spoke again on the Chicago case at the Saturday Club on 12 November.[82] The second letter was from James Dunphy of 75 Aungier Street who stated that he was evicting the Labour League because of the 'Chicago Anarchists' meeting.[83] Michael Hickie and F.J. O'Hagan, both members of the league, responded to these attacks on 26 October. Hickie denied, as *The Irish Times* had alleged, that the league was a branch of any English or American organization. The editorial had also referred to the Labour League as the 'Aungier Street Socialist League', perhaps remembering the Socialist League branch from the year before.[84] The loyalist newspaper *The Union* also editorialized against the league and concomitantly proved that the fear of 'foreign influences' was one shared by nationalism and unionism alike:

> It augurs badly for this unfortunate country to find Socialism creeping in. We have enough to contend with at present without implanting foreign seeds of social discord. Yet, if we may judge from the letters which have appeared within the last few weeks in the columns of the Irish newspapers, that germ of foreign growth — Socialism — has found its way into the very metropolis and attempts to take advantage of the present state of disorder to grow and thrive . . . Latter-day Socialism in reality is only another name for idleness and thriftlessness . . . the majority of its exponents are illiterate wanderers waiting for an opportunity to plunder in the universal ruin. What do they demand? Universal suffrage, to give them a finger in the regulation of other people's property; a withdrawal of capital from private sources in order to place it under public ownership, which would enable them to live comfortably on their neighbours; wages regulated by the State, the way the lazy and indolent would reap as much as the talented and energetic — taking all in all, a system in which the individual is entirely obliterated for the sake of community.[85]

A week after the Labour League's 'Chicago Anarchists' meeting the *Freeman's Journal* gave an unexpected boost to Irish anarchism when it interviewed Peter Kropotkin. A member of the Russian nobility, Kropotkin was considered one of the foremost leaders of the anarchist movement. In 1887 he was living in Britain where he had helped to establish an anarchist newspaper *Freedom*.[86] The interview, which referred to him as 'one of the most kind-hearted of men', focussed on Kropotkin's conversion to anarchism and on his attitude to the condemned men in Chicago. He roundly condemned the proposed executions and alleged that 'the chief accusation against them is that they are professing ideas of Anarchy'.[87] When questioned on what he understood by anarchism he answered simply: 'No Government.'

> We are Socialists, but while the State-Socialists tend towards a further increase of the Governmental powers we proclaim No Government as our ultimate aim — home rule — real, but not sham home rule — for each free organisation growing up for the satisfaction of any of the numberless needs of humanity; free play to the individual in a society where all inheritance of the past — i.e. private appropriation of land, machinery, and all necessaries for production — has disappeared.[88]

According to Kropotkin, in a class-divided society 'force is necessary for maintaining a quite abnormal state of things' but with the victory of socialism 'where no such division exists, force and Government become absolutely useless'.[89] It was a long interview which allowed the anarchist to expound his politics with little or no hostility emanating from the interviewer.

The eviction of the Labour League from Aungier Street accelerated the demise of the organization. It is clear that the membership of the league had contracted by October and it was no longer capable of organizing outdoor meetings. The National Labour League collapsed at some stage during November 1887.[90] In its early months it was an incontrovertible success and attracted large numbers to its demonstrations. Despite its advocation of particular social reforms, such as state provision of work for the unemployed, it would be a mistake to conclude that the league had a Janus-like public face. It cannot be safely assimilated into the labourist political tradition because from the very beginning its leaders were unambiguously revolutionist. The Labour League was a socialist organization that used issues like unemployment and housing to emphasize the societal distress caused by capitalism. It contended that such calamities could only be thoroughly resolved through social revolution. However, the league had developed as a response to a particular unemployment crisis and as this crisis receded so too did interest in the Labour League. Some prominent members, such as J.B. Killen and Allen Upward, were more interested in outdoor agitation than they were in indoor discussion meetings and seem to have drifted away as the league declined.

THE STATIC YEARS, 1888–90

With the collapse of the National Labour League the socialists quickly regrouped in the Dublin Socialist Club which was established in December 1887. For the next two years they mostly relied on indoor meetings and resumed a propagandist rather than an agitational role in Dublin's political life. The revival of the Saturday Club in the last months of 1887 also allowed the Dublin socialists, as J.E. McCarthy confirmed, to 'get hold of large and attentive audiences every Saturday afternoon'.[91] The club now held its meetings in the Central Lecture Hall at 12 Westmoreland Street. Unfortunately, the Saturday Club was not as important as it once had been and the *Freeman's Journal* no longer published weekly reports. It did, however, seem even more sympathetic to socialism. J.B. Killen and Thomas Fitzpatrick contributed to one of its debates on 12 November and on 31 December Fitzpatrick delivered 'an eloquent lecture' on socialism to the club.[92] Adam O'Toole, the former International member, spoke in support of Fitzpatrick and the discussion was continued the following week when

Samuel Hayes and Joseph Karpel contributed.[93] At this second meeting James Walker, of the Contemporary Club, made a well-received speech in favour of socialism. It was Walker who had invited William Morris to Dublin in 1886.

On 24 December 1887 both *The Commonweal* and *Justice* published notices announcing the formation of the Dublin Socialist Club. The notices were signed by John O'Gorman and George King, both previously in the Dublin branch of the Socialist League, and those 'desirous of joining' were asked to write to 21 St Ignatius Road in Dublin. In a circular the club stated its purpose to be that 'of propagating the principles of Socialism' and added that, although the 'acceptance of the general principles of Socialism' was 'the only qualification necessary for membership, any person joining will not be committed to a course of action of which he may disapprove'.[94] The Socialist Club was not as ambitious or successful a project as the National Labour League but McCarthy remained confident in his irregular articles for *Justice*. In February 1888 he wrote:

> Socialism is quietly and imperceptibly permeating Irish Nationalism. Some time ago home rule was considered by the unthinking masses a panacea for all the evils of capitalism and every other 'ism'. The workers appeared to think that self-government would double their wages and give secure employment. Now they are beginning to see that it alone will do nothing except gratify a mere sentimentality, but nevertheless it may be used as a means to an end. The man who will play the leading part in the near Irish future is undoubtedly Michael Davitt . . . The propaganda work of our creed is in the hands of earnest men. Tom Fitzpatrick is a host in himself, as anyone attending the Saturday Club can testify. *Justice* is now on the table of the reading room of the Mechanics' Institute every week.[95]

However, in an earlier article he had conceded that their speaking power was 'rather limited'.[96] McCarthy, himself, does not appear as a contributor to lectures or debates in many reports. His critical attitude to home rule was replicated two months later in another report from Dublin which declared that 'the Irish Nationalist movement is a purely middle-class affair, led by middle-class men, actuated by middle-class ideas'.[97] This may have been written by John O'Gorman who began to contribute to *Justice* in February.[98] O'Gorman wrote cynically in March that while Ireland 'is the shuttlecock between the political tricksters, the condition of the country is getting worse every day; thousands are out of employment in Dublin and all the towns; [and] the cry of distress is heard on every side'.[99] His negative attitude to home rule was made more explicit a few months later when replying to a Davitt supporter who had argued in *Justice* for support for legislative independence.

An 'Irishman' must either be non-resident or he is altogether unacquainted with the opinions of Irish Socialists. At their meetings, at the Saturday Club, at the Industrial League, often at the branch meetings of the National League, he might have heard the same opinions expressed over and over again. He considers home rule worthy of the support of Socialists because 'it will give Irishmen an opportunity of going in earnest for the social freedom'. Here again he shows what little, or rather how little, he knows of Ireland as it is today. Under any scheme of home rule that I have yet seen there would dominate in Ireland two of the most reactionary forces in human society — an impecunious peasant proprietary and a well-organised priesthood. How a socialistic agitation would be helped by either of these precious orders perhaps an 'Irishman' knows.[100]

It would seem that where nationalists relegated the importance of labour, Irish socialists at this time viewed home rule as a diversionary issue. Such an outlook necessarily placed them in an adversarial position within a political nation actuated primarily by anti-colonalist desire.

On 18 March the Socialist Club celebrated the anniversary of the Paris Commune at the old Labour League rooms at 2 Bachelor's Walk. Fitzpatrick chaired the meeting which was well attended and speeches were delivered by King, O'Gorman, Swords and Coulon. Coulon once again finished the evening by singing the 'Marseillaise'. A telegram of greetings from the Socialist League in London was read out.[101] The Dublin socialists had themselves sent a similar message to be read out at the celebrations in London.[102] This meeting would appear to be the only event organized by the club during 1888, and it seems that there was to be no series of lectures. Members of the group did, however, take advantage of any opportunities that were available to promote their politics. In April they were involved in a housing agitation against Dublin Corporation for shelving a plan to build dwellings for the working class.[103] On 17 April O'Gorman and Fitzpatrick attended a meeting of the Industrial League and argued that the corporation should build houses that when erected 'should be let at such a rent as would cover cost of construction and maintenance alone'. Nobody, they declared, should be 'allowed to reap a profit out of the necessities of the poor'.[104] According to *Justice* such an impact was made by Thomas Fitzpatrick's speech that no one spoke against him. O'Gorman spoke again at an Industrial League meeting at 75 Aungier Street on 22 May when he opened a debate on trade unionism.[105] On 5 June he lectured at the Industrial League on education when he advocated free and compulsory education that 'should be purely secular and industrial and technical'.[106] This extensive use of the Industrial League clearly shows that the socialists in Dublin had no objection to using the facilities of organizations which they had previously criticized.

The Dublin socialists remained in contact with both the Socialist League and the SDF. It is clear that they had drawn closer to the SDF. This may have been connected to the internal disputes that were convulsing the Socialist League at that time. Also, there were occasional encounters with wandering socialists such as the anarchist, Max Nettlau, who became a major historical source on the anarchist movement. He came to Dublin in April 1888 where he met Auguste Coulon and probably other socialists in the city.[107] The Dublin Socialist Club, however, lost three important members during 1888. By July Samuel Hayes was writing to the Socialist League from an address at 116 Chord Road in Drogheda, County Louth. This would appear to have been a permanent move as he ordered copies of *The Commonweal* to sell in the area.[108] Worse still, both Fritz Schumann and Thomas Fitzpatrick left Dublin in August 1888. On 18 August the International Union of Glass Bottlemakers in Dublin entertained Schumann at its rooms and presented him with a purse of sovereigns in recognition of the work he had done for them. Schumann was returning to his native Denmark. Fitzpatrick, who was present by invitation, addressed the gathering on the subject of internationalism.[109] The following day it was Fitzpatrick's turn to be bid farewell when the Socialist Club assembled to wish him well before his departure for London: '"Fitz" has always been an earnest, consistent propagandist of the cause, and his loss will be much felt here' read the report in *The Commonweal*.[110] From London Fitzpatrick travelled on to Chicago from where he sent back a report for *Justice* on the labour movement in that city.[111] He was to return to Ireland before the end of the following year.[112] The Dublin Socialist Club, meanwhile, tottered into 1889.

As he had with the Socialist League branch, the Frenchman, Auguste Coulon, made efforts to revive the club in the early months of 1889. The club took rooms at 16 Dawson Street and those interested in joining were requested to contact Coulon at that address.[113] On 18 March the Socialist Club hosted the annual Paris Commune celebration at its rooms and the group sent a telegram which was read out at the joint SDF–Socialist League celebration in London.[114] The Dublin gathering included R.G. Russell, a founder of the Dublin Democratic Association, and a new member, Adolphus Shields.[115] (Shields was the father of the well-known actors William Shields, better known as Barry Fitzgerald, and Arthur Shields, who were born in 1888 and 1896 respectively.) Coulon, an anarchist, had remained loyal to the Socialist League which may explain why from late March to September *The Commonweal* alone carried notices and reports of meetings in Dublin. It seems that Coulon may also have been the central figure behind the launch of the Progressist Club in February 1889.[116] This club was probably created by the Dublin socialists because of the apparent failure of the Socialist Club. Certainly it was made more accessible and was open to radicals who stopped short of declaring themselves socialists. The new club took rooms at 87 Marlborough Street and organized regular weekly lectures and debates.[117] It proved successful and engendered a new lease of life for Dublin socialism. It also drew in trade unionists like William Graham of the bottlemakers who previously had little connection with the socialist movement.[118] Lecturers at the Progressist Club included John O'Gorman, Adolphus Shields, George King, H. Sutton Frizelle, J. Landye (a former Internationalist), J.A. Cree, R.F. Wilson and Arthur Kavanagh.[119] Thomas Fitzpatrick also gave a lecture on his return to Ireland.[120] Other 'veteran' socialists who were similarly involved with the club included J.T. Toomey, Auguste Coulon and Samuel Hayes (who was at one meeting at least).[121]

Some of the lectures led to heated discussions such as one by George King on 27 April in which he asserted that 'home rule and peasant proprietary would not make any material change in the condition of the Irish workers'. According to *The Commonweal* his views were 'violently assailed'.[122] When King lectured again on 29 June on the 'Gospel of plenty' it was reported that there was a 'slight disturbance by two or three blatant Gaels'.[123] The topic of anarchism proved particularly popular and a debate which opened in November, 'Anarchism versus Democracy', was kept up for three evenings because of 'the great number desirous of speaking'.[124] The defenders of Marxism outnumbered the anarchists although *The Commonweal* suggested that the anarchists held their ground well in the debate. One of those who spoke for anarchism was Dr John Creaghe who had spent much of his life in Argentina. Creaghe was a leader of British anarchism and it is unclear why he was in Ireland in November 1889. It is possible that he had travelled over especially for the discussion.

The Dublin Socialist Club organized what appears to have been its penultimate event in August 1889 when O'Gorman (advertised as a Dublin Socialist Club speaker) addressed the Progressist Club on the International Workers' Congress that had been held in Paris.[125] O'Gorman had attended the Paris conference as the delegate of the Dublin bottlemakers.[126] He was also there as a representative of the Dublin Socialist Club.[127] The Paris conference had been a strange affair because of a division within European socialism on the issue of parliamentary reformism. A disagreement on the political direction of French socialism meant that two international congresses were organized for Paris in July 1889. They were the International Workers' Congress (supported by the gradualist French 'Possibilists', the British SDF and the TUC Parliamentary Committee) and the International Socialist Labour Congress (supported by the Marxists including the Socialist League).[128] John O'Gorman, probably under the influence of the SDF, attended the 'Possibilist' conference.

The final meeting held by the Socialist Club seems to have been on 11 November when it organized a commemoration of the anarchists executed in Chicago two years earlier. On 9 November *The Commonweal* stated that a 'Chicago comrade will address the meeting' and this turned out to be the recently returned Thomas Fitzpatrick who explained the history of the case to a large attendance at 87 Marlborough Street.[129] The Dublin Socialist Club would seem to have lapsed after this meeting and the propaganda was carried on through the more successful Progressist Club.

Outside Dublin socialism had still made little impact by the end of 1889. A correspondent from Cork had shown some interest in a letter to *Justice* in February that year. Stephen Foreman, with an address at 28 South Terrace, wrote: 'We must abolish the landlord, but after that the farmer must go. Something must be done, and who should begin if not the Socialists? There are doubtless many Socialists in Ireland, though I know none of them. I would ask your Irish readers, and any of your readers, to communicate with me as above. If not I shall take the initiative myself.'[130] Foreman's isolation is tangible. By September 1889 *The Commonweal* was available in Guy & Co. at 70 Patrick Street in Cork and it is tempting to suspect Foreman's involvement. Likewise, the paper was available in four shops in Lurgan, County Armagh, which indicates the presence of a sympathizer in the town.[131] Cork and Lurgan, however, were the only places outside Dublin selling *The Commonweal* in 1889.

Rev. Bruce Wallace, in Limavady, County Down, made a contribution to the socialist movement in May 1889 when he established his newspaper, *Brotherhood*. Wallace's paper had a wide circulation in Ulster and in Scotland. In his first issue on 11 May he made clear the mildness of his 'Christian socialism' by giving first place to land nationalization. Moreover, he openly declared his support for the Liberal Party because it had, he claimed, 'already entrusted so much political power to the working classes and has given such large instalments of justice'.[132] In a later issue he outlined the central difference between his group and the two British socialist organizations:

> We stand aloof from both the Social Democratic Federation and from the Socialist League (though we acknowledge that they are both doing much useful educational work), because we believe that whatever measure of Socialism the people are prepared for can be most smoothly and most rapidly introduced by means of the Nationalisation of the Land.[133]

Wallace and his followers were not convinced socialists but they were a radicalizing influence and *Brotherhood* published extracts regularly from both *Justice* and *The Commonweal*. This group was also responsible for bringing Henry George to lecture in the Ulster Hall in Belfast in early July 1889. Wallace chaired the meeting.[134] For socialists, however, George was by now *persona non grata* because of his complete lack of sympathy for those executed in Chicago. William Morris expressed the changed view in 1887: 'Henry George approves of this murder; do not let anybody waste many words to qualify this wretch's conduct. One word will include all the rest — TRAITOR!!'[135]

COULON'S POSTSCRIPT

Of those involved in Dublin socialism during the 1880s only one, Auguste Coulon, has come to the attention of historians of the British 'socialist revival'.[136] Coulon, a member of the Socialist League's Dublin branch and afterwards a steady socialist activist, left Ireland at the end of 1889 and briefly returned to France where he involved himself with left-wing politics. In January 1890 he moved to London where he had a brother and rejoined the Socialist League in North Kensington.[137] The league at that stage had altered considerably from the organization he had joined in late 1885. Between 1887 and 1888 a battle between an alliance of anti-parliamentarian Marxists and anarchists and the 'parliamentary faction' had ended in the departure of many leading Marxists who would no longer accept the objection to parliament and to 'palliatives'. The council of the Socialist League was not unhappy to see this outflow as it believed in 'the impossibility of propaganda by electioneering coexisting with the educational propaganda in the same body to any good purpose'.[138] The long-term consequences, nonetheless, of this exodus were to be entirely detrimental to Morris and the other libertarian Marxists in the league.

At that time, wrote John Bruce Glasier, the Edinburgh socialist, there was 'a sort of current of Anarchism rising in the Socialist Movement — a current which a year to two later threatened to carry away with it a large part of the more active propagandists'.[139] The league's anti-parliamentarianism attracted many anarchists and by 1890 the libertarian Marxists had completely lost control of the organization's council. Morris, unable to accept the antics of some of the anarchists, withdrew and ceased his substantial £500 a year subsidy.[140] The league began to decline as provincial branches, largely unconvinced by anarchism, started to contract. By the early 1890s the Socialist League had become very much a London organization run by the anarchists, many of whom appeared determined to confirm the caricature of anarchism as a movement of bombastic incendiaries. H.B. Samuels, probably the worst offender, wrote in *The Commonweal* in July 1890 reporting on a Leeds riot where police and the mayor had been attacked: 'The consternation and confusion baffles description; and if the people had only the knowledge (they had the pluck) the whole cursed lot would have been wiped out. As the horses and men picked themselves up, it was to be seen that many were bruised and bleeding but, alas! no corpses to be seen.'[141] Dr John Creaghe, writing in November 1890, suggested: 'Every man should take what he requires of the wealth around him, using violence wherever necessary, and when dragged before his enemies he should tell them plainly that he had done what he knows to be right and what he is proud of having done. His example will soon find imitators.'[142] Propaganda by deed. By 1893 Samuels was applauding a bomb thrown in a theatre in Barcelona 'because of the death of thirty rich people and the injury to others'.[143]

It was into this milieu that Coulon stepped when he arrived in Britain. He immediately threw himself into political activity and delivered an address for his branch of the Socialist League in April 1890 on the French revolution.[144] Moreover, Coulon developed the image of being an anarchist with rather violent tendencies, and involved himself in the dispute with the league's Hammersmith branch which was one of the last outposts of libertarian Marxism in the London organization.[145] (Morris and the Hammersmith branch eventually seceded in early November after Samuels declared that he had intended to 'polish off' the judge in the Sheffield trial of an anarchist if a guilty verdict was brought in.[146]) Coulon had a problem finding employment in London but he finally found a place in a school for the children of foreign socialists which had been opened by the leading anarchist Louise Michel in north Soho.[147] This position gave him an image of trustworthiness in London's anarchist circles — an image he was to use with bad effect. Coulon had become a paid informer for Scotland Yard.

In October 1891 Coulon began to organize bomb-making classes ostensibly as 'chemistry classes'. Then he established a bomb 'factory' in Walsall informing those he encouraged to participate that the bombs were for use in Russia. In early 1892 a number of Walsall anarchists were arrested, on Coulon's information, and charged with conspiring to manufacture bombs. One of those arrested, Joe Deakin, broke under interrogation and confessed his part while naming others.[148] Coulon's leading role was made clear in Deakin's confession but no action was taken against him. Meanwhile, Coulon was also writing the 'International Notes' section for *The Commonweal* and in the true style of the *agent provocateur*, he used the column to promote terrorism. 'No voice', he wrote, 'speaks so loud as Dynamite and we are glad to see it getting into use all over the place.'[149] David Nicoll, the editor, eventually dropped Coulon when 'he sent me a paragraph celebrating the blowing up of a cow in Belgium as a great and good revolutionary act'.[150] The outcome of the Walsall case was to be ten years' penal servitude for three anarchists, but it also meant the exposure of Coulon. He was widely denounced as a police agent. *The Commonweal* claimed that Coulon had been at work elsewhere and 'had twenty plots in hand; all distinct from each other, Coulon knew everything, the rest of the "conspirators" knew only what they were doing'.[151]

In the event, Auguste Coulon was never arrested by the police for his role in the Walsall conspiracy. He retreated to lodgings in London from where he issued erratic leaflets attacking his accusers. He lambasted the anarchist Cyril Bell, accusing him of being an *agent provocateur* and commented that 'his short-sightedness and deafness added to the repulsiveness of his manners make him an object of disgust'.[152] Another leaflet attacked Nicoll.

Coulon, needless to say, ended his connection with the socialist movement. It was all a rather disreputable postscript to his activity in Dublin.

THE IRISH SOCIALIST UNION AND 'NEW UNIONISM', 1890–91

The loss of the Dublin Socialist Club in November 1889 left social radicals in the city without an explicit socialist organization. The Progressist Club had by now become a more radical version of the Saturday Club, which had finally collapsed, but it was not an organizing centre. Arthur Kavanagh explained the situation at the end of December in a letter to *Brotherhood*:

> On Saturday evenings the rooms of the Progressist Club are crowded with workers anxious to hear the Socialist cause or some plank in its platform debated; and at the close of each meeting some formerly bitter opponents step forward and avow their conversion to the Socialist creed. The Club is doing excellent work – lecturing, debating, and distributing literature amongst the workers.
>
> But this has not been considered sufficient, and in addition to the Club a Socialist organisation for active propaganda work is about to be formed. A meeting to this end was held a few weeks since and a committee formed to report whether it would be better to form an independent branch or to affiliate with the Social Democratic Federation.[153]

This organizing committee met through December to discuss a replacement for the ephemeral Dublin Socialist Club and eventually an inaugural meeting was arranged for 4 January 1890 at the Progressist Club rooms in Marlborough Street. It was decided not to affiliate to the SDF and a crowded attendance agreed to form the Irish Socialist Union (ISU) with the objectives of amalgamating 'other Socialist organisations', establishing a socialist library, propagating socialist ideas, circulating socialist literature and organizing open-air meetings.[154]

It is clear that the ISU had loftier ambitions than the Socialist Club in terms of its designated mission and political purpose. The club had largely existed simply to hold socialists together during a difficult period. In contrast, the ISU from the beginning sought to play a more ambitious role in Irish politics. It referred to what was created on 4 January as the 'Central branch' of the Irish Socialist Union; it clearly had hopes of establishing other branches as the National Labour League had apparently done. Secondly, the use of the designation 'Irish' instead of 'Dublin' may have been a statement of intent. In addition, Arthur Kavanagh indicated that they intended to enter electoral politics: 'We are sanguine of having within twelve months' time one or two Socialist seats in the municipal council and if all goes well, a land nationaliser will contest one of the divisions of the city for

Parliament.'[155] Also, a willingness among socialists in Dublin to travel for lectures elsewhere was evinced in January when Joseph Karpel spoke in Belfast as a representative of Russian nihilism.[156] Notices in both *Justice* and *The Commonweal* in February announced the arrival of the ISU and its basis was declared to be the 'union on a common platform of representatives of the various schools of Socialistic thought with a view to the more effective propaganda of the principles on which all are agreed'.[157] Interestingly, with the formation of the broad-based ISU, the strangely named Progressist Club quickly evaporated. For the socialists its *raison d'être* was gone and it lapsed at the beginning of the summer.[158] In November the ISU organized its own series of weekly lectures and debates to replace the Progressist Club forum.[159]

The creation of the Irish Socialist Union came at an important juncture in British and Irish social history, and may have been partly a response to a more militant mood among labour activists. During 1889 and 1890 'new unionism' swept through the industrialized parts of Britain. For the first time unskilled workers, who constituted the bulk of the labour force, were responding to trade unionism and creating new unions to rival the old craft-based unions which had served as paragons of moderation for most of their existence. These new unions tended to be combative and were often led by convinced socialists. The National Federation of Labour was formed in 1886 and a year later Joseph Havelock Wilson helped found the National Amalgamated Sailors' and Firemen's Union. These were the harbingers of the general unions that were to take off so rapidly after 1889. Importantly, Dublin socialists were connected with both these unions. James Keegan, the American member of the National Labour League, had also been a member of the Sailors' and Firemen's Union. Indeed, as early as 1887 he was lecturing on socialism under its auspices in Dublin.[160] Keegan disappeared from the city at some stage in 1887 so it is quite possible that he operated as a travelling organizer for the newly established union. Likewise, both Adolphus Shields and William Graham were organizers for the National Federation of Labour. (Both were members of the ISU.) At the end of 1889 Arthur Kavanagh reported that Shields and Graham had collected 'hundreds' of names of those interested in joining this general union in Dublin: 'Our comrades are busy addressing meetings of workers every night and Mr Graham is pleading the cause of unprotected labour in the rooms of the Dublin Trades Council.'[161] William Graham was a long-time trade union activist and had helped form the Dublin Glass Bottlemakers' Trade Society in 1882.[162] He had also worked with Fritz Schumann in the creation of the International Union of Glass Bottlemakers in 1886.[163] Despite this link with the Socialist League he was never a member of the Dublin branch and seems to have remained outside socialist circles until the era of 'new unionism' during 1889 and 1890.[164]

The Dublin socialists' interest in industrial strife in Britain developed discernibly during 1889. This can be seen by the topics chosen for discussion at the Progressist Club from August that year through to May 1890. At least nine of the lectures given during that period were on issues of labour politics.[165] A drift away from revolutionism was suggested by other debates although the revolutionary perspective certainly remained the dominant trend. For instance, when Kavanagh spoke on 'Practical Legislation', advocating land nationalization, the eight-hour day and other such demands as acceptable objectives, he was assailed by O'Gorman, Fitzpatrick and two other socialists.[166] Nonetheless, there was a change in the way Dublin socialists operated. In 1887 the National Labour League, while seeking to organize labour, expounded socialist perspectives and agitated for social change. While many of the 'new unions' were led by socialists their objectives were labourist even if militant. In 1890 the socialists who advocated 'new unionism' in Dublin undoubtedly sought to empower workers but there were few explicit calls for fundamental social change. Moreover, the three Dublin socialists (Shields, Graham and T. Hamilton) who helped lead the struggle for general unionism all subscribed to a rather mild brand of socialism. Graham, it would seem, was only on the fringes; Shields was a supporter of the politically tepid Fabian Society; and Hamilton was a Christian socialist.[167] Men like Thomas Fitzpatrick maintained the old Socialist League line. At a debate at the City of Dublin Workingmen's Club on 9 April he asserted that 'labour and capital were two factors having nothing in common, and with interests diametrically opposed to one another'. He thought it 'a lamentable thing at the close of the 19th century to find labour setting itself to prop up the falling edifice of capital'.[168]

The 1889–90 strike wave in Britain was successful: 44 per cent of strikers won outright victories, 42 per cent forced their employers to compromise, and only 14 per cent experienced complete defeat.[169] There was also a significant shift in the pattern of participation with unskilled workers being particularly active. The increased industrial activity was stimulating also for the older craft unions: the Amalgamated Society of Engineers, for instance, went from a membership of 53,740 in 1888 to 71,221 in 1891.[170] Will Thorne, the SDF leader of one of the largest 'new unions', saw the socialist movement as centrally instrumental in fermenting the new trade union movement:

> It was the culmination of long years of Socialist propaganda amongst the underpaid and oppressed workers. Politics had been preached to them, vague indefinite appeals to revolution, but we offered them something tangible, a definite, clearly-lighted road out of their misery, a trade union that would improve their wages and conditions; that would protect them from petty tyranny of employers.[171]

In Ireland 1890 was also a year of strikes with the national newspapers reporting hectic labour activity all year. The new general unions established
themselves in Ireland although there was conflict with some existing labour
bodies. In Dublin Shields and Graham shifted their allegiance to Thorne's
union, the National Union of Gasworkers and General Labourers of Great
Britain and Ireland. Indeed, Shields became the gasworkers' union's Dublin
district secretary.

Despite this recent engagement with trade unionism the Irish Socialist
Union continued with its other activities as well. The regular lectures continued and two members, B. McGuinness and Fitzpatrick, went in February
1890 to a meeting of the Ratepayers' Association, 'a pettifogging association
of small shopkeepers and tenement house owners', and gave 'these worthies
a lesson on their duties'.[172] On 19 March the ISU hosted the annual Paris
Commune commemoration at 87 Marlborough Street where addresses were
delivered by King, Fitzpatrick, Kelly, Hamilton, O'Gorman and others.[173]
A short telegram from Ireland was read out at the celebrations in London:
'Dublin comrades join with you in honouring the men who bravely fought
and fell in the cause of human freedom. Vive la Commune.'[174] On the day
of the Commune meeting another event occurred which was to bring Shields
before the public as an advocate of 'new unionism'.

The Dublin United Builder's Labourers' Trade Union had for some weeks
unsuccessfully attempted to negotiate a general pay increase for its members.
On 19 March it called a strike and 2,000 labourers came out for an increase
of four pence an hour. The following evening the workers attended a union
meeting, chaired by Shields, at the Labourers' Hall, 117 Lower Clanbrassil
Street. Michael Canty, the Cork-born labour-nationalist organizer for the
Gasworkers' Union in Ireland, addressed the meeting and extended his support. Patrick A. Tyrrell, for the Amalgamated Society of Engineers, and
Graham, for the bottlemakers, also pledged their solidarity.[175] However, the
following day the workers came under immense pressure when Archbishop
William Walsh of Dublin had a letter printed in the *Freeman's Journal* which
supported the employers and accused the workers of intransigence.[176]
Walsh also wrote privately to the union asking for delegates to meet him
in order to organize 'a permanent committee of conciliation between the
working men and their employers'.[177] The union felt it would be churlish
to reject such an offer of mediation and a deputation went to meet him on
22 March. Following the meeting the members returned to Clanbrassil Street
and a march was held to Harold's Cross Green where Canty told them to
'stick to their demands and when they got home rule put a labour candidate
in Parliament'.[178] Another march from the Labourers' Hall to the Nine
Acres in the Phoenix Park was held the next day. Shields, who it seems was
also president of the Dublin United Builder's Labourers' Trade Union, took
the chair and admitted that public opinion would force them to accept an

arbitrator suggested by Archbishop Walsh. It was a pragmatic response to a difficult situation. After the rally the procession re-formed and went to the Mechanics' Institute for a meeting of the Gasworkers' Union. Canty, Graham, Shields and Hamilton spoke and attempted to induce the builder's labourers to join.[179]

Michael Davitt was appointed as the arbitrator and the men returned to work on 24 March.[180] Davitt worked out a deal between workers and employers and the strike was not resumed. *The Commonweal* in early April commented: 'As is usual in cases of arbitration, the men have gained very little; in fact, many of them will lose 1s. 6d. [one shilling and six pence] per week.'[181] When Davitt read this remark he was quick to write to the socialist paper to correct it and assert that the workers would actually get an increase on their previous wage.[182] His sensitivity and irritation at *The Commonweal* may have resulted from more than this off-hand remark. In Dublin he had run foul of members of the ISU in the week after the labourers' strike finished. During March, Shields had been in communication with Davitt on the labour question. He tried to persuade him to start a labour newspaper in Dublin; Davitt had in fact founded a paper in London. He also asked him to help lead the wave of 'new unionism' in Ireland and thereby strengthen the Irish labour movement. Davitt at first appeared sympathetic but when asked to preside at a labour demonstration planned for 30 March in the Phoenix Park he refused, claiming that he would not be in Ireland at the time. However, this proved an excuse and Shields discovered shortly before the rally that Davitt was in fact to be in Dublin on the day.[183] The outcome was a public confrontation between Davitt and the socialists.

The posters advertising the mass meeting, presuming that Davitt was obliged to preside, carried his name as the chairperson. On seeing himself publicly announced as the chair Davitt wrote an open letter to Shields via the Dublin *Evening Telegraph* where he made his reservations public. He claimed, rather improbably, not to know anything of the organizing union, the Gasworkers' Union, and he queried who its leaders were. The National Union of Gasworkers and General Labourers of Great Britain and Ireland, founded in March 1889, and which included Eleanor Marx among its leading figures, had been to the forefront of 'new unionism' in Britain. Davitt's feigned ignorance was simply a ploy, however, and his real objection was contained in his question on what the union 'proposes to do for the labour interests of Ireland which Irish labour organisations are unable to accomplish?' He continued:

> While the workingmen of Ireland, skilled and unskilled, are, in my opinion, most willing to co-operate with their brethren in Great Britain in the general cause of labour, there are reasons, obvious and substantial, why all Irish labour bodies should have the right to the unfettered management

of their own funds, and should not be compelled to resort to a strike or
any similar action because it may seem expedient or necessary to men
unacquainted with the peculiar economic conditions of Ireland to order
a resort to such a proceeding in England or Scotland.[184]

His problem was with the incursions of British unions into Ireland and he
warned Irish workers of the purported negative conditions that regulated
'the relations between the organized workers of Great Britain and their
necessarily less-numerous fellow workers of Ireland with whom they are
endeavouring to amalgamate'.[185] This attack on the Gasworkers' Union was
published the evening before the meeting but the attendance was still quite
strong, with between 8,000 and 10,000 present.[186]

James Poole, a middle-class supporter of labour, presided in place of
Michael Davitt. He demanded decent wages for working men, 'a decent
dwelling' and more leisure time. It was not a notably radical speech. Shields,
Hamilton, Dr Edward Aveling (who had come from London) and Canty
did somewhat better. Adolphus Shields lambasted Davitt and accused him
of displaying little interest in the Irish working class: they 'had as much
claim upon Mr Davitt as the labourers of England, Scotland and Wales (hear,
hear). But as he was a recognised leader of labour he should be at their head.
He [Shields] did not object to his helping the labourers of other countries.
Far from it; but they should remember that charity began at home'.[187] He
explained that he felt Davitt was obliged to preside at the meeting as he
was in the country and although he still saw Davitt as 'a friend of the working
class', he believed that he had made a mistake in not appearing. Dr Aveling
made oblique criticisms of the arbitration system and spoke in reply to
Davitt's questions on the Gasworkers' Union. He also pointed to the support that British workers had given to home rule as evidence of the usefulness
of collaborating with the British working class. In truth this carried an unfair imputation as Davitt had always been in favour of a political alliance
between workers in Ireland and Britain. His problem lay in his desire to
see an independent Irish labour movement which, with the British movement, would, he believed, 'strive harmoniously and effectively to advance
the general interests of the working classes of these islands'.[188] Davitt did
not want Irish labour dependent on, or acting as an outgrowth of, the British
labour movement. On 2 April the *Freeman's Journal* published a refutation
of Shields and Aveling by Davitt in which he wrote:

> All I ask for as an humble advocate of the cause of the Irish labour — in
> the matter of international relationship with the labour cause outside
> of Ireland — is, that we are not to be deprived of the principle of
> home rule in our Irish labour organisations which is conceded to us by
> our friends in Great Britain in the matter of the future government of our
> country.[189]

Davitt had a strong point here, but Shields also had a point in his reference to Davitt's neglect of Irish labour. In January 1890 Davitt had helped to found the ephemeral Irish Democratic Trade and Labour Federation but this labour-nationalist organization was one of his few serious engagements with Irish working-class politics. Most of his labour activity was in Britain. While Davitt would not publicly acknowledge it, his refusal to attend the Phoenix Park rally was also possibly related to an unwillingness to appear on the same platform as Dr Edward Aveling. In April 1887 they had both spoken at a huge anti-coercion demonstration in London but Davitt had refused to meet Aveling because of Aveling's declared atheism.[190]

The Gasworkers' Union recruited successfully in Ireland during 1890.[191] In a year of intense industrial unrest the union was particularly active in Dublin and Belfast. In addition, in line with a directive sent out by the socialist Second International it organized Ireland's first May Day labour demonstration in the Phoenix Park that year. Shields chaired and a crowd numbering thousands heard speeches from Michael McKeown, a leader of the 1889 Liverpool dock strike, P.A. Tyrrell and from William Foreman of the Amalgamated Society of Railway Servants which had been involved in a serious dispute in Ireland early in the year. John Whelan, of the Gasworkers' Union, called on people to vote working men into parliament.[192] On 27 July the union organized another mass demonstration in the Phoenix Park to celebrate the anniversary of the inauguration of the 'eight hours' movement. Six hundred coal-porters, accompanied by the Bray Brass Band, headed the procession from Beresford Place. The attendance in the park numbered about 10,000, according to the *Freeman's Journal*.[193] James Poole presided and Canty, Shields and Myles Kavanagh spoke. Shields criticized the Irish parliamentary party, alleging that when the Eight Hours Bill was brought before parliament not one of the Irish MPs had supported it. Again, the politics of Dublin radicalism manifested itself: 'They talked a lot about the farmer, but they did not consider the interests of the man in the cities at all.'[194]

It is unclear what role the other members of the Irish Socialist Union played in the success of the Gasworkers' Union. Certainly, those from a Socialist League background would have had reservations. It was the politics of labourism rather than socialism and there seems to have been no concerted effort by the socialists to capitalize on this labour ferment. In early May Thomas Fitzpatrick did deliver an address on 'The New Trade Unionism' but there is, unfortunately, no extant account of what he said.[195] We can assume that he was enthused by the labour demonstrations but the reformist parameters would undoubtedly have bothered him as an anarchist. The only ISU members that we can positively connect with the Gasworkers' Union are Adolphus Shields, William Graham and T. Hamilton. A meeting of the ISU on 3 May 1890 did express its approval of the May Day demonstration and adopt a resolution in favour of the 'eight hours' movement.[196]

While the general unions recruited well they did not, as Davitt's caution indicates, receive a universal welcome. The existing trades bodies were never likely to embrace perceived competition, even if those joining had previously been non-unionized, and the fact that the unions were British was also a factor. Amos Varian followed Davitt's lead in January 1891 when he argued for conciliation boards and complained in a riposte to William Foreman that 'Irish trades amalgamated with English trades unions forfeit their independence in all matters of vital importance to the society'.[197] When J. Havelock Wilson arrived in Waterford in September 1890 to organize a branch of the National Amalgamated Sailors' and Firemen's Union he found himself ostracized by the local trades.[198] Likewise, Michael Canty and the Gasworkers' Union clashed with the Dublin Trades Council in early October. The dispute centred on competing efforts to organize women workers in Dublin factories. A meeting in St Patrick's Hall in Lower Clanbrassil Street provided the initial battleground in the conflict when Canty and John Martin, president of the trades council, publicly quarrelled about the booking of the hall.[199] This debacle was followed by a flurry of letters in the press from both sides. Martin was less than contrite in a letter to the *Freeman's Journal*:

> It is not the first occasion Mr Canty tried to annoy and disparage in his own silly way the Dublin Trades Council (the sole ambition of the members of this organisation being to promote harmony between workingmen and employer, and encourage home industry).[200]

John Martin had already accused Canty of being a 'disunioner' and this was clearly his attitude toward the Gasworkers' Union as well. Also, in accentuating the moderation of the trades council he was in effect accusing the Gasworkers' Union of unnecessary aggressiveness.

On 3 November the Irish Socialist Union held a general meeting at 87 Marlborough Street and it would appear that a reassessment of the organization took place.[201] After this meeting the organization was usually referred to as the Dublin Socialist Union (DSU) and it introduced a series of weekly lectures to fill the vacuum created by the dissolution of the Progressist Club. The first lecture was held on 15 November when John O'Gorman spoke on human slavery.[202] Rather confusingly, the DSU used the 'Progressist Club' name when advertising its lectures in the *Freeman's Journal*.[203] This, however, was simply a flag of convenience and notices in radical and socialist papers confirm that these were Socialist Union lectures.[204] Five days before the opening lecture the DSU held a meeting to commemorate the 'judicial murder of our Chicago brethren'.[205] The room in Marlborough Street was decorated with anarchist slogans, and speeches were delivered by Fitzpatrick,

Graham, Hamilton, O'Gorman and by a German socialist named Werk-sleider.[206] In late November the group issued a circular which called on workers to recognize the need for internationalism and 'the consequent necessity for international organisation'.[207]

In January 1891 one of the weekly lectures provided an interesting window into contemporary Irish socialist thinking on the home rule question. The talk, 'Home Rule as a Social Panacea', was delivered by George King who was staunchly in favour of home rule before he joined the Socialist League in late 1885. Now he made biting criticisms of the policy although he admitted that 'under it some of the present suffering would disappear'. Concomitantly, however, he protested that 'it would only alleviate the sufferings of the few and place them in the ranks of the classes, leaving the great body of the people groaning under the same servitude as before'. Five other Dublin socialists spoke during the discussion and only one, Arthur Kavanagh, considered home rule to be a worthy objective. J.T. Toomey claimed that home rule would be detrimental to social progress because 'the masses of the people were at present led by their enemies' and these home rule politicians would continue to 'contrive to blind the workers to their own interests'. J.C. Collier, another Socialist Union member, flatly opposed home rule, and John O'Gorman contended that it would entail 'the rule of the farmer, the publican, the clergyman and the party politician . . . The farmer hoped to be able to get absolute possession of the land, and then ignore the claims of labour with the assistance of the other classes . . . just mentioned'. The publicans, he argued, would repeal all past temperance laws and the clergy, who sprang 'from the classes and imbibed class prejudice from their youth upwards, would also be enemies of progress'. Thomas Fitzpatrick thought that 'until the power of the priests was broken it would be dangerous to introduce Home Rule into Ireland'.[208] The singular advocate of home rule was Kavanagh who argued that the working class would be able to successfully push for social progress through an improved parliamentary system.

> As soon as the all-important question of home rule was settled, the intelligent electors of Ireland would demand these reforms. He objected to the manner in which the clergy had been spoken of. The clergy were uncompromising opponents of the publicans, and under a Home Rule legislature the clergy would justly use their influence in the temperance cause. That would be the first and most important step in the right direction. The clergy were not the enemies of progress. The patriotic priests of Ireland were always found fighting on the side of the people, except in cases of attempted revolution, where they did their duty in striving to prevent their flocks from being made the victims of British Government vengeance.[209]

Kavanagh evidently possessed a robust faith in parliamentary politics and, moreover, a highly defensive view of the clergy. The fact that his position on home rule failed to find supporters among Irish socialists is very interesting. Rather than pose an alternative, as James Connolly was later to do, Dublin socialists articulated a critique of home rule that objectively meant support for the prevailing colonial relationship, and markedly failed to confront its anti-democratic nature.

In early February the DSU held another meeting that provided evidence of the retreat of anarchism in the city of Dublin. The Socialist League had a strong anarchist contingent in its Dublin branch and its libertarian perspective had remained an influence throughout the late 1880s. By 1891, however, the troubled Socialist League was crumbling as a real force in British left-wing politics. At the Dublin meeting on 5 February King advocated Marxism in a lecture on individualism. Fitzpatrick opposed him from the anarchist standpoint but the majority of contributors clearly accepted King's position.[210] The diminished influence of anarchism was also reflected in a shift away from the Socialist League which was now almost entirely an anarchist organization. After February 1891 Dublin correspondence to *The Commonweal* ceased and it no longer carried notices of Socialist Union meetings.[211] *Justice* continued to print weekly notices and at the end of March it reported on the annual Commune commemoration which was held in Dublin on 19 March. According to the report addresses were delivered by Fitzpatrick, Hamilton, O'Gorman and two *émigré* socialists at the Socialist Union event.[212]

SOCIALISTS, PARNELL AND THE WORKING CLASS

In 1890 Adolphus Shields had failed in his attempt to enlist a nationalist leader, Davitt, into the leadership of the Irish labour movement. Had he succeeded it would have opened up important political possibilities. In 1891 the split in the Irish parliamentary party seemed to provide Shields with another unforeseen opportunity to recruit a national figure. Parnell had lost the leadership of the parliamentary party in December 1890 after heated discussions on the repercussions of the O'Shea divorce scandal. Only a minority of Irish MPs continued to support him and he found himself fighting for his political life in Ireland. Michael Davitt was one of the first to publicly criticize him and a concerted battle between the Parnellites and anti-Parnellites raged throughout 1891.[213] Parnell, himself, was to die at the age of forty-five in October that year but the division in the nationalist movement continued for many years afterwards. Indeed, the Irish nationalist MPs did not reunite as a single political party until 1900 under John Redmond.

In Dublin a 'Parnell Leadership Committee' was established in early 1891 and in towns and cities around the country local committees were set up. The National League continued under Parnell's control while a separate national organization was put in place by the majority of home rulers who opposed Parnell. Dublin became one of the Parnellites' few areas of strength and the Gasworkers' Union rallied to Parnell's defence. Three members of the union served on the Parnell Leadership Committee: Adolphus Shields, Myles Kavanagh and Frederick J. Allan.[214] Kavanagh was Dublin district assistant secretary while Fred Allan, a leading Fenian, was involved in organizing for the union during 1891. Allan remained a staunch Parnellite over the next few years.[215]

The Gasworkers' Union held a meeting on 28 February to celebrate the anniversary of the winning of the eight-hour day by Dublin's gasworkers. Shields, Canty and Myles Kavanagh spoke before a large crowd and, as usual, James Poole presided.[216] Shields announced their intention of organizing a labour conference to which Parnell would be invited. In an effort to ensure broad support for the proposed conference, the Dublin Trades Council was approached and asked to endorse the venture. At a special meeting of the council on 8 March it quickly transpired that support would not be forthcoming because of a desire to keep any such conference 'aloof from all political parties' and because of a barely concealed dislike of the organizing unions.[217] Fred Allan and Shields represented the Gasworkers' Union at the council meeting but came up against unbending opposition from the members including the vigorous Amalgamated Society of Railway Servants organizer, William Foreman. According to Allan: 'It is plain . . . that the Trades Council, or rather its executive, has allowed its political bias on the one hand and its unreasonable prejudice on the other, to draw it into antagonism to a project which is bound to benefit the labour movement in this country.'[218] Both Allan and Shields stressed the purportedly non-political nature of the conference and Shields accused the trades council of naked jealousy because the council would be 'playing second fiddle' at a conference called by unions 'composed principally of unskilled labourers'.[219]

Dublin Trades Council had a tradition of being non-political and its members clearly viewed the conference as a Parnellite enterprise. Despite Allan and Shields's protestations it is difficult to avoid the conclusion that it was precisely that. Parnell, never noted for his interest in labour issues, was reaching out to potential allies in his struggle with the home rule majority party. During 1891 his relations with both labour and the Fenians improved radically. Shields and the trade unionists, on the other hand, were greatly heartened by his new-found interest. On 14 March the labour conference was held in the Antient Concert Rooms in Dublin with Dr P.J. Neilan, of the Kanturk Democratic Labour Federation, presiding. Sixty-nine labour bodies from many parts of Ireland were represented although the majority appear to have come from Dublin and its adjacent counties. Neilan said that he saw the assembly as 'the first Irish Labour Parliament' and he suggested the continuance of that unity. A decision had already been taken on this question by Shields and others before the conference and they tabled a motion calling for the establishment of an Irish Labour League. This was accepted by the delegates present and a radical programme was voted on which pledged the new organization to nationalization of the land; manhood suffrage; triennial parliaments; payment of MPs; payment of election expenses; taxation of ground rents in towns and of unoccupied houses; the general promotion of Irish industry; promotion of the building of working-class housing by the state and the lowering of rent; the direct employment by local government of labour; an eight-hour day; state control of railways, canals, harbours, docks and all sources of transit; greater liberty for trade unions; evening sittings of all local boards; and removal of all taxation on necessary food.[220]

The acceptance of measures such as land nationalization by rural labourers' organizations is interesting. In addition, groups from areas as diverse as Athy, Kilkenny, Carlow, Waterford, Quilty West, Kanturk and Belfast united in accepting a programme with major radical connotations. There was a short discussion on education which led to the dropping of a clause in the programme on free and compulsory education. Poole had suggested that it be secular education but this was opposed by Allan who pointed out that such a clause would immediately bring them into conflict with the clergy. Canty argued that a suitable compromise could be found in simply excising the education demand from the proposed programme. Myles Kavanagh proposed a prepared list of names to form the executive of the Labour League, which included Shields, Allan, Poole and trade unionists from Belfast, Newry, Cork, Waterford and Kanturk. This was accepted and the new executive was given the right to co-opt.

Parnell arrived to address the conference during the afternoon. William Hey, representing the Belfast branch of the Gasworkers' Union, had sounded a note of caution about Parnell's presence during the morning session. Hey mentioned that some of his constituents looked 'slightly with fear at the prominence given to a certain gentleman on the paper that had been sent up to [them] . . . They said why was not Col. Saunderson [the unionist leader] consulted as well as Mr Parnell'. He argued that unless 'all political and religious questions were put aside this labour movement would be a failure'. Hey's equation of unionism and nationalism was not likely to be well received outside of parts of Ulster and John Whelan, while welcoming Hey's comments, held that they were 'highly honoured when they had one of the greatest statesmen of the age championing their cause in the British House of Commons'.[221]

In his speech Parnell repeated some of the points he had made in an earlier speech in Clerkenwell. He accepted the principle of land nationalization although his definition of this policy would have amused Davitt and Henry

George. In addition, he declared his support for the eight-hour day and with regard to the elements of the Labour League programme he said: 'All these are questions upon which any advanced thinker must be in agreement with you; and I am glad to concur with you, as a whole, in the very excellent programme of practical reform which you have drawn out.' Publicly recognizing the growing strength of the labour movement, he advocated progress by constitutional means:

> As regards the workingmen of Great Britain and of Ireland, I believe that their lot will be one of speedy and rapid improvement (hear, hear). The power which the Constitution gives to the masses — the political power which it gives — the power which it gives them of influencing the elections and of using their force by returning members of Parliament, is a growing and an increasing one, and all of us politicians are bound to recognise it; and even if we [did] not sympathise with you we must now sympathise with you in order to maintain our political existence (applause).[222]

Parnell received a tremendous reception and he was followed by the Parnellite MP, W.A. McDonald, who expressed his sympathy with the new organization. At the conclusion of the conference a procession to Beresford Place was hurriedly organized. Led by a quickly mustered Gasworkers' Union band the Parnellite demonstration wound its way through the streets of Dublin where Parnell received an enthusiastic reception: 'Cheer followed cheer at every few yards and no more striking or more impromptu procession has ever taken place in Dublin.'[223] The march was vast by the time it reached Beresford Place where a huge crowd was waiting. On Allan's motion James Poole was moved to the chair. Parnell, who was greeted by prolonged cheering, spoke and said that he had come from a meeting in the same building where the National League had been founded and where now had 'also been founded a great organisation for the workingmen of Ireland (cheers) . . . I, as an Irish Nationalist (cheers), believing in the future of my country, in the right of our country to nationhood, welcome these attempts of the workingmen to improve their condition, and promise you my hearty and cordial support, knowing that in the workingmen Ireland has her best army, her strongest and her bravest soldiers and her steadiest fighters for the National rights of Ireland (long and prolonged cheers)'.[224] The unionist *Irish Times* was dismayed by the emergence of the Irish Labour League and worried that Parnell was contriving to make himself the leader of both his own nationalist party and this new 'powerful intended organisation'. In future, the newspaper predicted, a parliamentary candidate would find that 'it will not be enough to hoist the flag of [Justin] McCarthy or Parnell to indicate his position; he must supplement his proclamation with the profession of a number of communistic principles, as to property of every sort, which the working men have chosen to impose upon other classes'.[225]

It was a late conversion for Parnell and some were less than convinced of his sincerity. After his speech at Clerkenwell the anti-Parnellite East Dublin Radical Club had said that it regarded 'Mr Parnell's newly-found love for the labourers as a mere election cry to catch their votes'.[226] Shields clearly thought otherwise and it is probable that the conservative conglomeration of forces opposing Parnell inspired some sympathy for him from anti-clerical socialists and Fenians. The SDF was pleased with Parnell's apparent conversion and *Justice* commented after the Dublin labour conference in a piece entitled, 'Parnell, the Democratic':

> Mr Parnell is doing good work, if only in the way of propaganda. The programme which he formulated on Saturday last at Dublin is practically the old palliative programme of the SDF; less women's suffrage and one or two other matters . . . What will the Liberals, and their new allies, the Catholic priests, do and say?[227]

Shields's hopes, however, were dashed in subsequent months when the Irish Labour League failed as a movement. In addition, Parnell spent virtually all his political energies in the months before his death fighting his opposition within the nationalist movement and thus was not able, or perhaps not willing, to expend much time on labour politics.

EIGHT HOURS AND LABOUR REPRESENTATION

Adolphus Shields and the Gasworkers' Union were ardent advocates of the Eight Hours Bill which was then being strongly promoted by the British 'new unions'. A debate on the 'eight hours' movement in the City of Dublin Workingmen's Club on 20 April provided him with an opportunity to voice his support for the measure. However, another member of the Socialist Union, J.T. Toomey, spoke against the bill and opined that all its objectives 'could be achieved by a change in the currency'.[228] Toomey, a man who spoke with a broad southern accent, had made this argument before.[229] In 1886 at a meeting of the Saturday Club he had delivered 'a strong eulogy on the use of paper money as a means of building up national prosperity'.[230] It was not a policy that would have much interested the Socialist League and, indeed, it may have been his deviant socialism that caused him to resign from the league branch in May that year after a short membership.[231] The Socialist League was not a broad church like later organizations such as the Socialist Club or the Socialist Union.

The Gasworkers' Union managed to forge an alliance with Dublin Trades Council in April, just a month after their clash, in order to organize the 1891 May Day demonstration. A delegate committee was established with members from at least twenty-seven Dublin labour bodies. Shields and Fred Allan represented the Irish Labour League; Michael Canty, Myles Kavanagh and Tim Donovan represented the Gasworkers' Union.[232] The procession to the Phoenix Park was impressive and the thousands who assembled for the rally were addressed from three separate platforms. The police estimated the attendance as 17,000.[233] Both Shields and John Whelan used the opportunity to indicate their support for Parnell although Whelan's strong comments evoked an interruption from John Martin of the trades council who was presiding at the platform. Other speakers included James Poole, William Field, Pete Curran, Fred Allan, William Foreman and William Graham. Poole signalled the temper of the gathering when he remarked that 'when Labour Day in May came to be merely an outing then he thought that men of intelligence would stay away, but today they were there because work had to be done'.[234] The demand for an eight-hour day was foremost among the resolutions passed and labour representation in parliament was also demanded by most of the speakers. Shields called on those present to join the Labour League. William Field, who was to be elected as a Parnellite MP in 1892, urged that nobody should vote for a parliamentary candidate who had not given a written pledge to promote the interests of the labour movement. He called for a vote for every working man: 'The laws had given them the right to labour all their lifetime and then to die in the work-house.'[235] Another large labour demonstration was held in Drogheda on the same day where Canty was among the speakers. Again, the demands for labour representation and an eight-hour day were to the fore.[236]

During 1890–91 the Gasworkers' Union in Ireland grew to a membership of 20,000–25,000.[237] With such strength in the country it is not surprising that it decided to hold its second annual conference in Dublin from 18 to 20 May 1891. A number of leading socialists arrived with the Gasworkers' Union delegates from Britain. Thorne, himself an SDF member, and Dr Aveling, Eleanor Marx and Pete Curran were among the socialists involved with the union. The conference was held in the Antient Concert Rooms and, despite objections from Davitt among others, Aveling was selected to chair. Aveling was also selected by the Dublin and Belfast branches to represent them at the Brussels International Congress later in the year. In the elections for the ten-person executive Marx polled the highest number of votes and such was her popularity that she was nominated for the presidency of the union although this was a position that held no interest for her.[238]

On Sunday 17 May, the day before the conference, the Gasworkers' Union organized a labour demonstration in the Phoenix Park. Shields, Allan and Canty were on the platform although English delegates made the speeches. Poole, who presided, moved two resolutions, the first of which called for the international organization of labour. The second resolution encapsulated the central political demands of the union:

> That this mass meeting of Dublin workers hereby pledges itself to sup-
> port at the forthcoming municipal and Parliamentary elections only those
> candidates who are in favour of manhood suffrage, an international legal
> eight hour day, payment of members of Parliament and local boards, and
> payment of all election expenses and greater liberty for labour com-
> bination.[239]

Thorne, in a subsequent address, called on Irish workers, particularly
women, to join the union, and declared that they had done in Ireland what
had never been done 'by the two political parties before, they had joined
the north and the south together. There was no bigotry existing between
the people of Ireland, who were really kept divided by the two political parties'.[240] Such a naïve view of the deep political division in Ireland was hardly conducive to a proper understanding of the very real problems that Irish
socialism confronted. Marx, in her speech, made a point that had seemingly escaped the attention of the entirely male leadership of the Irish Labour
League and of the Gasworkers' Union in Ireland:

> She was now supporting a resolution the terms of which she could scarce-
> ly be said to endorse. It was not 'manhood' suffrage but adult suffrage
> they wanted, for women should have a voice in the matter (hear, hear).
> Their union was helping in that direction. It was the only union where
> men and women were acting entirely side by side and to that fact she
> ascribed some of the great fruits of their organisation.[241]

There is no public record of any opposition to the exclusion of women from
the suffrage demand being voiced at the Labour League convention. It may
be that Shields, Graham and Poole (who was certainly in favour of votes
for women) felt that they would have no success if they pushed the demand
for women's suffrage. It could also be that the policy held no great interest
for them. Irish socialism cannot, until the twentieth century, be seen as
anything other than an entirely male enterprise. It did not have activists
such as Eleanor Marx or Jessie Craigen who were willing to force women's
rights onto the agenda.

   Marx made one of the most advanced speeches that afternoon. She argued
that the only way to get the eight-hour day and 'obtain the only real freedom
which was of value was by using the political power which they had in their
own hands'.[242] Aveling argued for home rule which was responded to by
cries of 'Parnell for ever' and Marx later recalled that 'no words were more
enthusiastically cheered than "Let Ireland be free, but let it be an Ireland
of free workers; it matters little to the men and women of Ireland if they
are exploited by Nationalist or Orangeman; the agricultural labourer sees
his enemy in the landlord, as the industrial worker sees his in the
capitalist"'.[243] These were probably Aveling's words and he also spoke

strongly in favour of Irish nationalists embracing internationalism. This Phoenix Park rally echoed the calls for labour representation and the eight-hour day which had become consistent demands since the rise of 'new unionism'. The Gasworkers' Union in Ireland was undoubtedly an empower-ing and radicalizing element of the labour movement and particularly assisted the growing movement for independent labour representation. Friedrich Engels, who was kept informed by Eleanor Marx, wrote of it in February 1891:

> The Gasworkers now have the most powerful organisation in Ireland, and will put up their own candidates in the next election, unconcerned over either Parnell or McCarthy. That Parnell is now so friendly with the workers, he owes to encounters with these same Gasworkers, who had no compunc-tions about telling him the truth. Michael Davitt, too, who had at first wanted independent Irish trades unions, has learned from them: their con-stitution secures them perfectly free home rule. To them the credit for giving impetus to the labour movement in Ireland.[244]

Engels briefly visited Ireland in September when he may have met Poole and other members of the Gasworkers' Union. He was mistaken regarding Gasworkers' Union election candidates. In 1891 the Dublin socialist and labour activists were asking candidates from existing parties to pledge themselves to support the interests of labour. In January 1893 the formation of the Independent Labour Party was to promote autonomous representation.

Meanwhile, with some of its members active with the 'new unions', the Socialist Union continued into 1892 with its weekly lectures. The themes very much reflected the concerns of the SDF in Britain with John O'Gorman lecturing on 'Individual Liberty and Socialism', Fitzpatrick on 'How to Realise Socialism', and Arthur Kavanagh talking on 'The Ideals of the Revolution'.[245] Despite the involvement of a number of its British members the SDF maintained a distance from the 'new unionism' movement and it would seem that the Socialist Union in Dublin did much the same thing.

NOTES AND REFERENCES

1 *Freeman's Journal*, 3, 8 Mar. 1886.
2 *Freeman's Journal*, 8 Mar. 1886.
3 Joseph Karpel to Socialist League, n.d. but early 1887, Socialist League Papers, IISH.
4 Auguste Coulon to Socialist League, 10 Feb. 1887, Socialist League Papers, IISH.
5 *The Commonweal*, 12 Mar. 1887. The paper was only available in Dublin at the following outlets: Wheeler, Earl Street; O'Brien, 22 Upper Ormond Quay; Carver, 41 Amiens Street; and Mannock, 9 Great Brunswick Street.
6 *The Commonweal*, 19 Mar. 1887.

7   *Justice*, 20 Nov. 1886.

8   *Justice*, 2 Apr. 1887.

9   *The Commonweal*, 12 Mar. 1887.

10 Gerard Moran, 'James Daly and the rise and fall of the Land League in the west of Ireland, 1879–82', *Irish Historical Studies*, vol. xxix, no. 114, Nov. 1994, p. 197; T.W. Moody, *Davitt and Irish Revolution, 1846–1882* (Oxford, 1981), pp. 351–3.

11 *Freeman's Journal*, 30 Nov. 1881; *Cork Examiner*, 30 Nov. 1881.

12 Ronald Bush, *The Genesis of Ezra Pound's Cantos* (Princeton, 1976), pp. 91–102; A.D. Moody, 'Pound's Allen Upward', *Paideuma*, vol. iv, no. 1, Spring 1975.

13 *The Commonweal*, 3 Sept. 1887.

14 *The Commonweal*, 11 Sept. 1886.

15 Auguste Coulon to H.H. Sparling, 22 Sept. 1886, Socialist League Papers, IISH.

16 John O'Gorman to Socialist League, 21 Dec. 1886, Socialist League Papers, IISH.

17 *The Commonweal*, 26 Mar. 1887; *Justice*, 26 Mar. 1887.

18 *The Commonweal*, 26 Mar. 1887.

19 *Justice*, 26 Mar. 1887; *The Commonweal*, 2 Mar. 1887.

20 *Justice*, 14 Mar. 1885.

21 Michael Gabriel to H.H. Sparling, 7 Mar. 1886, Socialist League Papers, IISH.

22 John W. Boyle, *The Irish Labor Movement in the Nineteenth Century* (Washington, 1988), p. 158.

23 *The Commonweal*, 19 Mar. 1887; *Justice*, 19 Mar. 1887.

24 *Justice*, 26 Mar. 1887.

25 John O'Gorman to Socialist League, 24 Mar. 1887, Socialist League Papers, IISH.

26 William Morris to E. Chapman, 13 Apr. 1885, Socialist League Papers, IISH.

27 *The Commonweal*, 17 May 1890.

28 ibid.

29 *The Commonweal*, 25 Feb. 1888.

30 *Freeman's Journal*, 10 Feb. 1886.

31 *The Commonweal* most often referred to this organization as the *Irish* Labour League but I use *National* Labour League because this is the name used in *Justice* and in its own advertisements in the *Freeman's Journal*.

32 John Quail, *The Slow Burning Fuse: The Lost History of the British Anarchists* (London, 1978), p. 69.

33 T.W. Grimshaw, 'A statistical survey of Ireland, from 1840 to 1888', *Journal of the Statistical and Social Inquiry Society of Ireland*, pt lxviii, 1889, p. 328.

34 *Freeman's Journal*, 7 Mar. 1887.

35 *The Commonweal*, 12 Mar. 1887.

36 *Freeman's Journal*, 7 Mar. 1887. In April 1882 J.B. Killen and T.D. Sullivan spoke together in Dublin at a 10,000-strong working-class demonstration against coercion. (*Cork Examiner*, 10 Apr. 1882.)

37 *Freeman's Journal*, 7 Mar. 1887.

38 ibid.

39 ibid.

40 ibid.

41 *Freeman's Journal*, 3 Mar. 1887.
42 *Freeman's Journal*, 7 Mar. 1887. In 1881, Tyrrell had been secretary of the Irish Home Manufacture Association. Both Amos Varian and J.B. Killen had also supported this association. (*Freeman's Journal*, 27, 28 Oct. 1881.)
43 *Freeman's Journal*, 2 Aug. 1887.
44 *Freeman's Journal*, 7, 14 Mar. 1887.
45 *Freeman's Journal*, 14 Mar. 1887.
46 *The Commonweal*, 19 Mar. 1887.
47 ibid.
48 *Freeman's Journal*, 14 Mar. 1887.
49 ibid.
50 *Justice*, 2 Apr. 1887.
51 *Justice*, 16 Apr. 1887.
52 *Freeman's Journal*, 21 Mar. 1887.
53 *Freeman's Journal*, 28 Mar. 1887.
54 *Justice*, 23 Apr. 1887.
55 *Justice*, 30 Apr. 1887.
56 *Freeman's Journal*, 2 May 1887.
57 *Justice*, 21 May 1887.
58 *Irish Times*, 26 Oct. 1887.
59 *The Commonweal*, 28 May 1887; *Justice*, 28 May 1887.
60 John O'Gorman to Socialist League, 24 Mar. 1887, Socialist League Papers, IISH.
61 *Justice*, 4 June 1887. Meanwhile, police detectives watched the socialists and informed their superiors that they believed J.B. Killen, James Keegan, J.E. Masterson and Thomas Fitzpatrick to be among the most prominent figures in the agitation. 'The Association', they reported, 'is not formidable at present, but may become so and is watched.' (DMP Files, 1887: Crime Dept. — Special Branch, Movement of Suspects, Dublin Police District, 16 May–7 June 1887, National Archives.) Joseph Edmundson Masterson was a former member of the Central branch of the Land League and had been a leading Land League activist in Dublin. Killen may have brought him into the National Labour League agitation.
62 *The Commonweal*, 4 June 1887; *Freeman's Journal*, 7 May 1887. House leagues had been formed in many towns in Ireland during the 'land war' and their primary role had been to combat rack-renting. (*Cork Examiner*, 11 Dec. 1880, 10, 24 Jan. 1881.) They had enjoyed a strained, although ostensibly mutually supportive, relationship with the Land League. See Thomas Brennan's letter to the Mitchelstown house league published in the *Cork Examiner*, 4 Feb. 1881.
63 *The Commonweal*, 4 June 1887.
64 *Freeman's Journal*, 4 June 1887; *The Commonweal*, 11 June 1887; *Justice*, 11 June 1887.
65 *The Commonweal*, 18 June 1887.
66 ibid.
67 *Irish Times*, 26 Oct. 1887.
68 *Justice*, 4 Aug. 1887; *The Commonweal*, 30 July 1887.
69 *Irish Times*, 26 Oct. 1886.

70 *Freeman's Journal*, 4 July 1887.
71 *The Union*, 18 June 1887.
72 *Freeman's Journal*, 7 Mar. 1887.
73 *The Commonweal*, 20 Aug. 1887.
74 ibid.
75 *The Commonweal*, 3 Sept. 1887.
76 *The Commonweal*, 22 Oct. 1887.
77 *Irish Times*, 21 Oct. 1887. We are indebted to the conservative *Irish Times* for the extant extracts from this early socialist manifesto which it published with the intention of 'exposing' the National Labour League.
78 *Freeman's Journal*, 20 Oct. 1887.
79 John Quail, op. cit., pp. 72–4.
80 *Irish Times*, 21 Oct. 1887.
81 *Irish Times*, 24 Oct. 1887.
82 *The Commonweal*, 19 Nov. 1887.
83 *Irish Times*, 24 Oct. 1887.
84 *Irish Times*, 21 Oct. 1887.
85 *The Union*, 19 Nov. 1887.
86 Martin A. Miller, *Kropotkin* (Chicago, 1976), pp. 166–7.
87 *Freeman's Journal*, 27 Oct. 1887.
88 ibid.
89 ibid.
90 The final notice for the National Labour League appeared in *Justice*, 19 Nov. 1887, advertising a meeting for 24 November with a plea to all readers to attend.
91 *Justice*, 10 Dec. 1887.
92 *Justice*, 7 Jan. 1888; *The Commonweal*, 19 Nov. 1887.
93 *Justice*, 7, 14 Jan. 1888.
94 Dublin Socialist Club circular (dated Dec. 1887) in the Socialist League Papers, IISH.
95 *Justice*, 18 Feb. 1888.
96 *Justice*, 10 Dec. 1887.
97 *Justice*, 28 Apr. 1888.
98 *Justice*, 25 Feb. 1888.
99 *Justice*, 24 Mar. 1888.
100 *Justice*, 2 June 1888.
101 *The Commonweal*, 24 Mar. 1888; *Justice*, 24 Mar. 1888.
102 Dublin Socialists to London telegram, 19 Mar. 1888, Socialist League Papers, IISH.
103 *Justice*, 28 Apr. 1888.
104 ibid.
105 *Justice*, 2 June 1888.
106 *Justice*, 16 June 1888.
107 See the note by Max Nettlau (dated 3 Apr. 1940) on the back of a letter from N. Devereux to Socialist League, 20 Apr. 1888, Socialist League Papers, IISH. N. Devereux, who had been a member of the Socialist League in Dublin, was possibly Nicholas Devereux who was mentioned in the UCD College Register in 1883. See 'Fathers of the Society of Jesus', *A Page of Irish History: Story*

of University College, Dublin, 1883–1909 (Dublin, 1930), appendix, p. 591. For Devereux's membership of the Dublin branch of the Socialist League in 1886 see George King to H.H. Sparling, 11 Dec. 1886, Socialist League Papers, IISH.

108 Samuel Hayes to Socialist League, 15 July 1888, Socialist League Papers, IISH.
109 *The Commonweal*, 25 Aug. 1888; *Justice*, 25 Aug. 1888.
110 *The Commonweal*, 25 Aug. 1888.
111 *Justice*, 29 Dec. 1888.
112 *The Commonweal*, 23 Nov. 1889.
113 *The Commonweal*, 9 Feb. 1889; *Justice*, 9 Feb. 1889.
114 *The Commonweal*, 23 Mar. 1889.
115 *Justice*, 23 Mar. 1889.
116 *The Commonweal*, 2 Feb. 1889.
117 *The Commonweal*, 20 Apr. 1889.
118 ibid.
119 *The Commonweal*, 20, 27 Apr., 4, 11, 18 May, 14 Sept., 19 Oct. 1889.
120 *The Commonweal*, 21 Dec. 1889.
121 *The Commonweal*, 1, 15 June, 12 Oct. 1889.
122 *The Commonweal*, 4 May 1889.
123 *The Commonweal*, 6 July 1889.
124 *The Commonweal*, 9 Nov. 1889.
125 *The Commonweal*, 10 Aug. 1889.
126 *The Commonweal*, 17 Aug. 1889.
127 Yvonne Kapp, *Eleanor Marx, Volume II: The Crowded Years, 1884–1898* (London, 1976), p. 312.
128 ibid., pp. 293, 311–12.
129 *The Commonweal*, 23 Nov. 1889.
130 *Justice*, 9 Feb. 1889.
131 *The Commonweal*, 29 Sept. 1889. The outlets in Lurgan were: Peter Duffy, 3 Market Street; James Kennedy, 30 High Street; W. Mahaffy, 20 High Street; Mary Carter, Middle-row.
132 *Brotherhood*, 11 May 1889.
133 *Brotherhood*, 1 June 1889.
134 *Brotherhood*, 13 July 1889.
135 *The Commonweal*, 12 Nov. 1887.
136 E.P. Thompson, *William Morris: Romantic to Revolutionary* (New York, 1976), pp. 590–3; John Quail, op. cit., *passim*.
137 E.P. Thompson, op. cit., p. 590. Thompson mistakenly claims that Coulon had worked 'for a few months with the Social Democratic Society in Dublin'.
138 *The Commonweal*, 9 June 1888.
139 John Bruce Glasier, *William Morris and the Early Days of the Socialist Movement* (London, 1921), p. 124.
140 John Quail, op. cit., pp. 97–8.
141 *The Commonweal*, 12 July 1890; John Quail, op. cit., p. 95.
142 *The Commonweal*, 29 Nov. 1890; John Quail, op. cit., p. 97.
143 *The Commonweal*, 25 Nov. 1893.
144 *The Commonweal*, 19 Apr. 1890.

145 John Quail, op. cit., p. 107.
146 ibid., p. 96. William Morris had endured quite a lot of anarchistic dementia by November 1890. In August the anarchists in the Socialist League had organized a 'Revolutionary Conference' at the Autonomie Club in London. Among the suggestions were that in the event 'of a crisis at home, the first thing to do was to fire the slums and get the people into the West-end mansions' (Charles Mowbray); that they 'should preach to the thieves, the paupers, and the prostitutes . . . The first act of the Revolution ought to be to open the prison doors' (Frank Kitz); and that they should advocate 'individual guerilla warfare . . . We should recognise individuality' (Pearson). The only issue actually decided by the conference was that there should be no chairperson or 'any such quasi-constitutional official'. See E.P. Thompson, op. cit., pp. 568–9.
147 John Quail, op. cit., p. 107; E.P. Thompson, op. cit., p. 590.
148 John Quail, op. cit., pp. 104–5.
149 The Commonweal, 5 Dec. 1891.
150 Quoted in John Quail, op. cit., p. 110.
151 The Commonweal, 16 Apr. 1892.
152 Quoted in John Quail, op. cit., p. 122.
153 Brotherhood, 11 Jan. 1890.
154 ibid.
155 ibid.
156 ibid.; John W. Boyle, op. cit., p. 182.
157 Justice, 8 Feb. 1890; The Commonweal, 15 Feb. 1890.
158 The Progressist Club did not meet after May 1890. It is probable that a summer recess was called but the club failed to resume for the 'winter session'.
159 The Irish Socialist Union began a series of regular weekly lectures in late November after its 'Chicago Anarchists' commemoration meeting on 10 November. See The Commonweal, 15 Nov. 1890 for notification of the first lecture.
160 Freeman's Journal, 7 Mar. 1887; The Commonweal, 20 Aug. 1887.
161 Brotherhood, 11 Jan. 1890.
162 Freeman's Journal, 16 Aug. 1882.
163 Graham also worked with Schumann during the 1886 Dublin bottlemakers' dispute. See John W. Boyle, op. cit., p. 176. Boyle is mistaken in ascribing Socialist League membership to William Graham.
164 He first attended the Progressist Club on 13 Apr. 1889. The Commonweal, 20 Apr. 1889.
165 The speakers were Thomas Fitzpatrick, George King, J. Wilson, T. Hamilton, Arthur Kavanagh and John O'Gorman who gave three of the lectures. The Commonweal, 21 Aug., 7, 14 Sept., 12, 19 Oct., 14, 28 Dec. 1889, 1 Mar. 1890; Justice, 3 May 1890.
166 The Commonweal, 25 Jan. 1890.
167 For Hamilton's Christian socialism see The Commonweal, 16 Nov. 1889; Freeman's Journal, 31 Mar. 1890.
168 Freeman's Journal, 10 Apr. 1890.
169 James E. Cronin, 'Strikes and power in Britain, 1870–1920', International Review of Social History, vol. xxxii, no. 2, 1987, p. 164.

170 Henry Pelling, *A History of British Trade Unionism* (Harmondsworth, 1967), p. 104.
171 Will Thorne, *My Life's Battles* (London, 1925), p. 76.
172 *The Commonweal*, 15 Feb. 1890.
173 *The Commonweal*, 25 Mar. 1890.
174 ibid.
175 *Freeman's Journal*, 19, 21 Mar. 1890.
176 *Freeman's Journal*, 21 Mar. 1890.
177 *Freeman's Journal*, 22 Mar. 1890.
178 *Freeman's Journal*, 23 Mar. 1890.
179 *Freeman's Journal*, 24 Mar. 1890; *The Commonweal*, 5 Apr. 1890.
180 *Freeman's Journal*, 25 Mar. 1890.
181 *The Commonweal*, 5 Apr. 1890.
182 *The Commonweal*, 19 Apr. 1890.
183 *Freeman's Journal*, 31 Mar. 1890.
184 *Evening Telegraph*, 29 Mar. 1890.
185 ibid.
186 *The Commonweal*, 5 Apr. 1890.
187 *Freeman's Journal*, 31 Mar. 1890.
188 ibid.
189 *Freeman's Journal*, 2 Apr. 1890.
190 Yvonne Kapp, op. cit., p. 198.
191 John W. Boyle, op. cit., pp. 109–14; Emmet O'Connor, *A Labour History of Ireland* (Dublin, 1992), pp. 50–1.
192 *Freeman's Journal*, 5 May 1890.
193 *The Commonweal*, 2 Aug. 1890.
194 *Freeman's Journal*, 29 July 1890.
195 *Justice*, 3 May 1890.
196 *Justice*, 10 May 1890.
197 *Freeman's Journal*, 15 Jan. 1891.
198 *Freeman's Journal*, 20 Sept. 1890. Havelock Wilson was accompanied by William Foreman.
199 *Freeman's Journal*, 4, 6 Oct. 1890.
200 *Freeman's Journal*, 7 Oct. 1890.
201 *Justice*, 1 Nov. 1890.
202 *Justice*, 15 Nov. 1890; *The Commonweal*, 22 Nov. 1890.
203 For examples of the use of the 'Progressist Club' name see *Freeman's Journal*, 15, 21, 28 Jan. 1891.
204 See the notices in *The Commonweal*, *Justice* and the *Belfast Weekly Star* during 1891.
205 *Justice*, 1 Nov. 1890; *The Commonweal*, 22 Nov. 1890.
206 *The Commonweal*, 22 Nov. 1890.
207 *Justice*, 29 Nov. 1890.
208 *Belfast Weekly Star*, 24 Jan. 1891. All the preceding quotes are taken from this report of the meeting.
209 ibid.
210 *Belfast Weekly Star*, 14 Feb. 1891.

211 The final notice of a Dublin Socialist Union meeting in the now flailing Socialist League paper was in the February 1891 edition.

212 *Justice*, 28 Mar. 1891.

213 On the 'Parnell split' see F.S.L. Lyons, *The Fall of Parnell* (London, 1960), and Frank Callanan, *The Parnell Split, 1890–91* (Cork, 1992).

214 *Freeman's Journal*, 6, 9 Feb. 1891.

215 Paul Bew, *Conflict and Conciliation in Ireland, 1890–1910* (Oxford, 1987), p. 19.

216 *Freeman's Journal*, 2 Mar. 1891.

217 *Freeman's Journal*, 9 Mar. 1891.

218 ibid.

219 *Freeman's Journal*, 10 Mar. 1891.

220 *Freeman's Journal*, 16 Mar. 1891.

221 ibid.

222 ibid.

223 ibid.

224 ibid.

225 *Irish Times*, 16 Mar. 1891.

226 *Belfast Weekly Star*, 17 Jan. 1891.

227 *Justice*, 21 Mar. 1891.

228 *Freeman's Journal*, 21 Apr. 1891.

229 For Toomey's accent see *Freeman's Journal*, 8 Jan. 1886.

230 *Freeman's Journal*, 28 Dec. 1886.

231 For Toomey's resignation from the Socialist League see George King to H.H. Sparling, 11 Dec. 1886, Socialist League Papers, IISH.

232 *Freeman's Journal*, 21 Apr. 1891.

233 DMP Files 1891: Chief Superintendent's Office, 4 May 1891, National Archives.

234 *Freeman's Journal*, 4 May 1891.

235 ibid.

236 ibid.

237 Eleanor Marx, who was on the executive of the union, claimed in August 1891 that Irish members amounted to some 25,000. Thorne in his memoirs refers to an Irish membership of 20,000. Yvonne Kapp, op. cit., p. 484; Will Thorne, op. cit., p. 144.

238 Yvonne Kapp, op. cit., p. 477.

239 *Freeman's Journal*, 18 May 1891.

240 ibid.

241 ibid.

242 ibid.

243 Yvonne Kapp, op. cit., p. 484.

244 Friedrich Engels to F.A. Sorge, 11 Feb. 1891, published in Karl Marx and Friedrich Engels, *Ireland and the Irish Question: A Collection of Writings* (New York, 1972), p. 353.

245 *Justice*, 28 Mar., 2 May, 27 June 1891.

6.

Labour Socialism, 1892-96

While the Dublin Socialist Union survived into 1892 it is clear that the propagandist revolutionism of most of its members was incapable of providing an attractive alternative to that 'something tangible' offered by Will Thorne and the 'new unions'. It was during this period that the middle-class Fabian Society extended its membership to include Irish and British working-class socialists and labour activists swept up in the euphoria of industrial conflict.[1] The Fabians espoused a vague socialism that recoiled from Marxism and the notion of irreconcilables in a class struggle for a new society. 'I am a Socialist because I believe in Evolution', said Annie Besant, a leading Fabian organizer.[2] According to Besant, the capture 'of Radical organisations already existing should be the first object of the Labour Party'.[3]

The Fabian Society was an integrative organization which was not even clearly in favour of the foundation of an autonomous party of the working class. Permeation of the Liberal Party, argues Hobsbawm, was perhaps the closest thing to a consistent policy held by the Fabians.[4] Their socialism was essentially liberal thought infused with philosophical idealism. It was reformist and, more importantly, 'practical' in that it put great stress on the efficacy of legislative change. On Ireland the Fabians avoided a definite stance on the issue of legislative independence and, unlike the SDF and Socialist League, they were not seen as ardent home rulers.[5] Indeed, in its politics the Fabian Society was often openly pro-imperialist. As a sort of half-way house between Radicalism and revolutionary socialism, the Fabians attracted many on the left-wing of the Radical movement in the late 1880s and early 1890s. Rev. Harold Rylett, who had moved back to his native

England by 1890, was a supporter and a friend of the leading Fabian, Sidney Webb.[6] In 1891, Eleanor Marx rather coldly characterized the Fabians as 'middle-class folk too honest to be contented with the present conditions of society; too educated to throw in their lot with the Salvation Army; too superior to identify themselves wholly with the profane vulgar'.[7] In fact the London-based leadership proved decidedly nonchalant with regard to the provincial working-class members won between 1890 and 1892 and did little to prevent the slippage that saw many branches defect *en masse* to the Independent Labour Party (ILP), in particular, and other socialist bodies after 1892.

FABIANISM AND IRISH SOCIALISM

In some ways the Fabians in Ireland did little more than lay the ground-work for the branches of the ILP that briefly blossomed in three Irish cities between 1892 and 1895. Certainly, the society provided a vehicle for those moderate socialists who felt uncomfortable with the politics of the SDF. In Belfast a Fabian Society was established in February 1891 thus providing that city with its first socialist organization. The society, however, collapsed early in 1892.[8] Its chairman, not unexpectedly (as he was perfect material for the Fabian Society), was Rev. Bruce Wallace, the land nationalizer and admirer of the Liberals. Other members included William M. Knox, John Murphy, W.T. Anderson, Alexander Stewart and R.H. Feagan.[9] Wallace's *Belfast Weekly Star* was used to promote the group and those interested were invited to contact Anderson at 25 College Street.[10] The *Belfast Weekly Star*, much like *Brotherhood*, espoused a social radicalism with a Christian and moral overtone: 'Men who waste their money and their leisure in public-houses, in gambling and in other demoralising pastimes, deserve no increase of wealth or leisure.'[11] Wallace moved to Britain in 1891 and this absence may have precipitated the demise of the Belfast society.[12] Some of its members quickly involved themselves with establishing the ILP in the city.

In Dublin a branch of the Fabians was formed in 1892 and, to some extent, it seems to have displaced the Dublin Socialist Union. The DSU held lectures weekly at 87, Marlborough Street until 31 March 1892.[13] Thereafter it would appear to have lapsed although it is very possible that it continued for some time longer, like the Dublin Socialist Club, as a loose base for the capital's socialists. It had unquestionably failed in terms of its initial objectives, and this may be ascribed largely to a divergence between most of its members and those, such as Adolphus Shields, who became involved with the wave of 'new unionism'. It is unclear what happened to activists like Thomas Fitzpatrick but between 1892 and 1895 we see the rise of labour socialism in Ireland and the obscuration of revolutionary socialism.

The emergence of the Fabians in Dublin was undoubtedly a symptom of this change.

Prominent Fabians first appeared in Dublin on the coat-tails of the 'new unions'. In July 1890, I. Cohen of the Fabian Society had been present on the platform at the Gasworkers' Union demonstration in the Phoenix Park in support of the 'eight hours' movement.[14] Likewise, Annie Besant was organizing women workers in the country later that year and in early October she gave a lecture on 'Class War' in Dublin. In her speech she confined herself to calling for the 'municipalisation' of industry and she remarked knowingly that 'teetotalism would be useless without the abolition of land-lordism'.[15] Clearly, this was not 'clear-cut' socialism as understood by former members of the Socialist League. When the Dublin society was formed two years later it contained a number of active trade unionists, including Adolphus Shields who remained a member until the collapse of the society in 1899. James Sexton, the union leader, named Shields in his memoirs in the context of finding in Dublin shortly before 1900 'the nucleus of a Socialist body in the form of a Fabian Society, chiefly composed of officials at Dublin Castle and men employed on the editorial side of the Irish newspapers'. Shields, at that stage, was working as a printer for the *Freeman's Journal*. 'The members of the Society', wrote Sexton, 'had set up a guest house in which they lived and to which all known Socialists were welcome.'[16] The Dublin Fabians were represented by two speakers at the 1893 Phoenix Park May Day demonstration. James J. Nolan spoke on plat-form number three as the official representative of the society and Shields spoke on platform number two as a delegate of the Typographical Association.[17] By 1893 Shields was no longer representing the Gasworkers' Union which had suffered serious setbacks in Dublin in the preceding years.[18]

On May Day 1894 the Fabians had a more substantial input into the Dublin labour demonstration. The parade, and rally in the Phoenix Park, attracted an attendance of almost 10,000 and the Dublin Fabian Society had its own section in the march. Robert Dorman and W.J. Phillips, both members, spoke from the platform. Dorman proposed a long resolution which demand-ed manhood suffrage; the eight-hour day; promotion of trade unionism; assimilation of the borough and parliamentary franchise; labour represen-tation in parliament and on local boards; and payment of MPs by the state. He also castigated the action of the House of Lords in halting the Employers' Liability Bill and said that he thought that 'the time has arrived when the Trades Unions of the Kingdom should demand the reform, reconstruction, or, if necessary, the abolition of that non-representative assembly'.[19] Dor-man, in calling for an eight-hour day, stressed the educative and ethical value of such a reform:

It gave the worker time for recreation, time for educating himself, and getting a knowledge of the world and the things that were taking place about him; and not only that but it gave the working-man who was the father of a family an opportunity for performing the duties of his position as a parent required of him.[20]

Robert Dorman played an important role in the early history of modern Irish socialism. During the mid-1890s, almost alone, he revived outdoor meetings in Dublin. He was born in Dublin in 1859 and joined the British navy as a boy but was invalided and discharged in 1880. As a life-insurance inspector he spent much time moving around the country. Politically he was a Christian socialist and his commitment survived through to the 1920s when as a member of the ILP he could be found holding forth at the Custom House steps in Belfast where he settled in 1912.[21] In the late 1920s he held a Labour seat in the Northern Ireland Senate at Stormont.[22]

REPRESENTING LABOUR, 1892–94

In February 1892 Dublin Trades Council formed a committee 'with a view to have Irish workers represented direct in the next Parliament' and on 'all municipal boards and councils'.[23] The motion establishing the committee was moved by a delegate from the Sailors' and Firemen's Union and seconded by the bricklayers' representative and 'new unionist', John Whelan. An election was shortly due and within days of its meeting the trades council handed over its hall to William Field, the Parnellite labour-nationalist, for an address on 'Work and Workers'. Field urged the necessity for a 'universal union of workers' which could 'control the world' but he balanced this socialistic-sounding statement with a dismissal of revolution and an advocation of parliament as a means of redress. He also called for working men to be elected to the Westminster parliament in order to promote and safeguard the interests of the working class.[24] In the event, that year's general election saw labour-nationalist candidates returned for the first time. Four, if we include Michael Davitt, were elected; the others were Field, Eugene Crean and Michael Austin. Crean and Austin were both trade unionists and, like Davitt, anti-Parnellite nationalists.[25]

While these elections were noted and welcomed by most sections of the labour movement there still existed a strand of trade unionism that yearned for the election of labour representatives whose central priority was labour issues and not nationalism or unionism. 'New unionism' and the labour ferment of 1890–91 had greatly encouraged many of those who sought independent labour representation. Moreover, throughout the early 1890s the developing demand in the resurgent labour movement for independent political representation had led to the formation of local political labour bodies across Britain. Traditional labourism was joined by a more radical labour socialism as a moderate non-Marxian socialist movement emerged which embraced the parliamentary road to social change. This labour socialism needs to be examined if we are to properly understand the ideological shift that Irish socialism experienced between 1892 and 1895.

Irish socialism during this period must be viewed in the context of the British 'socialist revival' and in the context of developments on the political left in Britain generally. Separatism had yet to take off as an overpowering force in Irish politics and nationalists, by and large, were content to fight for a federal arrangement with the colonial power. Likewise, Irish socialists were little influenced by separatist ideas and tended to see themselves as part of the wider British socialist movement. Indeed, as we have seen, most Irish socialists were lukewarm, if not hostile, toward home rule which they saw as the empowerment of the priesthood and the native bourgeoisie. With social radicalism so weak in Ireland they tended to look to Britain for sustenance. Moreover, the proximity of the two countries meant that the labour movements were closely linked and often enjoyed a shared experience.

Stephen Yeo has suggested that a change occurred in British socialism during the mid-1890s.[26] According to Stuart Macintyre, this can best be represented as a transition from the millennial fervour of the 1880s to 'a more fragmented socialist movement which was more attentive to short-term pragmatic considerations'.[27] In essence, the Marxian revolutionism of the 1880s was overtaken, although not superseded, by a labour socialism that was ethical rather than scientific. This labour socialism, even though partially a product of Marxism, was reformist and focussed on the achievement of political representation within the existing system. The SDF had never been anti-parliamentarian in the sense that the Socialist League had been but it was never lured into viewing parliamentary legislation as anything other than a half-measure. The Independent Labour Party and the labour socialists, in contrast, believed that real social change could be effected with legal methods and within a system of representative democracy. It would be wrong, however, to draw a strict doctrinal line between members of the ILP and members of the SDF and other socialist bodies. Often membership of a socialist body depended simply on what particular organization existed in the locality, and where a number existed the rank-and-file often moved easily back and forth between them. Political sectarianism had yet to develop into the art form that it became in later years. The ILP was consciously a broad socialist party. 'It is sometimes charged against the ILP', Keir Hardie wrote in 1908, 'that it has never formulated its theory of socialism. That is true and therein lies its strength.'[28] In fact, its greatest attraction probably lay in its 'pragmatism' and in its attention to the trade union movement.

The first substantive link in the chain that led to the formation of the ILP in 1893 appeared when James Keir Hardie, a former Scottish miner, contested a by-election in Mid-Lanark in April 1888. Four months later the Scottish Labour Party was founded with Hardie as its chief spokesperson. In 1892 Hardie was elected as an Independent Labour MP. His election boosted the expanding support for the establishment of an Independent Labour Party and within eight months in 1892–93, forty-four ILP branches were created without the assistance of official organizers.[29] By the time of the inaugural conference in Bradford many local sections were already in place. Independent Labour candidates had also gained election to a number of local boards and councils in the years before 1892; thus Hardie's election appeared to belong to a developing momentum. The SDF leadership, however, was not convinced that a new socialist party was required. In August 1892, *Justice* proclaimed:

> We say . . . that outside the SDF there is at present no Independent Labour Party. If out of existing elements it is possible to form one we wish it good speed, confident that the result will demonstrate that there is no logical basis for independent political action, except in Social Democracy. But, in view of our past experiences, remembering how many men have been lost to the Social-Democratic movement through the formations of evanescent, nebulous, and invertebrate independent parties in the past, we submit that the position of the SDF is not yet likely to be filled by any other body, and adjure our comrades to stand by the Red Flag of Social Democracy and uncompromising political independence.[30]

The official ILP image of the SDF, in turn, was of 'a dry, dogmatic, irrelevant Marxism, wholly out of touch with working-class experiences'.[31] Nonetheless, when the new party was formally inaugurated in January 1893 six SDF branches, all from Lancashire, attended the conference in Bradford.[32] Co-operation among the rank-and-file was strong. Labour socialism, however, did present a cogent alternative to the Marxism of the SDF. Its short-term ambitions appeared achievable where the long-term objectives of the SDF promised a struggle that seemed to offer no immediate benefits.

THE ILP IN BELFAST

Belfast began its socialist tradition with Fabianism and moved easily into labour socialism. It was the first city in Ireland to establish an ILP branch and it was also one of those areas that formed a section of the ILP prior to the Bradford conference. The first meeting of the 'Belfast Labour Party' was held in the Engineers' Hall in College Street on 29 September 1892.[33] Leading members included the ex-Fabians, William Knox and Alexander

Stewart. The latter, a founder of the Dublin Democratic Association in 1885, was probably a key mover in the enterprise. He was active in the Amalgamated Society of Engineers which controlled the Engineers' Hall, and, moreover, had been much involved with independent labour politics in Britain where in 1889 he was elected to a local board in Newcastle-on-Tyne as a labour candidate.[34]

Over the next twelve months the branch, according to Stewart, 'met with a considerable amount of opposition' and a number of the original members dropped out.[35] Also, despite holding a number of meetings little impact was made and the branch was largely ignored by the press. In September 1893, however, the Belfast ILP came out of obscurity when it took advantage of Belfast's hosting of the annual conference of the British Trade Union Congress (TUC). On Sunday 3 September, the day before the TUC met, the Belfast ILP organized a conference in the Crown Chambers Hall, Royal Avenue, to which adherents of the ILP, SDF, Fabian Society and other labour organizations were invited. There were quite a few British socialists in Belfast for the congress and the ILP meeting was well attended with Keir Hardie, Pete Curran, Ben Tillet, Fred Brocklehurst, H.H. Champion, Dr Edward Aveling and Leonard Hall among the prominent socialists present. In a long report the following day the *Belfast News Letter* named the current Belfast ILP committee: W.S. Roberts (president), T. Miller jnr (secretary), W.H. McAllister (treasurer), Alexander Stewart and William Knox.[36] Stewart presided at the conference where a local member, J.H. Gilliland, put a series of motions that aptly demonstrated the intent of the organization. Aside from 'domination in the House of Commons', Gilliland's proposal demanded

> Equal adult suffrage, labour representation on all public Boards and in Parliament, elections to be all on one day, permanent ballot, providing for a second voting, payment of official election expenses, a permanent ballot law applied to all cases, and the references of all great cases to the people.[37]

Aveling clearly felt the need to advance the discussion and he proposed his own motion 'in favour of the nationalisation of the whole means of production' which he believed would go 'to the root of the whole question'. However, it is not clear that the Belfast ILP in general showed such a radical approach. Later in the day, Stewart presided at a meeting on the Custom House steps near Donegall Quay where Aveling and Tillet addressed a crowd of over 3,000 on labour rights.

Once the congress had begun the ILP branch busied itself on the fringes. After the day's deliberations were adjourned on 5 September a large meeting of delegates was organized by the ILP at which a circular was drawn up advocating independent labour representation and advertising a discussion to be held the following day. A few hours after this delegate meeting the local ILP branch held its own meeting where speeches were delivered by TUC delegates. Hardie was present and the branch passed a motion praising his exertions for the labour movement.[38] On 6 September a long and heated discussion on labour representation and socialism was held at the congress. Keir Hardie met trenchant opposition when he moved a motion that effectively asked the TUC to support the ILP. It read:

> That in the opinion of this Congress the claims of labour in Parliament should be asserted irrespective of the convenience of any political party; and to secure this it is necessary that Labour members in the House of Commons should be unconnected with either the Liberal or Tory Party and should sit in opposition to any Government until such times as they are strong enough to form a Labour Cabinet.[39]

This was too much for the non-socialist trade unionists and after an acrimonious debate the motion was rejected by 119 votes to 96. Nonetheless, the thinness of the margin was encouraging.

On Saturday 9 September, the conclusion of the TUC proceedings was marked with a huge trade union demonstration through the city to a rally in Ormeau Park. Thousands attended but the event was marred by working-class division on the question of home rule. To many loyalists, British labour leaders were anathema because of their support for legislative independence. A number of speakers were severely heckled for being supporters of home rule and John Burns MP, who had voted for the measure, was forced to flee. Will Thorne also came under attack apparently because he wore a trade union sash containing the colour green.[40] One SDF speaker, perhaps Thorne, had 'his eye cut open' during the scuffles.[41] Moreover, a counter demonstration of loyalists attracted a substantial crowd of 5,000.[42] Anti-socialism was an important component of the loyalist/unionist political perspective and its conservative adherents were to be a perennial source of trouble for Belfast socialists. Indeed, the Orange orators presented a decidedly more physical challenge than Catholic social conservatism presented in the rest of the country.

The day after the Ormeau Park rally Stewart presided at a less turbulent meeting at the Custom House steps where Hardie, Aveling and Tillet addressed a large crowd. This moderate success was followed the next Sunday by a similar meeting with local ILP speakers but the 'attempt to introduce a Socialistic and Secularist platform' led to a 'Socialistic disturbance' according to the *Belfast Evening Telegraph*.[43] A loyalist mob attacked the meeting and chased William Knox when he attempted to distribute socialist leaflets. Knox was rescued after a police baton charge.[44] On 20 May 1894 Henry Alexander of the London SDF received a similarly unpleasant reception when he spoke alongside William Walker, of the Belfast ILP, to an audience of 600 at the Custom House steps.[45] Hardie's *Labour Leader* carried a brief notice of this meeting but *Justice* was more expansive in its report:

> Alexander was nearly having a rough experience when he addressed a Belfast meeting on Socialism last Sunday week. He alluded to something concerning William the Conqueror, whom the audience took to mean William III, for there is but one William to an Orange crowd, and that is he of Orange — whereat there was much vigorous and prolonged applause. But happening casually to mention Home Rule it was found advisable to close the meeting if broken heads were to be avoided. There is evidently a good field for Socialist propaganda in Belfast![46]

In point of fact, William Walker, a twenty-four-year-old trade unionist and the branch's most effective outdoor speaker, had to be kept under continuous police protection in 1894–95 because 'of his advocacy of the principles of Socialism'.[47] In 1911 he recalled that they had 'preached the Gospel of Socialism . . . faced [with] the batons of the police; the deacon poles of the Orangemen; the assaults of the hooligans; the execration of the rabble'.[48] Nonetheless, they continued and Walker and John Murphy, also an ILP member, made a significant radical contribution as members of Belfast Trades Council although it remained largely the domain of traditional labourism.[49] In December 1894 the Belfast ILP made a new departure when T. Miller jnr gave the first address in a series of indoor public meetings.[50] These continued in 1895.

During February and March 1895 soup kitchens were opened in Belfast to deal with the distress caused by a rise in unemployment in the city. The ILP decided that the time was 'again opportune to place before the citizens of our city the cause and true remedy for the state of things that prevailed' and so, on 24 February, Walker and another member, William Rice, returned to the steps of the Custom House and made socialist speeches to a crowd of over 2,000.[51] They were well received and they returned over the next three Sundays until their audience had grown to as many as 10,000 people. Such success clearly roused the ire of Belfast's anti-socialists. On 31 March a loyalist mob was waiting for the socialists when they arrived, with about 100 grouped around the speakers' post. Arthur Trew, an anti-nationalist and anti-Catholic demagogue, led the charge and Walker was forced to give his address 'amid singing, shouting and bawling'. After fifteen minutes the steps were abandoned and the socialists led a crowd of about 4,000 in a parade through the city centre. They again returned to the Custom House the following three Sundays and survived unscathed thus lulling them into the false belief that the worst was over. However, the next week the ILP found itself 'forestalled by 500 roughs, game for anything, from pitch-and-toss to manslaughter'. Walker and his comrades attempted to hold their meeting but were carried off the steps 'at least a dozen times, only to be dragged back by willing hands'. At one stage, the loyalists grabbed Walker, a Protestant, and attempted to throw him into the harbour amid shouts of 'Three cheers for King William' and 'To hell with the Pope!'[52] The socialists beat a hasty retreat. On 5 May the Belfast ILP held yet another meeting at the Custom House when Walker spoke for fifteen minutes on 'Municipal Socialism'. According to the *Belfast News Letter* he was confronted by a 'hostile crowd' of about 4,000 which 'endeavoured to get hold of him'.[53] Singing 'God Save the Queen' and 'Rule Britannia' and shouting 'No Socialism here!', the crowd made the meeting impossible and were twice baton-charged by the police in a scene that went on for some eighty minutes.[54] At the beginning of June *The Clarion*, a British socialist weekly, carried a report from Belfast:

> We think it advisable to discontinue the Custom House meetings until the spirit of the pious and immortal William cools down a bit. On Saturday evening, however, we went to the Queen's Bridge. As usual bigotry and brutality were well represented in the audience; but amidst cries of 'Throw him in the dock!', 'You're a Home Ruler!', 'Drown him!', Walker held his ground and said all that he went there to say. A large crowd followed us through the streets, but we divided, Walker jumping on a tram car, and they dispersed.[55]

In 1896 the ILP managed to hold meetings once more but the organization never really regained its momentum.[56] Loyalist opposition continued and on 22 February the *Labour Leader* reported yet another assault on the socialists when Dan Irving, of the Lancashire SDF, was severely heckled at the Custom House steps and an attempt was made to rush the platform. In March, John Bruce Glasier, a leading ILP member, visited Belfast and briefly raised morale although he did not address any outdoor public meetings. At the end of the year the remnants of the branch held a conference to organize for the future. However, the Belfast ILP quietly lapsed in early 1897.[57] A number of years later Arthur Trew, the sectarian loyalist demagogue, bragged (with perhaps some justification) that he was responsible for 'the overthrowal of the local society of Socialists'.[58] Other factors may also have assisted in the demise of the branch. Most importantly, the diminution in Belfast's membership reflected a general trend which saw a high tide in terms of the membership base of the ILP in 1894–95 and a significant falling away in 1895–96.[59] Disappointment after the labour electoral failures and the loss of Keir Hardie's seat in the 1895 general election was an important factor that was widely noted at the time. The ILP regained some strength in 1896–97 but not all areas had the problems faced by its Belfast members.

LABOUR AND SOCIALISM IN DUBLIN, 1894–96

Unlike Belfast, Dublin did not immediately respond to the clarion call of the ILP and a branch was not established until late 1894. Socialist propaganda continued in the city, nonetheless, and from the beginning of 1894 the local Fabian Society provided a forum for discussion at its weekly lectures in the Central Lecture Hall on Westmoreland Street.[60] Also, there were intermittent visits to the city by SDF and ILP speakers from Britain. Russell Smart, a leading ILP member and a commercial traveller by occupation, visited Dublin three or four times in the first months of the year. According to William Orr, a socialist activist in the city, Smart was looked on as an 'old friend' by Dublin socialists.[61] At the end of April, Dublin Trades Council hosted the first conference of the Irish Trades Union Congress at its hall in Capel Street.[62] Some 119 delegates attended from the trades councils of Dublin, Belfast, Cork, Limerick and Drogheda, representing over 21,000 trade unionists directly and 39,000 indirectly.[63] William Walker was present as a Belfast delegate.[64] Also in the city was Russell Smart who gave a lecture on socialism immediately after the conference concluded. 'He . . . astonished us all', commented Orr, 'by the manner in which he electrified our slow moving Trades Council and delegates from all parts of Ireland'.[65]

Another visitor to the city was the London SDF organizer Henry Alexander. In April, *Justice* mentioned that Alexander, who like Smart was a commercial traveller, would shortly be visiting Belfast, Cork, Dublin and Derry and suggested that anybody in those cities 'desirous of helping to form branches of the SDF' should write to the SDF headquarters in London. Perhaps aware of previous efforts, the paper sardonically added: 'Some special jollification ought to be arranged to celebrate the establishment of the first branch of the SDF in Ireland, whenever that event comes off.'[66] In the event, there was no need to uncork the champagne bottles as the SDF failed once again to make any important inroads. Alexander did, however, speak at meetings in Dublin and Belfast. In Belfast he was lucky to escape intact when objection was taken by some of his audience to his support for home rule. In Dublin, he got a better reception when he spoke at a Fabian Society meeting on 'Why Irishmen should be Socialists'. At this 24 May lecture Alexander was well received and a lively discussion followed in which Robert Dorman and Arthur Kavanagh, as well as Alexander Duncan and Patrick Shelley of Dublin Trades Council, participated.[67] Alexander, interestingly, was also sympathetic to the ILP and offered, at one stage, to lecture for them on his travels.[68] In the second week of July a Glasgow SDF member named Coulson arrived in Dublin and 'practically started in Dublin the outdoor propaganda of undiluted Socialism' by addressing a large meeting at the Custom House steps: 'The convincing manner in which he drove home the truth of the Gospel of Humanity was evidenced by the eagerness with which his bag-full of literature, including a few dozen copies of *Justice*, was bought up.'[69] The following day Coulson addressed another meeting and William Orr fancied that among the converts was an old police sergeant who warmly shook the speaker's hand at the end of the lecture and expressed a hope that he would be back in Dublin soon. Orr was enthused by this procession of speakers:

> During the past couple of months Russell Smart, Alexander (London) and Coulson (Glasgow), have been in Dublin doing excellent work, which, if followed up energetically, should make the city on the Liffey an excellent centre, as recent exposures of the rottenness and insincerity of both sections of the Nationalist Party have disgusted the workers with it, while Liberalism and Conservatism have practically no following at all . . . What we suffer from here is an almost total absence of outdoor speakers, most of our local men being in positions which preclude their coming into the open.[70]

This problem with speakers was an old one for Dublin socialists.

Without doubt, Russell Smart must have created an interest in the ILP in Dublin and Alexander would have encouraged this interest. It is also possible that socialist trade unionists like Adolphus Shields had by 1894 come into contact with Belfast members of the organization. Shields would certainly have known British ILP members from the days of 'new unionism'. In addition, Murtagh Lyng, a Dublin socialist, came into contact with the ILP while on a visit to Liverpool and brought back some of the party's literature.[71] This material seemingly encouraged the Dublin socialists to contact Keir Hardie to ask him to speak in the city.[72] Hardie was also influenced during 1894 to visit Dublin by James Connolly, then a leading Edinburgh socialist and member of the ILP. Connolly informed Hardie that there was the nucleus of a labour movement in Ireland which 'only needs judicious handling'. He agreed that both the Parnellites and anti-Parnellites were simply 'middle class parties interested in the progress of Ireland from a middle class point of view'. Their advanced attitude on the agrarian question, he suggested, was 'an accident' arising out of 'the political situation and would be dropped tomorrow if they did not realise the necessity of linking up the Home Rule agitation to some cause more clearly allied to their daily wants than a mere embodiment of the nationalist sentiment of the people'.[73] Connolly contended that Hardie should make a strong labour speech in Dublin, the heart of Parnellism, 'without reference to the two Irish parties, but . . . anti-monarchical' and thereby force the hand of the Parnellite leader, John Redmond: 'If you can show them it would be [in] their interest politically to support us they will do so.'[74] In practical terms, he gave Hardie the address of a 'Mr Doyle', 6 Swifts Row, Lower Ormond Quay, in Dublin who

was a member of the local Fabian Society and suggested that he ask them
to organize a meeting to 'bring this matter to a head'.[75]

On 29 October a meeting was held at 47 York Street in Dublin 'to form
an Independent Socialist (Labour) Party'.[76] A few days later the *Labour
Leader* carried a short piece by Tom Mann in which he announced that Hardie was about to visit Ireland in order to firmly establish the ILP in the
country.

> The Irish question is the English, Scotch and Welsh question too, i.e. How
> to completely dislodge and effectually get rid of the monopolists of the
> essentials of life, that the people, as a people, may come by their own.
> Let us hope our Irish brothers will make common cause with us, and so
> allow in their and our struggle against Landlordism and Capitalism.[77]

Hardie arrived in Dublin at the end of the first week of November and addressed three successful public meetings in the city as well as launching a
local branch of the ILP. The first meeting, on Thursday 8 November, saw
a remarkable coming together of socialists, trade unionists and labour-
nationalists. Held in the Trades Hall in Capel Street, it was chaired by the
president of the Dublin Trades Council, Thomas O'Connell. On the platform were other members of the trades council: E.L. Richardson (vice-
president), John Simmons (secretary), John Fitzpatrick, P.A. Tyrrell and
others. Also present were William Field MP and a number of Dublin
socialists: Adolphus Shields, W.J. Phillips, James Nolan, George King and
John O'Gorman.[78] O'Connell, in introducing Hardie, extended him a *'céad
míle fáilte'* and said:

> The reason they should give him a thorough welcome was because he was
> an advanced Home Ruler, a friend of Amnesty, and by his assistance he
> had got one of the delegates from Ireland appointed as a member of the
> Parliamentary Committee of the Trades Congress and another a member
> of the Federation Committee.[79]

O'Connell was also president of the Irish Trades Union Congress and plainly
saw Hardie as a useful ally in Britain. Hardie was not enticed by O'Connell's comments to speak on home rule and instead made a bland speech
on trade unionism. The ILP was only referred to briefly and the reason
for this became obvious when Richardson spoke at the end of Hardie's lecture. According to Richardson, 'lest capital should be made of the matter',
Hardie was invited to speak solely on the labour question. William Field,
in a short contribution, was at pains to explain that he was there that evening 'as an Irishman and a Home Ruler above all things'.[80]

Two days later Hardie launched the Dublin branch of the ILP at a meeting
in the Rotunda. O'Connell chaired once again and Hardie gave a speech

in which he accentuated his support for home rule and stated that the ILP supported the policy as a principle not as an expediency.[81] He rather contradicted this point in the *Labour Leader* a week later when he remarked that 'at the recent municipal elections branches of the Irish National League passed resolutions not to support ILP candidates under any circumstances. It cannot be expected, if this continues, that the ILP will wax enthusiastic over the Irish Question'.[82] Evidently, home rule could be dropped because of pique. At the Rotunda meeting Field, once again, indicated home rule as his actuating priority but members of the Trades Council, including Patrick Shelley, supported the motion in favour of establishing the ILP in the city.[83] The following day Hardie spoke alongside Robert Dorman at an open-air meeting by the Custom House in Beresford Place. In a more explicit address he told a large crowd that the Irish nationalist MPs were following a mistaken policy in supporting Liberal candidates against those from the independent labour movement.[84] After his Dublin meetings Keir Hardie travelled on to Waterford city where he inaugurated another branch of the ILP. In his report for the *Labour Leader* Hardie praised the Sunday meeting in Beresford Place as the best of the three he had spoken at in Dublin:

> It was a remarkable gathering. Not only did the great concourse of people drink in the new gospel with avidity, but they displayed an amount of enthusiasm which I have rarely seen equalled, and never exceeded. Everything I have seen in the Metropolis of Ireland has borne out my first impression, that the artisan class is ripe for the change implied in the adding of Labourism to Nationalism.[85]

The Dublin branch began life with a membership of forty-seven which quickly rose to over fifty.[86] Applications for membership were also apparently received from Cork and Kilkenny although a branch was never established in either place.[87] The branch quickly split, however, on the issue of support for the Irish parliamentary party. On 24 November, the *Labour Leader* reported that 'the political question has been fought once and for all, and the branch understands itself on that point'. This was too sanguine a view and the following week the paper reported:

> A big fight took place in the Dublin branch over the question of non-membership in any other party and in the end the recommendation of the Rules Committee was endorsed which was that persons joining the ILP must give up connection with every other political association. On this being carried the minority left the meeting, but as 37s. [thirty-seven shillings] was taken in entrance fees after they left a good start must have been made.[88]

Adolphus Shields and Robert Dorman appear to have been the leading figures in the Dublin ILP although Dorman seems to have spent some of the subsequent months in Waterford assisting the branch there. This absence may have been related to his job as a life-insurance inspector. James Nolan, in an article for the *Labour Leader*, pointed to one problem facing the Dublin socialists:

> The working men in Dublin are Parnellite almost to a man, and it will take some time before they can see that that political party will not bring their cause as working men forward . . . and every reader of the *Labour Leader* should know that Michael Davitt represents no one but himself, and has no claim to speak for workers in Ireland.[89]

This palpable antipathy to Davitt was far milder than some advice Hardie had received from T. Harrison, a painter, from Clonmel in County Tipperary earlier in the year. After commending the ILP he wrote:

> But my principal reason for addressing you is to warn your Party against Mr Michael Davitt. I see it reported in the papers he is likely to be put up for a seat in England.
>
> Be certain, he will make an attempt to lead your Party under God knows how many excuses. Shun him, he is a *fraud*. He ruined us here by attempting to organise a labour party and deserted at a beck from the Irish Catholic Clergy. Several strikes he attempted to settle and he succeeded in only making a perfect muddle. In some cases when invited to speak he even didn't answer our letters. The present Irish Party have completely sold us — so don't mind what you do to them.
>
> But, above all, keep Davitt out or your party will live to rue the day ye took him in.[90]

Harrison's advice was unnecessary in any case as Davitt viewed the ILP as dangerous to the interests of home rule and labour, and he maintained this position until the end of the century in spite of Hardie voting with the Liberals for the second Home Rule Bill in 1893. Hardie, in turn, abhorred Davitt's conduct toward Parnell.[91]

The Dublin ILP took rooms in late December at 2 Bachelor's Walk where the National Labour League had met in 1887. Meetings to discuss socialism were held every Wednesday, Friday and Sunday evenings.[92] Lectures were organized for the Sunday meetings and W.J. Phillips gave the first on 16 December when he spoke on 'Poverty'. He dealt with this rather broad remit as it affected Dublin and advocated the building of houses for the working class by the corporation and the municipalization of the trams and the gas supply. P.J. Tevenen, the Irish secretary of the Amalgamated Society of Railway Servants, was present and participated in the discussion.[93] The day before this ILP meeting, George King gave a talk entitled 'Some Objections to Socialism' at the Fabian Society in the Central Lecture Hall in which he argued for class politics.[94] The second ILP Sunday lecture was on 23 December when Adolphus Shields spoke on 'Home Rule and the ILP'.[95] In early December Russell Smart had lectured in Dublin on ILP policy and had come under sustained attack from ardent nationalists.[96] Shields clearly felt it was necessary to give a clear exposition of their position. At the meeting, which was chaired by Robert Dorman, Shields argued:

> Surely no useful function was performed by the present Capitalist Home Rule parties which could not be performed equally well by a Labour Home Rule Party. The Independent Labour Party thought Home Rule desirable, but if it gave the Irish worker no better conditions than his English brother sweltered under, it was not the kind of Home Rule to emancipate the wage slaves of Ireland.[97]

His admiration for Parnell was obvious; he mentioned Parnell's acceptance of the Irish Labour League programme in 1891 and expressed his belief that

> If Parnell had lived ere this there would have been an alliance of Irish and English workers formed on an avowedly revolutionary basis for the over-throw of every form of tyranny and oppression.[98]

On why the ILP had been formed in Dublin, Shields maintained that pursuit of home rule provided part of the motivation. It was

> Firstly, that it was the duty of the Irish workers to take hold of the political machinery in order that it might not be used against their brothers the world over; secondly, because by it they might secure economic liberty — freedom to live, freedom to labour, and freedom to enjoy the fruits of their labour; and, thirdly, because it was only by a practically united demand a Home Rule measure worth having could be obtained, and such unity could best be secured by a Home Rule party run in the interest of the wealth producers.[99]

In May 1895 the ILP organized the annual labour demonstration when the Dublin Trades Council opted out. The council claimed that it was unable to take part because of the expenditure necessary for the annual conference of the Irish Trades Union Congress to be held in Cork the following month. In fact, even after the Dublin demonstration had been arranged the president of the trades council absented himself and spoke at the May Day rally in Drogheda.[100] Without the participation of the trades council the event was smaller than it had been in previous years but, nonetheless, two platforms were required to address the thousands who attended. The ILP, led by Shields, the branch secretary, had its own section in the parade headed by a red banner with the motto, 'Workers of the world, unite!' Shields presided on one of the platforms in the Phoenix Park and among the speakers were trade unionists, such as P.J. Tevenan, and the two ILP speakers, Robert

Dorman and Laurence Strange.[101] Strange represented the Waterford section of the ILP. Michael Canty, the 'new unionist', was also present and marched with the coal labourers.

By July, however, the Dublin branch was on the decline apparently because of consistent opposition from the home rule movement: 'We are now entering a new era as far as Socialism is concerned in Dublin. Our comrades have seen the wisdom of (for the present) dropping all attacks on other political parties, and setting themselves to work to educate people in the principles of Socialism.'[102] This was an admission of defeat and it was only a matter of time before the branch collapsed. According to William O'Brien, who knew former members in the late 1890s, the ILP recruited several members of the Dublin Trades Council but made little real progress:

> In carrying on propaganda they met with criticism of the body because it was a branch of a British organisation, and also the only literature they had for sale at propaganda meetings was all written from an English point of view and printed in England.[103]

By the end of 1895 the ILP branch had dissolved and by the beginning of 1896 a Dublin Socialist Society was formed. This organization was in the tradition of the Dublin Socialist Club and the Dublin Socialist Union and was open to socialists of all description. Shields became secretary of the new body.[104]

LAURENCE STRANGE AND THE WATERFORD ILP

When Keir Hardie completed his weekend engagements in Dublin in November 1894 he left for Waterford city where he was due to speak on Wednesday at a meeting to launch a local ILP branch. The main instigator behind this branch was Laurence Charles Strange, a solicitor who lived in Tramore but worked in the city.

Laurence Strange had been involved with the home rule movement for a number of years but his politics were decidedly left-wing and after the Parnell split he maintained a distance from both factions of the parliamentary party. This was a difficult thing to do in Waterford which was one of only nine constituencies to elect a Parnellite MP in the 1892 general election. Political divisions were deep and those who failed to manifest explicit support for John Redmond, the Parnellite MP, were viewed suspiciously as possible McCarthyites.[105] By 1894, the Parnellites were also known as Redmondites (because of Redmond's leadership) and the majority party took the name of its leader, Justin McCarthy. Laurence Strange attempted independence. In terms of social politics he was an SDF sympathizer from at least 1892 and his socialism was influenced by Marxism in the sense that he argued for a scientific view of the world.[106] At the beginning of 1892 he made a large donation toward the SDF 'Free Speech Defence Fund' and, again, in April 1894 he gave a guinea toward Hyndman's election expenses while proffering advice on the conduct of the campaign.[107] In December 1892 he had a letter published in *Justice* that called for the release of Fenian prisoners.[108] Nine months before, *Justice* had printed another letter from Strange that indicated his very real despair over poverty and unemployment. At the time, Waterford city was dealing with an upsurge in unemployment and a local relief committee assisted over 400 people out of a population of just 20,000. 'Many of those assisted', wrote Strange, 'are able-bodied young men and the cry is always "want of work"'.

> It seems to me that where a man is willing to work, and by reason of inability to procure work is reduced to a starving condition, it is equitable that such a one should help himself to food sufficient to satisfy his appetite. The law sends a man to gaol for throwing himself into the Thames should he be picked out alive, but surely it is difficult to draw a line between the would-be-suicide who seeks a speedy death 'neath the muddy water of the river and the poor wretch who with food within his reach permits himself to die of hunger.
>
> Some folk may say it is meritorious on the part of the starving pauper to pass a bread shop and not take a loaf. The self-denial on the part of the starving pauper might be placed to his credit were it a moral obligation and not the arm of the law which held him in check. It may be said, 'If you had a bread shop yourself how would you like to have your loaves stolen?' I should not like it, but taking the situation from the other fellow's stand-point, neither should I like to starve.[109]

This would have been frightening talk for the 'respectables' of Waterford, but such opinions did not make him an unpopular figure and in 1894 he served on Waterford Corporation.

Strange resigned from the corporation in October shortly before he helped to organize the ILP in the town. He cited a number of reasons, including the corporation's failure to extend the municipal franchise, and he declared that he would never consent 'to accept a seat in the Council unless as the nominee of a citizens committee'.[110] He also complained of the system by which a majority vote 'is secured on what is called "Party lines" irrespective of the merits of the matter under discussion'.[111] In truth, his name had recently been removed from the Burgess Roll and he would have gone out naturally in November.[112] His resignation allowed him to raise some issues before his departure. At the end of October, Strange spoke alongside Davitt at a meeting of agricultural labourers in Dungarvan and called on those present to join the labour-nationalist Irish Land and Labour Association.[113]

This organization had been founded on 15 August and its objectives included improved housing, welfare and working conditions for labourers.[114] The Parnellite *Waterford News* saw it as a vehicle for Michael Davitt and advised its readers to 'give Michael the cold shoulder'.[115] Strange, in his speech, called on workers to transcend the division in the Irish party and unite on issues of common concern. He told them that

> As long as they merely came to meetings . . . and left the meeting to discuss the rights and difficulties of labour in a haphazard sort of way they could never arrive at a proper conception of the labour movement. They should, he said, educate themselves. They should consider the way the labour movement is going ahead in France, Belgium, Germany and other countries where the question was dealt with from a purely scientific stand-point.[116]

Keir Hardie arrived in Waterford on Monday evening, 12 November, to a tremendous reception. His 7.30 p.m. train was met by a large crowd and, accompanied by a local band, 2,000 people followed his wagonette in a torch-light procession from the train station to the hall of the Waterford Federated Trades and Labour Union in William Street.[117] This body was essentially the local trades council and represented 400 of the town's workers.[118] At the local Trades Club Hardie was introduced by Strange to a number of local trade unionists, and addressing the crowd he thanked them for their welcome 'to this your ancient city'. Hardie's comment produced a shout of 'This Parnellite city!' from someone in the crowd.[119] But, he continued:

> We believe in the righteousness of the cause we are espousing and are determined, God helping us, to trust no rich man's party but to unite the common people of all nationalities in a warfare against class privilege, class monopoly and class injustice which have been the ruin of not only the workers of Ireland but of the workers of every other country.[120]

Following this rally Hardie went to Tramore where he stayed the night as Strange's guest.

Two days later Hardie addressed a crowded meeting in the Large Room of the City Hall. Strange, amid loud applause, was moved to the chair and in opening the proceedings he asked workers to 'consider this matter from a Christian and scientific stand-point'.[121] Others present included Robert Dorman, the ILP's Irish organizer, and members of the trades council. Hardie, in his speech, pointed to the common interests of Irish and English workers and he opined that so far society had been 'the heaven of the rich, the purgatory of the wise and the hell of the poor'.[122] On socialism, he said: 'They heard a great deal about Socialism being preached. It was used as a bogey, but what they preached was only practical Christianity as distinguished from theoretical Christianity.'[123]

The meeting was a success and Hardie left behind the nucleus of an ILP branch when he departed from Waterford. On the following Monday, the inaugural meeting of the branch was held in the William Street Trades Club. Circulars were distributed throughout the city and about fifty tradesmen and labourers assembled for the meeting which was chaired by Michael Cashin, president of the Federated Trades and Labour Union. Also present were Strange, Robert Dorman, Stephen J. Farrell, Patrick Walsh and Thomas Francis Meagher.[124] Twenty-five members were enrolled and Thomas F. Meagher gave the party position on home rule.[125]

> If they had Home Rule in the morning would the Irish House of Commons be a representative one from a working-man's point of view? He said distinctly it would not. If we got Home Rule in this country — and Mr Strange and the party with which he was associated were quite satisfied that we should get Home Rule — we want no second chamber. We want the one and only chamber to be elected on manhood suffrage.[126]

Meagher, a member of the Waterford ILP, like many radicals of the time failed to envisage women as part of the suffrage demand. His attention to home rule followed his comments at Hardie's lecture where he had commended the speaker for advocating the policy in England.[127] Strange explained the rules and constitution of the ILP to the gathering and he attempted to answer some questions that had been raised since Hardie's visit regarding the ILP and home rule. He assured his audience that the branch had no intention of interfering with Redmond or with the home rule movement.

> If John Redmond or Tim Healy or John Dillon came down tomorrow to contest the city and a labour representative sought their suffrages they would be bound to support their own man, but if John Redmond or anybody else came forward and there was no labour representative of course they were at liberty to support whatever candidate pleased them.[128]

It is clear that nationalist sensibilities were aroused. Robert Dorman moved to assuage these fears and reminded the meeting that Keir Hardie 'and his followers were Home Rulers long before William Ewart Gladstone and his present Cabinet were converted to Home Rule by Parnell'.[129] His invocation of Parnell was undoubtedly deliberate.

On 28 November the branch held another public meeting and it was reported that thirty-seven members attended with about sixty others also present.[130] Patrick Walsh presided and Strange gave an address on socialism in which he challenged anybody who disagreed with him to meet him in open debate.[131] On 4 December, Dorman was the main speaker at another meeting in the Trades Club where he used the Bible to bolster an ethical argument for labour socialism. After mentioning the Book of Proverbs, he continued:

> Trades unionists have as their object the removal of at least some of the poverty which, according to Solomon, is the destruction of the poor, and they have as their object the obtaining of such a rate of wages as will enable the worker to procure such food as is convenient for himself and those depending on him . . . Who can tell how large a proportion of the vice, crime, immorality, and drunkenness is due to the low standard of living which many of our fellow-men and women, otherwise abundantly endowed intellectually and morally, are compelled to conform to?[132]

Once again, Meagher spoke on home rule, criticizing the acrimony within the home rule movement as likely 'to retard the progress of Home Rule for Ireland' and he defended the ILP against hostility emanating from the nationalist press: 'They had been told by certain journals that on this question they should stand aside. If they were not allowed to voice their opinions now what privileges would be accorded them by the gentlemen who run these journals under Home Rule.'[133]

In addition to public meetings the ILP used local newspapers to generate debate on social issues. The *Waterford Daily Mail* was particularly sympathetic and it watched the branch's progress 'with deep interest' while recommending its readers attend the meetings.[134] On 20 November the paper published a letter from the ILP on poor housing in which the branch argued that the 'working classes have the power to end this sad state of affairs by their votes'.[135] A more controversial letter from Laurence Strange was carried a few days later.

> Owing to the temperament of the Irish, Ireland is about the last place where a movement based on scientific theory will dominate; but even here we have indications which ought to enlighten the most obtuse . . . To calm the fears of the nervous let it be understood that the present movement does not mean — as the ignorant would suggest — the taking of wealth already acquired; it merely means the enactment of laws to prevent the future spoilation of the workers.[136]

The letter created a debate, with letters on the issues raised being published over subsequent weeks.[137] A Parnellite priest, Fr Murphy of Kilmanagh, provided Strange with his most strident opposition. He denied that the Irish were peculiarly adverse to scientific thinking and he repudiated the idea that laws should be open to change by majorities: 'Laws, for instance, safeguarding the interests of religion, the rights of parents, of married persons, of individual liberty and property may not be changed at will by the mass of the governed, or in any other way.'[138] Murphy returned to these sentiments in a later letter when he provided what he considered to be a concrete example of democratic tyranny.

> For instance, the new school of 'Revolted Women', as the women form the
> majority of the population in all civilised countries, aspire to take the govern-
> ment of the different countries into their own hands. According to Mr
> Strange's abstract German principles, whenever they find that they possess
> a majority of votes, they will 'have the right to alter any form of laws at
> will'. Consequently, they will have the right to pass laws to compel the
> men to rock the cradle, cook, knit, darn, dust the rooms, look after the
> slops, and attend to all womanly household duties . . . Our future rulers
> of revolted women, governing on the abstract German principle of the rule
> of the majority, may pass laws to mutilate a certain proportion of male
> babies, and keep a certain proportion, and feed them as long only as they
> are useful, after the example of the hive-bee republics.[139]

Prospects for men in a democratic society looked decidedly grim. Fr Murphy
later accused Strange of harbouring 'un-Catholic and illogical assumptions'
and he recommended that workers look to the Catholic Church for
solace.[140] Strange responded to the priest but eventually decided that the
ongoing argument was pointless.[141] Robert Dorman also contributed to the
Waterford Daily Mail and other local papers with letters which ranged from
complaints about 'the sanitary arrangements of Brown's Lane Gateway' to
letters in January 1895 on temperance and indigenous industry.[142] In one
letter he underlined the restrictive nature of the municipal franchise: 'We
have been years struggling (and rightly so) for the interest of Home Rule,
and yet we are shut out from all voice in the local government of our native
land.'[143] In 1895 the ILP was to run candidates in Waterford's local
elections.

Within weeks of its formation the ILP branch had become an important
part of the city's political life. It had won the support of the Waterford
Federated Trades and Labour Union and was generally believed to represent the views of many working-class people. Certainly, the involvement of
a local politician, Laurence Strange, and of several prominent trade unionists
gave it an image of seriousness. Strange, and the trades council, were also
attentive to the interests of the rural labouring class and Strange continued
his support for the Irish Land and Labour Association.[144] This prompted
allegations that the labour activists were guilty of anti-Redmondism.[145] Indeed, by the end of January 1895 the branch was already feeling the pressure
of nationalist political division and when Strange wrote to Tom Mann to
inform him that the Waterford ILP was unable to provide a proposed £5
donation to party funds because the branch was 'insignificant in numbers'
he also added: 'You have no idea of the difficulty in this country of keeping
any labour organisation free from the party political strife which has now
lasted for over three years.'[146]

Later in the year the branch put forward two candidates, Strange and J.J.
Rogers, in the Waterford municipal elections. Unfortunately, Strange was

disqualified before the election because of a technical error in his nomination papers and Rogers, the less well-known candidate, received only fifteen votes out of a poll of 109.[147] Both candidates stood again in the 1896 municipal elections and Strange polled forty votes which brought him close to defeating the Mayor of Waterford who polled forty-nine votes. Once again, Rogers fared badly, garnering nineteen votes.[148] As Emmet O'Connor points out, Rogers does not seem to have been a serious candidate and he even failed to vote himself.[149] The Waterford ILP disappeared after this election disappointment and Strange moved with other members toward Redmondism. He was re-elected to the local council in 1897 and in 1899 he became Mayor of Waterford. Organized socialism did not revisit the city until the second decade of the twentieth century.[150] Strange became a member of the Irish Socialist Republican Party in the late 1890s but he was never really active and a branch of the party was never formed in Waterford.[151]

The ILP rapidly became the largest socialist organization in Britain but its success in Ireland was fleeting, although it did manage to re-establish itself in Belfast at the beginning of the twentieth century. Its image as a British party caused it some problems in Dublin and in Waterford, while Hardie's open support for home rule did not help it in Belfast. There seems to have been little unity between the Belfast branch and those in Waterford and Dublin, and the three branches at no stage co-ordinated their activity in Ireland. This was a serious organizational failure and accentuated their role in Ireland as merely provincial branches of a British organization. Had they operated together as an Irish ILP they may have provided the country with the beginnings of a significant socialist party.

NOTES AND REFERENCES

1   E.J. Hobsbawm, *Labouring Men: Studies in the History of Labour* (London, 1986), pp. 253–4.
2   Quoted in Willard Wolfe, *From Radicalism to Socialism: Men and Ideas in the Formation of Fabian Socialist Doctrines, 1881–1889* (New Haven and London, 1975), pp. 262–3.
3   ibid., p. 259.
4   E.J. Hobsbawm, op. cit., p. 253.
5   A.M. McBriar, *Fabian Socialism and English Politics, 1884–1918* (Cambridge, 1966), p. 119.
6   Sidney Webb to Beatrice Potter, 19 Sept. 1890, in Norman MacKenzie (ed.), *The Letters of Sidney and Beatrice Webb. Volume One: Apprenticeships, 1873–1892* (Cambridge, 1978), pp. 190–1.
7   Quoted in Yvonne Kapp, *Eleanor Marx. Volume II: The Crowded Years, 1884–1898* (London, 1976), pp. 483–4.

8 John W. Boyle, *The Irish Labor Movement in the Nineteenth Century* (Washington, 1988), p. 179.
9 ibid., p. 179; *Belfast Weekly Star*, 28 Feb. 1891.
10 *Belfast Weekly Star*, 28 Feb. 1891.
11 ibid.
12 John W. Boyle, op. cit., p. 158n.
13 *Justice*, 26 Mar. 1892.
14 *Freeman's Journal*, 28 July 1890.
15 *Freeman's Journal*, 7 Oct. 1890.
16 James Sexton, *Sir James Sexton, Agitator: An Autobiography* (London, 1936), p. 155.
17 *Freeman's Journal*, 2, 8, May 1893; *Irish Times*, 8 May 1893.
18 John W. Boyle, op. cit., p. 114; Dermot Keogh, *The Rise of the Irish Working Class: The Dublin Trade Union Movement and Labour Leadership, 1890–1914* (Belfast, 1982), pp. 102–3; Arthur Mitchell, *Labour in Irish Politics, 1890–1930* (Dublin, 1974), pp. 16–17.
19 *Freeman's Journal*, 7 May 1894.
20 *Irish Times*, 7 May 1894.
21 Bob McClung, 'Senator Bob Dorman', *Labour Opposition*, Aug. 1925. It is implied in this article that Dorman was born in Belfast but according to himself (*Waterford Daily Mail*, 17 Nov. 1894) he was a native of Dublin.
22 John W. Boyle, op. cit., p. 190n.
23 *Freeman's Journal*, 29 Feb. 1892.
24 *Freeman's Journal*, 2 Mar. 1892.
25 Emmet O'Connor, *A Labour History of Ireland, 1824–1960* (Dublin, 1992), p. 57.
26 Stephen Yeo, 'A phase in the social history of socialism, c. 1885–1895', *Bulletin of the Society for the Study of Labour History*, vol. xxii, 1971, pp. 6–8.
27 Stuart Macintyre, *A Proletarian Science: Marxism in Britain, 1917–1933* (London, 1986), p. 48.
28 Stephen Yeo, 'Notes on three socialisms', in Carl Levy (ed.), *Socialism and the Intelligentsia, 1880–1914* (London, 1987), p. 244.
29 Stephen Yeo, 'A new life: the religion of socialism in Britain, 1883–1896', *History Workshop*, no. 4, Autumn 1977, p. 28.
30 *Justice*, 6 Aug. 1892.
31 David Howell, *British Workers and the Independent Labour Party, 1888–1906* (Manchester, 1983), p. 284.
32 ibid., p. 292.
33 *Belfast News Letter*, 4 Sept. 1893.
34 Bob McClung, 'Alex Stewart', *Belfast Labour Opposition*, July 1925.
35 *Belfast News Letter*, 4 Sept. 1893.
36 ibid.
37 ibid.
38 *Belfast News Letter*, 6 Sept. 1893.
39 *Belfast News Letter*, 7 Sept. 1893.
40 Austen Morgan, *Labour and Partition: The Belfast Working Class, 1905–23* (London, 1991), p. 62.
41 *Labour Leader*, 15 Dec. 1894.

42 *Belfast News Letter*, 11 Sept. 1893.
43 *Belfast Evening Telegraph*, 18 Sept. 1893, quoted in Austen Morgan, op. cit., p. 62.
44 *Belfast News Letter*, 18 Sept. 1893.
45 *Labour Leader*, 26 May 1894.
46 *Justice*, 2 June 1894.
47 Bob McClung, 'William Walker', *Belfast Labour Opposition*, March 1925. On Walker, see John W. Boyle, 'William Walker', in John W. Boyle (ed.), *Leaders and Workers* (Cork, 1966).
48 Quoted in Austen Morgan, op. cit., p. 62.
49 On the ILP and Belfast Trades Council see Henry Patterson, *Class Conflict and Sectarianism: The Protestant Working Class and the Belfast Labour Movement, 1868–1920* (Belfast,1980), pp. 33–40.
50 *Labour Leader*, 22 Dec. 1894.
51 *Justice*, 6 July 1895.
52 ibid.
53 *Belfast News Letter*, 6 May 1895.
54 *Justice*, 6 July 1895.
55 *The Clarion*, 1 June 1895.
56 *The Clarion*, 18 Jan., 15 Feb., 15 Mar. 1896.
57 John W. Boyle, *Irish Labor Movement*, p. 187.
58 Quoted in Austen Morgan, op. cit., p. 62.
59 David Howell, op. cit., pp. 328–9.
60 *Justice*, 13 Jan. 1894.
61 *Justice*, 28 July 1894.
62 John W. Boyle, *Irish Labor Movement*, pp. 144–5.
63 ibid., p. 149.
64 ibid., p. 150.
65 *Justice*, 28 July 1894.
66 *Justice*, 28 Apr. 1894.
67 *Justice*, 2 June 1894. Alexander Duncan, interestingly, had (with William Graham) helped to form the Dublin Glass Bottlemakers' Trade Society in 1882 and was its founding president. (*Freeman's Journal*, 16 Aug. 1882.)
68 Carl Levy, 'Education and self-education: staffing the early ILP', in Carl Levy (ed.), op. cit., p. 157.
69 *Justice*, 28 July 1894.
70 ibid.
71 William O'Brien, *Forth the Banners Go: Reminiscences* (Dublin, 1969), p. 6.
72 ibid., p. 6.
73 James Connolly to Keir Hardie, 3 July 1894, ILP Archives, BLPES.
74 ibid.
75 ibid.
76 *Justice*, 27 Oct. 1894.
77 *Labour Leader*, 3 Nov. 1894.
78 *Freeman's Journal*, 9 Nov. 1894.
79 ibid.
80 ibid.

 81 *Freeman's Journal*, 12 Nov. 1894.
 82 *Labour Leader*, 17 Nov. 1894.
 83 *Freeman's Journal*, 12 Nov. 1894.
 84 ibid.
 85 *Labour Leader*, 17 Nov. 1894.
 86 *Waterford Daily Mail*, 14 Nov. 1894; *Labour Leader*, 24 Nov. 1894.
 87 *Waterford Daily Mail*, 14 Nov. 1894.
 88 *Labour Leader*, 1 Dec. 1894.
 89 *Labour Leader*, 15 Dec. 1894.
 90 T. Harrison to Keir Hardie, 20 Feb. 1894, ILP Archives, BLPES.
 91 T.W. Moody, 'Michael Davitt', in John W. Boyle (ed.), op. cit., p. 54.
 92 *Labour Leader*, 22 Dec. 1894.
 93 ibid.
 94 ibid.
 95 *Labour Leader*, 29 Dec. 1894.
 96 *Labour Leader*, 8 Dec. 1894.
 97 *Waterford Daily Mail*, 1 Jan. 1895.
 98 *Labour Leader*, 29 Dec. 1894.
 99 ibid.
100 *Freeman's Journal*, 6 May 1895.
101 ibid.
102 *The Clarion*, 3 Aug. 1895.
103 William O'Brien, op. cit., p. 6.
104 ibid., p. 8.
105 Emmet O'Connor, 'The influence of Redmondism on the development of the labour movement in Waterford in the 1890s', *Decies*, no. 10, January 1979, p. 39.
106 See his comments in the *Waterford Daily Mail*, 22, 30 Nov. 1894.
107 *Justice*, 9 Jan. 1892, 14 Apr. 1894.
108 *Justice*, 10 Dec. 1892.
109 *Justice*, 16 Mar. 1892.
110 *Waterford News*, 3 Nov. 1894; *Waterford Daily Mail*, 26 Oct. 1894.
111 *Waterford Daily Mail*, 26 Oct. 1894.
112 *Waterford News*, 27 Oct., 3 Nov. 1894.
113 *Waterford News*, 3 Nov. 1894.
114 Dan Bradley, *Farm Labourers: Irish Struggle, 1900–1976* (Belfast, 1988), pp. 26–42.
115 *Waterford News*, 27 Oct. 1894.
116 *Waterford News*, 3 Nov. 1894.
117 *Waterford Daily Mail*, 14 Nov. 1894; *Waterford News*, 17 Nov. 1894.
118 *Waterford News*, 24 Nov. 1894.
119 *Waterford News*, 17 Nov. 1894.
120 ibid.
121 *Waterford Daily Mail*, 17 Nov. 1894.
122 *Waterford News*, 17 Nov. 1894.
123 ibid.
124 *Waterford News*, 24 Nov. 1894.
125 *Labour Leader*, 1 Dec. 1894.

126 *Waterford Daily Mail*, 21 Nov. 1894.
127 *Waterford Daily Mail*, 17 Nov. 1894.
128 *Waterford News*, 24 Nov. 1894.
129 ibid.
130 *Waterford Daily Mail*, 1 Dec. 1894; *Labour Leader*, 8 Dec. 1894.
131 *Labour Leader*, 8 Dec. 1894.
132 *Waterford Daily Mail*, 12 Dec. 1894.
133 ibid.
134 *Waterford Daily Mail*, 18 Dec. 1894.
135 *Waterford Daily Mail*, 20 Nov. 1894.
136 *Waterford Daily Mail*, 22 Nov. 1894.
137 *Waterford Daily Mail*, 27, 28, 29, 30 Nov., 4, 6, 9, 11, 14 Dec. 1894.
138 *Waterford Daily Mail*, 27 Nov. 1894.
139 *Waterford Daily Mail*, 6 Dec. 1894.
140 *Waterford Daily Mail*, 14 Dec. 1894.
141 *Waterford Daily Mail*, 9 Dec. 1894.
142 *Waterford Daily Mail*, 19 Dec. 1894, 14, 22 Jan. 1895.
143 *Waterford Daily Mail*, 4 Dec. 1894.
144 *Waterford News*, 12 Oct. 1895.
145 Emmet O'Connor, 'The influence of Redmondism', p. 39.
146 Lawrence Strange to Tom Mann, 28 Jan. 1895, ILP Archives, BLPES.
147 *Waterford News*, 30 Nov. 1895.
148 *Waterford News*, 28 Nov. 1896.
149 Emmet O'Connor, 'The influence of Redmondism', p. 41.
150 ibid., p. 41.
151 On Strange's membership of the ISRP see the list of early members in 'ISRP 1896–1904, Notes on formation of and of movements which preceded it', William O'Brien Papers, NLI.

EPILOGUE

Towards a Socialist Republicanism

The history of Irish socialism after 1896 has received considerable scrutiny in the many biographical and political studies of James Connolly.[1] J.W. Boyle, in his study of nineteenth-century Irish labour, has also provided a useful survey of socialism in the immediate post-1896 era.[2] It is not the intention of this epilogue to rehearse that material but rather to accentuate the enormity of the redirection prompted by the political thought of Connolly and the Irish Socialist Republican Party (ISRP). After 1896 a version of Marxism emerged that has remained potently influential on the Irish left ever since.

THE ARRIVAL OF JAMES CONNOLLY

In 1887 the National Labour League won an audience of some significance in Dublin city but, by and large, the propagandist *modus operandi* of 1885–90 had placed Irish socialists in a position of relative isolation. This abstract propagandism was largely an inheritance from the Socialist League branch. The engagement with labour politics between 1890 and 1895 brought them away from this isolation and socialists played leading roles in the politicization of the Irish labour movement. However, traditional labourism continued to dominate and trade union candidates put forward in municipal contests usually reflected this reality. Dublin Trades Council moved directly into electoral activity in 1895 when it formed an electoral association and in the same year it ran its first official candidate in the local elections. Belfast had already moved in the same direction in a politicization that was partly presaged by the nomination of Alexander Bowman, secretary of the trades council, as the Liberal candidate for a parliamentary seat in 1885.

As the labour movement was developing this political direction Irish socialism was in a weak state and unable to pose a radical alternative to labourism. By 1896 the branches of the Independent Labour Party had collapsed or were in the process of collapsing. Socialists in the capital city had retreated to an inconspicuous Socialist Society and outdoor propaganda was left to Robert Dorman who spoke regularly to attentive crowds from the steps of the Custom House.[3] The immediate prospects for socialism in Dublin seemed dim and the Socialist Society appeared to offer no real way forward. However, in mid-December 1895 *Justice* had published an appeal advertising the services of the leading Edinburgh socialist, James Connolly.[4] Connolly, secretary of the Scottish Socialist Federation and an ILP member, was down on his luck and in need of employment to support his young family. Members of the Dublin Socialist Society noticed this advertisement and after discussion it was decided to communicate with Connolly. Adolphus Shields and Robert Dorman wrote a joint letter offering him one pound per week if he agreed to transfer to Dublin and act as an organizer for the society.[5] Connolly's parents were both Irish and he had always felt a deep affinity with the country so he eagerly accepted the offer.

Connolly arrived in Dublin in early May 1896. It is not clear whether Shields and Dorman knew what to expect and it is possible that they attached too much importance to his ILP membership. In fact, Connolly owed his primary allegiance to the Marxist SDF tradition and while he admired and supported Keir Hardie he did not place the same emphasis on parliamentary and municipal elections. In 1894 and 1895 he had stood as a socialist (rather than as an Independent Labour) candidate in local elections in Edinburgh. He wrote of his candidature:

> The return of a Socialist candidate does not mean the immediate realisation of even the programme of palliatives commonly set before the electors. Nay, such programmes are in themselves a mere secondary consideration of little weight, indeed, apart from the spirit in which they will be interpreted. The election of a Socialist to any public body is only valuable in so far as it is the return of a disturber of the political peace.[6]

Within a short time of arriving in Ireland Connolly forced the demise of the Dublin Socialist Society. According to Thomas Lyng, a member of the society, he confronted the leaders, 'pulverised them in debate, preached socialism unblushingly to them, shattered their little organisation, and from the fragments he founded a small Irish Socialist Republican Party'.[7] There is undoubtedly an element of retrospective hyperbole in Lyng's account but Connolly certainly convinced Dorman, if not Shields, and others of the necessity to move beyond the Socialist Society.

The ISRP was founded on 29 May in Ryan's public house at 50 Thomas Street. The motion to form the new body was moved by Robert Dorman and seconded by another ex-ILP member, Thomas Lyng.[8] Only six others, including Connolly, were present at this meeting. A committee was appointed: Connolly (secretary), Dorman (treasurer), Lyng (finance), and a man named Whelan (librarian). Whelan, who soon disappeared from the scene, may have been the bricklayer and 'new unionist', John Whelan. The object of the new organization was declared to be the establishment 'of an Irish socialist republic and the consequent restoration of social democracy in the island'.[9] Rooms were rented at 67 Middle Abbey Street and the ISRP began recruiting.

What the twenty-seven-year-old Connolly had initiated marked a huge step away from the perspective on legislative independence held previously by Irish socialists. The home rule politics of the ILP had undoubtedly assisted in this process. The ILP branches in Dublin and Waterford (not in Belfast) had during their short existence articulated support for home rule rather than the studied indifference offered by bodies like the National Labour League and the Irish Socialist Union. The ISRP, however, moved beyond the ILP and declared for separatism. This declaration connected with the beginnings of a resurgence of republican separatism and a cultural nationalism that fed it. W.B. Yeats saw the Parnell split as a dividing line in the history of Irish nationalism. He wrote:

> The modern literature of Ireland, and indeed all that stir of thought which prepared for the Anglo-Irish war, began when Parnell fell from power in 1891. A disillusioned and embittered Ireland turned from parliamentary politics; an event was conceived; and the race began, as I think, to be troubled by that event's long gestation.[10]

The defeat of the home rule bills was undoubtedly an important factor also. But, certainly, the internecine warfare within the Irish parliamentary party led some people to question the efficacy of constitutional nationalism. By the time the ISRP was founded republican separatism was stronger than it had been for some time. In a manifesto issued shortly after its foundation the party declared its primal object to be the securement of a socialist republic. Among other principles it believed

> That the subjection of one nation to another, as of Ireland to the authority of the British Crown, is a barrier to the free political and economic development of the subjected nation, and can only serve the interests of the exploiting classes of both nations.
>
> That, therefore, the national and economic freedom of the Irish people must be sought in the same direction, viz., the establishment of an Irish Socialist Republic, and the consequent conversion of the means of

production, distribution and exchange into the common property of society, to be held and controlled by a democratic state in the interests of the entire community.[11]

The ISRP positioned itself against the home rulers who it believed offered a 'sham' solution and against republicans who abjured social change. 'If you remove the English army tomorrow', wrote Connolly in January 1897, 'and hoist the green flag over Dublin Castle, unless you set about the organisation of the Socialist Republic your efforts would be in vain.'[12]

Much of the ISRP programme followed that of the SDF. However, the stance taken on the national question and British colonialism went considerably beyond any position ever taken by the SDF. Indeed, in 1892 *Justice* had indicated a softening of the SDF line on home rule when it advocated partition on sectarian grounds.

> It does seem to us very strange that the Liberal press and the Liberal Party should consider it an essential part of home rule that Ulster, with all its history and traditions, should be placed under the control of Roman Catholic Ireland of the South and West. We are, as we have always been, Home Rulers, in the sense that we would leave Irishmen to manage their own affairs . . . But we cannot, for the life of us, see why 3,000,000 or 4,000,000 Catholics in the South and West should dominate Ulster simply because Ireland is an island, anymore than we can comprehend why Spain should dominate the Low Countries because Europe is a continent.[13]

The SDF seemed to accept the idea of an island divided on a sectarian basis and, moreover, rather artlessly viewed the province of Ulster as a religiously homogeneous entity. It was a strange policy for a Marxist organization. It was also an attitude liable to encourage Belfast socialists like William Walker who opposed the very notion of Irish home rule.

A second innovative element in the ISRP's politics lay in the object agreed at the foundation meeting on 29 May. Aside from the establishment of a socialist republic, the founding members sought the 'restoration' of social democracy. This was a theme that Connolly was to develop over the following years. According to the ISRP what it required was, in truth, nothing more than a return to the system that prevailed before the victory of colonialism, albeit with alterations in keeping with modern life. Connolly's argument, which he presented in *Erin's Hope: The End and the Means* in March 1897, was that a Celtic communism had existed in Ireland as late as the seventeenth century and only disappeared as a direct result of colonial oppression. He claimed that the 'democratic organisation of the Irish clan' foreshadowed the 'more perfect organisation of the free society of the future'.[14] This recruitment of history was an important weapon with which to confront Irish nationalism, whatever about its dubious historical veracity.

In his pamphlet, Connolly presented the Irish middle class as enemies of this 'traditional' culture and he attacked home rule:

> Beginning by accepting a social system abhorrent to the best traditions of a Celtic people . . . [the middle class] next abandoned as impossible the realisation of national independence. By the first act they set the seal of approval upon a system founded upon the robbery of their countrymen, and by the second they bound up the destinies of their country with the fate of an Empire in the humiliation of whose piratical rulers lies the Irish people's only chance of national and social redemption. As compensation for this gross betrayal the middle class politicians offer — Home Rule.[15]

He contended that Ireland's salvation could only be achieved by the working class and within a system of socialism. 'We mean to be free', he wrote, 'and in every enemy of tyranny we recognise a brother, wherever be his birthplace; in every enemy of freedom we also recognise our enemy, though he were as Irish as our hills.'[16] For the ISRP the Irish parliamentary party belonged to the latter category.

BUILDING THE ISRP

The party was publicly launched at the Custom House steps in Dublin on 7 June 1896 at an open-air meeting chaired by Alexander Blaine, a former Parnellite MP. Connolly and Robert Dorman were the speakers. Blaine himself declined to join the new organization.[17] Over the next few months the ISRP slowly built up a membership of just over forty men — there were no female recruits. Among those who joined were Murtagh Lyng, the former ILP member, and Arthur Kavanagh, the 'veteran' socialist.[18] Dorman's friend, Laurence Strange, also took out membership but he did little for the party. In April 1897 he refused to organize a public meeting for the ISRP in Waterford while writing to the secretary 'in a very hopeless manner of the prospects of Socialism in the city'.[19] George King and John O'Gorman both became supporters of the organization and made donations towards the party paper, *Workers' Republic*, which was first published in August 1898.[20] The ISRP made repeated efforts to get King to lecture but it is not clear if he ever did.[21] According to William O'Brien, who joined in 1899, King and O'Gorman were former members of the Dublin branch of the First International.[22] This means that they had been active in left-wing politics for twenty-four years by 1896. Their age may explain why they never joined the party although political considerations might also have played a part. O'Gorman, in particular, had always viewed the national question as a diversion to be rejected. In March 1899 both were present at the ISRP's annual Paris Commune celebration. Toasts were made including one to the 'Memory of the Dead', which was responded to by John O'Gorman, and one to 'The Social Revolution', which was responded to by George King.[23] O'Gorman died in June 1902 and King joined him around the same time.[24]

Not all Dublin socialists, however, welcomed the ISRP or James Connolly. Shields is not listed among the initial members of the party and he seems to have withdrawn to the Fabian Society. He does seem to have had a brief membership in 1898.[25] It is possible that family commitments caused Shields to decrease his socialist activities: he and his German wife eventually accumulated a family of eight children and money was never plentiful in the Shields household. His son Arthur, who was born in 1896, recalled in later years that they 'moved house rather a lot, about twelve times in all. We were always having to move because nothing could be paid'.[26] He also remembers his father being friendly with Connolly, although he was undoubtedly referring to the years before 1916. Another 'veteran' socialist, J.T. Toomey, was openly hostile and William O'Brien recalled a comment he made to him about Connolly: 'Look here young man, a curse descended on Ireland the day James Connolly put his foot on it.'[27] It would be remarkable if such hostility did not exist towards Connolly's new departure. Outside of Ireland the ISRP received some support and Dr Edward Aveling was admitted into membership in late 1896.[28] Eleanor Marx also offered her support.[29]

The ISRP was never a large organization. William O'Brien states that the number of members in Dublin at any given time was about fifty, of whom only half were really active. Only fifteen would regularly turn up for the weekly meetings.[30] In the long term the ideas of the organization turned out to be more influential than the organization itself. Nonetheless, the ISRP did make something of an impact and incontrovertibly reinforced the growing separatist movement. In fact, unlike the ILP, it paid scant attention to trade unionism and concentrated its mind on the anti-colonialist movement.[31] Connolly displayed his SDF background in this area and in his pessimistic assessment that 'on the industrial plane the power of the master's purse will nearly always win'.[32] (Ironically, in later years he radically revised this view and played a leading role in the Irish trade union movement.) Every Sunday after 7 June Connolly and Dorman returned to the Custom House and preached their socialist message. Within a few weeks they expanded this method of propaganda and regular weekly stands were also occupied in the Phoenix Park on Sundays and at St James's Fountain every Tuesday. These outdoor meetings continued until October when Dorman departed for Limerick city where he was to unsuccessfully attempt to establish a branch.[33] With Dorman gone the ISRP was obliged to train other members in the art of public speaking. Apart from Connolly the most able and active members included Edward W. Stewart, Thomas Lyng, Murtagh Lyng, Daniel O'Brien, Thomas O'Brien and W.J. Bradshaw.[34] The Lyngs and the O'Briens were brothers and another O'Brien, William, later joined and also became a leading activist. Outdoor lecturing was complemented by indoor meetings and in December 1896 Connolly addressed the Fabian Society on 'Why We Are Revolutionists'.[35]

In his endeavour to trace a radical tradition in Irish history, Connolly organized the publication of James Fintan Lalor's writings in late 1896 and the pamphlet received a favourable review in the republican paper *Shan Van Vocht*.[36] Lalor, a separatist and social radical in the 1840s, was later to receive a prominent position in Connolly's book, *Labour in Irish History*.[37] In October, articles which would form part of his pamphlet, *Erin's Hope: The End and the Means*, appeared in the *Labour Leader* in which he put forward his thesis on Celtic communism. He concomitantly argued for separatism and internationalism and highlighted their compatibility in the context of relations between Ireland and Britain.

> The interests of labour all the world over are identical, it is true, but it is also true that each country had better work out its own salvation on lines most congenial to its own people. No Irish revolutionist worth his salt would refuse to lend a hand to the Social Democracy of England in the effort to uproot the social system of which the British Empire is the crown and apex, and in like manner, no English Social Democrat fails to recognise clearly that the crash which would betoken the fall of the ruling classes in Ireland would sound the tocsin for the revolt of the disinherited in England.[38]

In late 1896 and early 1897 Alice Milligan, editor of the *Shan Van Vocht*, accepted and published articles by Connolly on the relationship between nationalism and socialism in Ireland. Milligan later lectured for the ISRP and her eighteen-year-old brother became a member of the organization.[39] The ISRP also developed links with the republican separatist, Maud Gonne. On the other hand, T.W. Rolleston, who had once shown some interest in the Socialist League, wrote acknowledging receipt of party material but 'expressing [his] belief that Ireland could only be governed by a strong monarchy'.[40]

At the beginning of January 1897 the party became aware that a nationalist committee had been established to organize a commemoration of the 1798 rebellion the following year.[41] It was agreed to join in the celebrations and send delegates to the organizing committee.[42] In addition, the ISRP formed a Rank and File '98 Club, with Thomas O'Brien as secretary, and undertook the publication of extracts from the writings of leading United Irishmen. This club attracted separatists and social radicals who were not impressed with the political moderation shown by the official committee.[43] Coincidentally, 1897 happened to be the year of Queen Victoria's diamond jubilee and this provided a useful moment for the ISRP and its new-found allies.

On 21 June, the day preceding Jubilee Day, the party organized a mass meeting in Foster Place under the slogan 'Down with Monarchy: long live the Republic!' A crowd of about six thousand attended. Connolly chaired and a resolution demanding a republic was proposed by Edward W. Stewart and seconded by Patrick Shelley of the Dublin Trades Council. Maud Gonne also spoke and a procession was held afterwards to the ISRP rooms in Middle Abbey Street where Connolly addressed the crowd from a window.[44]

On Jubilee Day the ISRP organized a dramatic demonstration through the streets of Dublin. At the front of the march was a black coffin inscribed with the words 'British Empire', and, according to William O'Brien, they carried 'ten banners bearing a motto . . . giving the number who died in the Famine, the number who were forced to emigrate and things of that kind. It wound up by saying "from British Rule, O Lord deliver us"'.[45] Maud Gonne and W.B. Yeats, who were both involved with the Fenians at this time, participated in the demonstration which attracted thousands. By the time it reached O'Connell Bridge over the Liffey the police had baton-charged and intense street-fighting was raging. Over two hundred people were consequently treated in hospital.[46] At the bridge Connolly ordered the coffin to be thrown into the river, shouting 'Here goes the coffin of the British Empire. To Hell with the British Empire!'[47] He was arrested and spent the night in a cell. Gonne paid his fine the next morning and he was released.

These events set the tone of ISRP activities over succeeding years. In 1898 the party was very involved in the 1798 centenary celebrations that were to play such a powerful role in the vitalization of republican separatism.[48] The organization also took a proactive position in the anti-Boer War campaign at the end of the century.[49] However, while supporting separatism the ISRP was careful not to be drawn away from its objective of a socialist republic and it maintained its distance from the nationalist movement. The profile achieved during 1897–99 did little to increase the membership of what was essentially a Dublin organization. Indeed, there were some serious losses such as Robert Dorman who resigned from the party in June 1897.[50] In Belfast and Cork, branches were established on a precarious basis and neither lasted long. The Cork branch was the first organized manifestation of socialism in the city since the International had come under severe clerical attack in 1872. Once again, the Catholic Church proved instrumental in the demise of Cork socialism, when the ISRP branch came under sustained attack from local clergy.[51] In Belfast the collapse of the ILP branch in early 1897 left a vacuum that was soon filled by a Belfast Socialist Society. The ISRP made a number of efforts to convince the Belfast socialists to form a branch but it was not until September 1899 that this happened and its existence was short.[52] Many in Belfast held a view of internationalism similar to that which had once dominated socialism in Dublin. In 1916, Robert Lynd, a former member of the Belfast Socialist Society, recalled their attitude to Connolly. The society, he wrote, met 'in a dusty upper room, illuminated by candles stuck in empty gin-bottles'.

> One of the members used to bring copies of Connolly's paper, the *Workers' Republic*, to sell at our meetings. But most of us, I think, were indifferent to what we regarded as sentimental Nationalism. We rejected almost unanimously a proposal to adopt as our colours orange and green and as our crest the clasped hands of the United Irishmen. We were doctrinaire Internationalists in those days and scarcely realised, as many of us do now, that Imperialism equally with capitalism means the exploitation of the weak by the strong.[53]

The anti-imperialist politics of the ISRP were always in danger of being conflated with nationalism by socialists eager to underscore their internationalism and their disdain for national chauvinism.

SOCIALIST REPUBLICANISM

In terms of its membership the ISRP was probably no bigger, and perhaps smaller, than some of the socialist organizations that had existed in Ireland before it. However, it displayed a willingness to think in grand terms and its hectic activity led to remarkable overestimations of the numerical strength of socialism in Dublin.[54] In addition, in August 1898 the party brought out a weekly paper, *Workers' Republic*, that was to survive in a sporadic manner until shortly before Connolly left for the United States in 1903. Moreover, candidates from the party contested local elections in Dublin from 1899 although they generally fared badly. With the possible exception of the labour socialists who had run for the ILP in Waterford, these were Ireland's first thoroughly socialist candidates. The election campaigns allowed the ISRP to argue publicly the politics of class struggle but the *Workers' Republic* was undoubtedly far more important in terms of spreading the socialist-republican message.

The first issue of the *Workers' Republic* appeared on 13 August 1898, in time to take advantage of the 1798 centenary celebrations. Two days later the Wolfe Tone memorial foundation stone was laid in Dublin by a committee dominated by home rulers. The ISRP took up this contradiction in the leading article of the first issue.

> Our Home Ruler leaders will find that the glory of Wolfe Tone's memory will serve, not to cover, but to accentuate the darkness of their shame. Wolfe Tone was abreast of the revolutionary thought of his day, as are the Socialist Republicans of our day. He saw clearly, as we see clearly, that a dominion as long rooted in any country as British dominion in Ireland can only be dislodged by a revolutionary impulse in line with the development of the entire epoch.[55]

For the ISRP the contemporary 'revolutionary impulse' was socialism, or more precisely, Marxian socialism. The paper later returned to the question of Wolfe Tone with a comment that exemplifies the politics of socialist republicanism.

> A monument to such a man can only be erected by a free people . . . Let Ireland seek help where Wolfe Tone found it, viz., in the ranks of the democracy in revolt; wherever the Socialist banner flies, there gather the true friends of freedom, there let us take our stand, and there let us prepare to raise the only worthy monument to the pioneers of freedom — the realisation of the freedom for which they fought.[56]

The politics developed by the ISRP introduced a new vocabulary into the Irish left. Socialist republicanism was Marxian, revolutionist, strongly anti-imperialist and rooted in a sense of historical place. This last characteristic was important in the struggle to win some influence within the separatist movement. History and pantheons had become powerful elements in the Irish nationalist tradition by the late nineteenth century. Connolly and the ISRP showed that they could also appropriate history as a political weapon. However, this attempt to play nationalism at its own game ultimately proved unsuccessful and the socialists did not win hegemony over the separatist movement. Irish socialism, nonetheless, remained deeply influenced by the ideas of Connolly over the subsequent century and, with his execution after the 1916 Rising, he became mythologized as the founder of modern Irish socialism.

NOTES AND REFERENCES

1   Most biographies and studies of Connolly include some material on socialist organization after 1896 but the most informative are C.D. Greaves, *The Life and Times of James Connolly* (London, 1961), and a short study that focusses very much on the ISRP, particularly in Cork, by Seán Cronin, *Young Connolly* (Dublin, 1978). Cronin's book has been unfairly ignored, perhaps because of its popular format.
2   John W. Boyle, *The Irish Labor Movement in the Nineteenth Century* (Washington, 1988), pp. 192–215.
3   C.D. Greaves, op. cit., p. 59.
4   *Justice*, 14 Dec. 1895.
5   Seán Cronin, op. cit., p. 27.
6   Quoted in C.D. Greaves, op. cit., p. 52.
7   Quoted in ibid., p. 59. Kieran Allen mistakenly asserts that Lyng's remarks refer to the Dublin Fabian Society. They do not; indeed, the Fabian Society (led by Adolphus Shields) survived until at least 1899. Kieran Allen, *The Politics of James Connolly* (London, 1990), p. 15.

8   ISRP minutes, 29 May 1896, William O'Brien Papers, NLI.
9   ibid.
10 W.B. Yeats, *Autobiographies* (London, 1955), p. 559.
11 'Programme of the ISRP', in Desmond Ryan (ed.), *Socialism and Nationalism: A Selection from the Writings of James Connolly* (Dublin, 1948), pp. 185-6.
12 *Shan Van Vocht*, January 1897.
13 *Justice*, 14 May 1892.
14 James Connolly, *Erin's Hope: The End and the Means* (Dublin, 1968), p. 8.
15 ibid., p. 11.
16 *Workers' Republic*, 5 Aug. 1899.
17 Seán Cronin, op. cit., pp. 31-2. William Morris met Alexander Blaine, while he was a serving MP, in February 1888 and in a private letter had commented that he 'seemed a very good fellow, and almost a socialist'. William Morris to Jane Alice Morris, 19 Feb. 1888 in Philip Henderson (ed.), *The Letters of William Morris* (London, 1950), p. 279.
18 'ISRP 1896-1904, Notes on formation of and of movements which preceded it', William O'Brien Papers, NLI.
19 ISRP minutes, 15 Apr. 1897, William O'Brien Papers, NLI.
20 ISRP minutes, 5 Dec. 1898, William O'Brien Papers, NLI. O'Gorman and King are also listed in 'The *Workers' Republic* Publication Guarantee Fund 1898', William O'Brien Papers, NLI, where their addresses are given as 16 Leinster Road in Rathmines (O'Gorman) and 8 Mid-Mountjoy Street (King).
21 ISRP minutes, 5, 19 Dec. 1898, William O'Brien Papers, NLI.
22 'ISRP 1896-1904, Notes on formation of and of movements which preceded it', William O'Brien Papers, NLI.
23 ISRP minutes, 19 Mar. 1899, William O'Brien Papers, NLI.
24 See the notes written alongside O'Gorman and King's names in the list of 'Useful Addresses' held by the Socialist Party of Ireland (founded March 1904), William O'Brien Papers, NLI.
25 ISRP minutes, 7 Nov. 1898; and see also the ISRP membership cards, William O'Brien Papers, NLI.
26 See the interview with Arthur Shields republished in E.H. Mikhail (ed.), *The Abbey Theatre: Interviews and Recollections* (London, 1988), pp. 156-7. Arthur briefly involved himself with politics and was a member of the Irish Citizen Army during the 1916 Rising in Dublin. Afterwards he was interned in Frongoch camp.
27 'ISRP 1896-1904, Notes on formation of and of movements which preceded it', William O'Brien Papers, NLI.
28 ISRP minutes, 8 Oct. 1896, William O'Brien Papers, NLI.
29 Eleanor Marx to Secretary, ISRP, 4 Mar. 1898, William O'Brien Papers, NLI. Also, see Connolly's remarks in *Forward*, 1 July 1911: 'And within a month of its formation in 1896 she [Marx] wrote to the Dublin organisation offering us whatever help it was in her power to give.' Quoted in Desmond Ryan (ed.), op. cit., p. 29; William O'Brien, *Forth the Banners Go: Reminiscences* (Dublin, 1969), p. 5.
30 William O'Brien, op. cit., p. 5.
31 Kieran Allen, op. cit., pp. 18-19.
32 Quoted in ibid., p. 18.

33 C.D. Greaves, op. cit., p. 64.
34 William O'Brien, op. cit., p. 5.
35 Samuel Levenson, *James Connolly: A Biography* (London, 1973), p. 47; C.D. Greaves, op. cit., p. 64.
36 C.D. Greaves, op. cit., p. 65.
37 James Connolly, *Labour in Irish History* (Dublin, 1967). On Lalor see David Buckley, *James Fintan Lalor: Radical* (Cork, 1990).
38 Quoted in C.D. Greaves, op. cit., p. 67.
39 C.D. Greaves, op. cit., pp. 68–9. ISRP minutes, 10 Dec. 1896, William O'Brien Papers, NLI.
40 ISRP minutes, 10 Dec. 1896, William O'Brien Papers, NLI.
41 ISRP minutes, 7 Jan. 1897, William O'Brien Papers, NLI.
42 ISRP minutes, 21 Jan. 1897, William O'Brien Papers, NLI.
43 C.D. Greaves, op. cit., p. 71.
44 Seán Cronin, op. cit., pp. 48–9.
45 William O'Brien, op. cit., p. 9.
46 Seán Cronin, op. cit., p. 49.
47 C.D. Greaves, op. cit., p. 72.
48 ibid., pp. 80–2.
49 Seán Cronin, op. cit., pp. 53–7.
50 ISRP minutes, 17 June 1897, William O'Brien Papers, NLI.
51 Seán Cronin, op. cit., pp. 59–66.
52 ISRP minutes, 18 Sept. 1899, William O'Brien Papers, NLI.
53 Robert Lynd, 'Introduction' (1916) to James Connolly, *The Reconquest of Ireland* (Dublin, 1934), pp. xix–xx.
54 William O'Brien, op. cit., p. 5.
55 *Workers' Republic*, 13 Aug. 1898.
56 *Workers' Republic*, 5 Aug. 1899.

Conclusion

Socialism in Ireland between 1881 and 1896 was undoubtedly a minority taste. When a major autonomous party of the working class arrived at the beginning of the twentieth century its political and social ethos owed more to the tradition of labourism than it did to socialism. Despite the relative success of the political ideas of the ISRP the motivating ideology of the Irish Labour Party, formed in 1912, was rooted in labourist reformism with a perfunctory nod towards the socialism of James Connolly. The Irish Labour Party, in many ways, resembled the Labour Party in Britain and in the pre-1914 international labour movement the British state (Britain and Ireland) was unique in western Europe in that it alone produced no mass working-class party based on a Marxist or rejectionist ideology.[1]

The reasons for this are complex and have more to do with the years after 1896 but, certainly, an opportunity to entrench socialism, and connect in a substantial manner with the working class, did exist during the first decade or so of the 'socialist revival'. The explanations differ as to why Marxism, in particular, failed to take root in Ireland and Britain but we can point to at least one shared subjective problem. The 'sectish' Marxism expounded by Hyndman and the SDF, and later by Morris and the Socialist League, was too narrow and dogmatic to allow the development of a workable strategy of engagement with the working class. During the period of 'new unionism' (1889–91) those SDF members who involved themselves did so largely as individuals while Hyndman and the main body of the organization stood back, unable to comprehend the empowering aspect of this labour ferment. Indeed, for the historian it is a pleasure to turn to German or French socialism after examining the banality and aridity of socialist theory in late nineteenth-century Britain. Only William Morris stands out as a thinker of any importance or originality. However, while the Socialist League avoided many of Hyndman's chauvinistic inclinations its attitude to the labour movement was even more dismissive than that of the SDF. The Socialist League had little time for what it saw as struggles for mere palliatives and this view ultimately proved debilitating. In Ireland a leading Socialist League member, as we have seen, went as far as to undermine (through argument) a campaign against rack-renting landlords in Dublin.[2] And this at a time when roughly one-third of the population of Dublin city lived in slum housing.[3] Socialism in Ireland arguably got off to a bad start because of the source of the import. British Marxism, with all the weaknesses that hindered its growth at home, was never likely to win the mind of the Irish working class. It was not until 1896 that an 'Irish' Marxism evolved which attempted, however unsuccessfully, to deal with Irish particularisms.

Ireland was unlike other western European countries in which mass working-class parties did develop during the period covered in this study. It had parallels, to a limited degree, in Spain and Italy in terms of national culture but its colonial status ensured the existence of a revolutionary potential that Marx and Engels had observed. The state and the governing élite were unpopular and national politics was dominated by issues that were hardly conducive to the welfare of the British Empire. Home rule and the disestablishment of landlordism were both subversive demands. Socialism in Ireland, therefore, was faced with a competing and potent oppositional ideology in the form of nationalism. Nationalism, with its implicit and explicit advocation of pan-class alliances, was probably the greatest obstacle that confronted modern socialism. However, there is no tidy monocausal explanation for the feebleness of socialism in late nineteenth-century Ireland. Three significant objective factors demand examination: the agrarian nature of Irish society; the strength of religion as a political force; and the nationalist movement.

LAND

Ireland at the end of the nineteenth century remained a largely agrarian society. In this it differed enormously from Britain which had led the industrial revolution and where, by 1891, the agricultural sector contributed only one-thirteenth of gross national income.[4] Moreover, a consistent decline in the rural population meant that by 1911 only about 20 per cent of people in Britain lived in the countryside.[5] In contrast, as late as 1914, only one-third of Irish people resided in towns or cities with a population of 2,000 or more.[6] Indeed, in 1914 as much as 43 per cent of the Irish labour force was still employed in agriculture.[7] At the end of the nineteenth century Ireland was largely free of industrialization with the exception of Belfast and the north-east of the country. Dublin was primarily a commercial and administrative centre and, unlike Belfast, factory production was not the predominant occupation. Those engaged in industrial activity in the capital city were principally unskilled workers and old-style craft workers.[8] Guinness was the largest employer.

With a narrow industrial base, Ireland does not easily fit the profile of a country amenable to modern socialism. As J.A. MacMahon has pointed out, the 'social question' in Ireland (in the 1880s and 1890s) meant the land question and the plight of the urban working class tended to be overlooked.[9] This led to a degree of urban–rural tension, particularly in Dublin, with urban radicals questioning a perceived overemphasis in national politics on the problems of rural Ireland. This tension, nonetheless, should not be overstressed. The Land League managed to establish a significant organization in Dublin and it attracted the support of many urban radicals and socialists, such as Amos Varian and J.B. Killen. With the replacement of the Land League by the National League in 1882 the agrarian question received less attention from nationalist politicians but it incontrovertibly remained just one step behind home rule in terms of national priorities.

How did the urban-based socialists relate to the rural population and its concerns? The short answer is that they did not except in a very formal sense. The policy of land nationalization was an intrinsic element of the socialist programme during this period and, in so far as rural concerns were considered, that was it. Moreover, there was no substantial attempt to reach out to rural Ireland and convince land activists of the value of land nationalization beyond the short campaign waged by Davitt and George in 1882.

It could be said that the socialists showed good sense in not wasting their energy on such a doomed campaign. We could easily extrapolate from Davitt's retreat in 1882 and accept his sagacious belief that there was no prospect of winning over the agrarian movement to a policy of land nationalization outside of a home rule parliament. Davitt, arguably, had an insider view not possessed by the initially optimistic Henry George. However, Davitt also possessed something else — an overriding nationalism. Undoubtedly, if Davitt had persevered he would have split the Land League and damaged nationalist unity. He was aware of this probability and of the concomitant probability that he would most likely find himself on the minority side of the division. Being primarily a nationalist, he opted to defer to Parnell rather than pursue his social policy on the land question. Therefore, his retreat merely highlights the determining nature of his nationalism and the strength of the tenant-farmer element in the Land League. If land nationalization was to gain adherents in the countryside it would not have found its constituency there but among labourers and, perhaps, small farmers.

In 1881, Peter O'Leary, who was influential in the rural labourers' movement, declared at a meeting between labourers' delegates and the leadership of the Land League, including Parnell, that he believed land nationalization to be 'the only true and real solution' of the labour question.[10] More importantly, ten years later a number of labourers' organizations did form a brief alliance with Dublin radicals in the short-lived Irish Labour League. Convened by Adolphus Shields, a leading Dublin socialist, and other radical members of the Gasworkers' Union, it provides an example of the possibilities of political alliance between urban and rural radicals. The programme adopted was advanced and labourers' bodies from Kanturk, Kilkenny, Carlow and other areas voted for the inclusion of the policy of land nationalization. The presence of Dr P.J. Neilan of Kanturk at the conference was particularly important. It was he who initiated the labour-nationalist organization in Munster which with Davitt's support formed into the Democratic Trade and Labour Federation early in 1890.[11] Moreover, Kanturk and north-west Cork had, since the late 1860s, been the primary nursery of rural labourer agitation and organization.

Whether the socialists would have had any success in rural Ireland is still very much an open question. With such a weak position in the cities it is perhaps not surprising that rural labourers were ignored to the degree that they were. For much of the late nineteenth century socialists struggled to maintain their slight existence in urban Ireland.

RELIGION

'In dealing with Ireland', wrote James Connolly in 1910, 'no one can afford to ignore the question of the attitude of the clergy.'[12] Certainly, the progress of Irish socialism cannot be read without realizing the political strength of organized religion in Ireland. Much of the opposition to the Irish branches of the International in 1872 emanated from Catholics roused by the death of clerics in the Paris Commune the year before. Likewise, William Morris, after his visit to the Dublin branch of the Socialist League in 1886, left with the impression that religion was the primary obstacle to socialism in Ireland.[13] He saw both the Protestant and Catholic churches as problematic. In the mid-1890s the Belfast members of the ILP discovered the virulence of Protestant anti-socialism when they were repeatedly beaten and battered from the streets of the city by loyalist mobs.

The problem in Belfast was politico-religious as many of those attacking socialism also subscribed to the politics of unionism/loyalism which took its fundamentals from British conservatism. The Orange orators combined anti-Catholic sectarianism with a belief in Empire and in the prevailing social formation. Nationalists and socialists were equally seen as a threat to the existing *status quo*. In fact, one of the central reasons for attacking the ILP branch derived from the knowledge that most leaders of the British socialist movement supported home rule for Ireland.

In the rest of the country the Catholic Church nurtured an environment of antagonism to the politics of social radicalism. However, while we can point to individual clerics who attacked socialism, it would be an overstatement to claim that the Catholic Church mounted a concerted campaign against socialist doctrines. In 1872, in the wake of the death of the Archbishop of Paris, the Church unquestionably struck out against socialism across Europe and the Commune later became a battering-ram whenever socialism was discussed. By 1885, when the Dublin Democratic Association emerged, the Church was less agitated by the spectre of socialism in Ireland. Indeed, according to MacMahon, it was only after 1907 that the clergy began to appreciate the 'dangers' of social agitation to any great degree.[14] This is not meant as a contradiction of those late nineteenth-century Dublin socialists who pointed to the hostility of the Church as a primal difficulty. Rather, it is to underline the deeper sense in which Catholicism and religious sensibilities were embedded in the people. There was no real tradition of anticlericalism in Ireland and those socialists, such as Fritz Schumann, who openly declared their atheism ran the risk of political and social ostracism. The Church was a popular Church. There was no real need for a concerted campaign against socialist doctrines because most Catholics knew that they were expected to reject such allegedly pernicious ideas.

The Catholic Church was a pervasive influence in nineteenth-century Ireland. Its suppression under the Penal Laws had made it a victim of colonialism and the later political movement for Catholic emancipation had brought it and Irish nationalism into a close communion. It could claim links with the people that the Catholic Church in France, to its cost, was unable to do. Moreover, while it maintained a strict moderation in politics, it suffered from no damaging connections to an unpopular political regime.[15] They had in Ireland, claimed the Land Leaguer Andrew Kettle in 1881, 'the most democratic priesthood in Europe, a priesthood taken altogether from the ranks of the people, having no connection with the aristocratic alien class that claimed not alone to rule the people but to rob them'.[16] This was a widely held belief in late nineteenth-century Ireland. Philip Johnson, the rural labourers' leader and friend of Dr Neilan, argued in the same year as Kettle that the priests and people were 'cemented together by a bond of blood, and evil would be the day and blasted the cause that would dare to separate them'.[17] The social conservatism expounded by Catholic clergy and instilled in a devout people undoubtedly created considerable difficulties for those promoting the politics of socialism.

NATIONALISM

Nationalism, in the real sense of that term, was born in the nineteenth century but the demand for Irish national independence can be traced back, at least, to the republicans of the 1798 rebellion. Irish nationalism, as it developed, could look to a long history of dissatisfaction with the colonial power and, in time, nationalist historians would conflate Irish history into one momentous struggle for national freedom. For socialists the nationalist movement presented a number of problems.

In a nation striving for legislative independence, socialists needed to develop a textured analysis that allowed for an understanding of the political potential of the national question. Instead, it is arguably true that before 1896 most Irish socialists whistled past the central political issue of the day. In some ways this is surprising and indicates a rather linear conception of internationalism. However, the primary nationalist bloc, the home rule movement, was conservative on social issues and was hostile to manifestations of social radicalism. Henry George quickly discovered that the Irish parliamentary party was a most conservative body when it addressed issues other than home rule and peasant proprietorship. On the other hand, it was rather myopic of Irish socialists to ignore colonialism because of the social conservatism of constitutional nationalism. In effect, such an attitude necessarily ensured political marginalization in late nineteenth-century Ireland. The branches of the ILP, unlike preceding socialist groups, spoke strongly in support of home rule in both Dublin and Waterford but the tone was tangibly defensive and more the result of local pressures. In truth, the energy of the ILP in Ireland was primarily expended on labour issues and home rule was left to the home rule movement. Moreover, the ILP suffered from the contradiction that it was a British party operating in Ireland.

Irish nationalism was an oppositional ideology that left little space for competitors. It virtually monopolized political discontent and it provided vehicles for social unrest in the Land League and in a variety of labour-nationalist organizations from 1881 onwards.[18] Nationalism was also a factor in habituating rural labourers and the urban working class to occupying a subordinate location in Irish society. It offered no challenge to class stratification and did much to dissuade the working class from constituting itself as a self-conscious subject acting politically in its own collective class interest. Workers were asked to identify with the 'nation' rather than with their 'class'. James Connolly attempted to overcome this after 1896 when he argued that workers in a colonized country should identify with *both* their 'class' and their 'oppressed nation' and struggle for a socialist resolution. Before 1896 Irish socialists either tailed the home rule movement (like the ILP) or simply failed to develop *any* strategy for dealing with the problems presented by the strength of nationalism. Such an attitude inevitably meant conveyance to the margins of Irish political life.

In conclusion, we can say that socialism in Ireland had to deal with a myriad of subjective and objective obstacles which it proved incapable of overcoming. Problems of theory were not confronted until 1896 and even then it was only a partial examination that failed to uncover many fundamental weaknesses inherited from British Marxism. The objective difficulties impeding nineteenth-century socialism remained through the early decades of the twentieth century and were not overcome by socialists. The labour movement, on the other hand, did manage to establish independent labour representation and the Irish Labour Party secured a place in the Irish political system.[19] While socialists failed to develop a real movement between 1881 and 1896 it would be inaccurate to assert that they had no impact in Ireland. They provided voices of dissent in 1887 when Dublin's unemployed sought to articulate their grievances. Later still, they played significant roles in the politicization of the labour movement and they were instrumental in introducing 'new unionism' to Ireland. They argued for social change and, at times, confronted the nationalist movement with its lack of attention to the urban working class. If nothing else, their existence fractures the notion that for everybody 'nation' came before 'class'.

NOTES AND REFERENCES

1   Ross McKibben, *The Ideologies of Class: Social Relations in Britain, 1880–1950* (Oxford, 1991), p. 1; Dick Geary, *European Labour Protest, 1848–1939* (London, 1984), p. 15.

2   See Michael Gabriel's comments on the campaign against rack-renting in *Freeman's Journal*, 11 Jan. 1886. On the other hand, it must be said that from the time of the Dublin Democratic Association onward some Dublin socialists did attempt to take up the issue of poor housing.

3   L.M. Cullen, *An Economic History of Ireland since 1660* (London, 1987), p. 166.

4   E.J. Hobsbawm, *Industry and Empire: An Economic History of Britain since 1750* (London, 1968), p. 164.

5   ibid., p. 287.

6   Cormac Ó Gráda, *Ireland: A New Economic History, 1780–1939* (Oxford, 1994), p. 213.

7   ibid., p. 383.

8   A.C. Hepburn, 'Work, class and religion in Belfast, 1871–1911', *Irish Economic and Social History*, vol. x, 1983, p. 35.

9   Joseph A. MacMahon, 'Catholic clergy and the social question in Ireland, 1891–1916', *Studies*, vol. lxx, no. 280, Winter 1981, p. 264.

10 *Freeman's Journal*, 17 Sept. 1881. O'Leary repeated his call for land nationalization at a session of the Land Convention of the Land League and was responded to with loud cheering. (*Freeman's Journal*, 19 Sept. 1881.)

11 D.D. Sheehan, *Ireland since Parnell* (London, 1920), p. 172; Dan Bradley, *Farm Labourers: Irish Struggle, 1900–1976* (Belfast, 1988), p. 26. Dr P.J. Neilan, who

chaired the conference of the Irish Labour League, had been involved in labour issues since at least 1880 when he had been associated with Philip F. Johnson, Peter O'Leary and others in organizing rural labourers in north-west Cork. Neilan had also been secretary of the Kanturk Land League. (*Cork Examiner*, 23, 27 Dec. 1880.)

12   James Connolly, *Labour in Irish History* (Dublin, 1969), p. 86.

13   *The Commonweal*, 8 May 1886.

14   Joseph A. MacMahon, op. cit., pp. 264–5. On the Catholic Church and Irish socialism see also Emmet Larkin, 'Socialism and Catholicism in Ireland', *Studies*, vol. lxxiv, no. 293, Spring 1985.

15   Sheridan Gilley, 'The Catholic Church and revolution', in D.G. Boyce (ed.), *The Revolution in Ireland, 1879–1923* (Dublin, 1988), *passim*.

16   *Cork Examiner*, 20 May 1881. Kettle went on to assert that, therefore, they had 'a power blessed by God and sanctioned by religion'. His audience may have regarded these comments as particularly apposite at a time when parish priests and local curates were cramming themselves onto Land League platforms.

17   *Cork Examiner*, 1 Aug. 1881.

18   Irish Labour League (1881–82), Democratic Trade and Labour Federation (1890) and the Irish Land and Labour Association (1894).

19   On the development of independent labour representation in Ireland see Arthur Mitchell, *Labour in Irish Politics, 1890–1930* (Dublin, 1974).

Bibliography

ARCHIVE MATERIAL

1 Chief Secretary's Office Registered Papers (CSORP) (1886) National Archives, Dublin
2 Michael Davitt Papers, Trinity College, Dublin (TCD)
3 Dublin Metropolitan Police (DMP) Files (1882–91), National Archives, Dublin
4 Henry George Papers, New York Public Library (NYPL)
5 Independent Labour Party (ILP) Archives, British Library of Political and Economic Science (BLPES)
6 Marx Papers, International Institute of Social History, Amsterdam (IISH)
7 William Morris Papers, British Library (BL)
8 William O'Brien Papers, National Library of Ireland (NLI)
9 Andreas Scheu Papers, International Institute of Social History, Amsterdam
10 Socialist League Papers, International Institute of Social History, Amsterdam

NEWSPAPERS

Belfast News Letter
Belfast Weekly Star
Brotherhood
The Clarion
The Commonweal
Connaught Telegraph
Cork Constitution
Cork Examiner

Daily News
Daily Press
Daily Telegraph
Evening Telegraph
Freeman's Journal
Irish Times
Irish World
Justice
Labour Leader
Labour Opposition
Manchester Examiner and Times
The Nation
Pall Mall Gazette
The Radical
Shan Van Vocht
The Times
Ulster Examiner
The Union
United Ireland
Waterford Daily Mail
Waterford News
Workers' Republic

THESES

Boyle, John W., 'The rise of the Irish labour movement, 1888–1907', PhD thesis, Trinity College, Dublin, 1961

d'Alroy Jones, Peter, 'Henry George and British socialism, 1879–1931', MA thesis, Victoria University of Manchester, 1953

Hazelkorn, Ellen, 'Karl Marx and Friedrich Engels: the Irish dimension', DPhil thesis, University of Kent, 1980

McDonnell, Brendan, 'The Dublin labour movement, 1894–1907', PhD thesis, University College, Dublin, 1979

Morgan, Austen, 'Politics, the labour movement and the working class in Belfast, 1905–1923', PhD thesis, Queen's University, Belfast, 1978

O'Higgins, Rachel, 'Ireland and Chartism: a study of the influence of Irishmen and the Irish question on the Chartist movement', PhD thesis, Trinity College, Dublin, 1959

BOOKS AND ARTICLES

Allen, Kieran, *The Politics of James Connolly* (London, 1990)

Anderson, W.K., *James Connolly and the Irish Left* (Dublin, 1994)

Archbold E., and H.W. Lee, *Social-Democracy in Britain: Fifty Years of the Socialist Movement* (London, 1935)

A.U. [Allen Upward], 'The socialist candidate', *Dublin University Review*, June 1886

Bailey, William F., 'The coming socialism', *Dublin University Review*, Dec. 1885

Baker, Bill, 'The Social Democratic Federation and the Boer War', *Our History*, Summer 1974

Barker, C.A., *Henry George* (New York, 1955)

Bartlett, Thomas, and David Hayton (eds.), *Penal Era and Golden Age: Essays in Irish History, 1690–1800* (Belfast, 1979)

Bax, E.B., *Reminiscences and Reflexions of a Mid and Late Victorian* (London, 1918)

Bax, E.B., Victor Dave and William Morris, *A Short Account of the Commune of Paris* (London, 1886)

Benewick, Robert, R.N. Berki and Bhikhu Parekh (eds.), *Knowledge and Belief in Politics: The Problem of Ideology* (London, 1973)

Bevir, Mark, 'H.M. Hyndman: a rereading and a reassessment', *History of Political Thought*, vol. xii, 1991

'The British Social Democratic Federation, 1880–85: from O'Brienism to Marxism', *International Review of Social History*, vol. xxxvii, no. 2, 1992

'Fabianism, permeation and Independent Labour', *Historical Journal*, vol. xxxix, no. 1, Mar. 1996

Bew, Paul, *Land and the National Question in Ireland, 1858–82* (Dublin, 1978)

C.S. Parnell (Dublin, 1980)

Conflict and Conciliation in Ireland, 1890–1910 (Oxford, 1987)

'James Connolly and Irish socialism', in Ciaran Brady (ed.), *Worsted in the Game: Losers in Irish History* (Dublin, 1989)

Blunt, Wilfred Scawen, *The Land War in Ireland: Being a Personal Narrative of Events* (London, 1912)

Bolger, Patrick, *The Irish Co-operative Movement: Its History and Development* (Dublin, 1977)

Boos, Florence (ed.), 'William Morris's socialist diary', *History Workshop*, no. 13, Spring 1982

Boos, Florence and C.G. Silver (eds.), *Socialism and the Literary Artistry of William Morris* (Missouri, 1990)

Bourke, Marcus, *John O'Leary: A Study in Irish Separatism* (Tralee, 1967)

Boyce, D.G., *Nationalism in Ireland* (London, 1982)

Nineteenth-century Ireland: The Search for Stability (Dublin, 1990)

Boyce, D.G., (ed.), *The Revolution in Ireland, 1879-1923* (Dublin, 1988)

Boyce, D.G., Robert Eccleshall and Vincent Geoghegan (eds.), *Political Thought in Ireland since the Seventeenth Century* (London, 1993)

Boyd, Andrew, *The Rise of the Irish Trade Unions 1729–1970* (Tralee, 1972)

Boyle, John W., 'William Walker' in John W. Boyle (ed.), *Leaders and Workers* (Cork, 1969)

The Irish Labor Movement in the Nineteenth Century (Washington, 1988)

Boyle, John W., (ed.), *Leaders and Workers* (Cork, 1966)

Bradley, Dan, *Farm Labourers: Irish Struggle, 1900–1976* (Belfast, 1988)

Brady, Ciaran, (ed.), *Worsted in the Game: Losers in Irish History* (Dublin, 1989)

Briggs, Asa and John Saville (eds.), *Essays in Labour History, 1886–1923* (London, 1971)

Brown, Malcolm, *The Politics of Irish Literature: From Thomas Davis to W.B. Yeats* (Washington, 1972)

Buckley, David, *James Fintan Lalor: Radical* (Cork, 1990)

Bush, Ronald, *The Genesis of Ezra Pound's Cantos* (Princeton, 1976)

Callanan, Frank, *The Parnell Split, 1890–91* (Cork, 1992)

Challinor, Raymond, *The Origins of British Bolshevism* (London, 1977)

Clark, Samuel, *Social Origins of the Irish Land War* (Princeton, 1979)

Clark, Samuel and James S. Donnelly (eds.), *Irish Peasants: Violence and Political Unrest, 1780–1914* (Dublin, 1983)

Clarkson, J.D., *Labour and Nationalism in Ireland* (New York, 1926)

Cody, Seamus, 'May Day in Dublin: 1890 to the present', *Saothar*, vol. v, 1979

Cole, G.D.H., *A Short History of the British Working Class Movement. Volume II: 1848–1900* (London, 1927)

  Socialist Thought: Marxism and Anarchism, 1850–90 (London, 1957)

Cole G.D.H., (ed.), *A New View of Society and other Writings of Robert Owen* (London, 1927)

Collins, Henry, 'The Marxism of the Social Democratic Federation', in Asa Briggs and John Saville (eds.), *Essays in Labour History, 1886–1923* (London, 1971)

Collins, Peter, 'Irish labour and politics in the late nineteenth and early twentieth centuries', in Peter Collins (ed.), *Nationalism and Unionism: Conflict in Ireland, 1885–1921* (Belfast, 1994)

Collins, Peter, (ed.), *Nationalism and Unionism: Conflict in Ireland, 1885–1921* (Belfast, 1994)

Connolly, James, *The Reconquest of Ireland* (Dublin, 1934)

  Labour and Easter Week 1916 (Dublin, 1949)

  Socialism and Nationalism (Dublin, 1951)

  The Workers' Republic (Dublin, 1951)

  Erin's Hope: The End and the Means (Dublin, 1968)

  Labour in Irish History (Dublin, 1967)

Conway, Stephen (ed.), *The Collected Works of Jeremy Bentham*, Volume 9 (Oxford, 1989)

Craig, E.T., *An Irish Commune: The Experiment at Ralahine, County Clare, 1831–33* (Dublin, 1983)

Cronin, James, 'Strikes and power in Britain, 1870–1920', *International Review of Social History*, vol. xxxii, no. 2, 1987

Cronin, Maura, *Country, Class or Craft? The Politicisation of the Skilled Artisan in Nineteenth-century Cork* (Cork, 1994)

Cronin, Seán, *Young Connolly* (Dublin, 1978)

Cummins, Ian, *Marx, Engels and National Movements* (London, 1980)

Cullen, L.M., *An Economic History of Ireland since 1660* (London, 1987)

Cunningham, John, *Labour in the West of Ireland: Working Life and Struggle, 1890–1914* (Belfast, 1995)

Curtin, Nancy J., *The United Irishmen: Popular Politics in Ulster and Dublin, 1791–98* (Oxford, 1994)

Curtis, L.P., *Coercion and Conciliation in Ireland, 1880–92* (Princeton, 1963)

Daly, Mary E., *Dublin: The Deposed Capital, 1860–1914* (Cork, 1984)

Daly, Seán, *Ireland and the First International* (Cork, 1984)

D'Arcy, Fergus, 'The artisans of Dublin and Daniel O'Connell, 1830–47', *Irish Historical Studies*, no. 66, 1970

'The National Trades Political Union and Daniel O'Connell, 1830–1848', *Éire–Ireland*, vol. xvii, no. 3, 1982

'Marx, Engels and the Irish question', in Kevin B. Nowlan (ed.), *Karl Marx: The Materialist Messiah* (Cork, 1984)

'Unemployment demonstrations in Dublin, 1879–82', *Saothar*, vol. xvii, 1992

D'Arcy, Fergus, and Ken Hannigan (eds.), *Workers in Union: Documents and Commentaries on the History of Irish Labour* (Dublin, 1988)

Davis, Richard, *The Young Ireland Movement* (Dublin, 1987)

Davitt, Michael, 'The Irish social problem', *Today*, no. 4, Apr. 1884

The Fall of Feudalism in Ireland (London, 1904)

De Laveleye, Emile, 'The progress of socialism', *Contemporary Review*, Apr. 1883

Democratic Federation, *Socialism Made Plain: Being the Social and Political Manifesto of the Democratic Federation* (London, 1883)

Documents of the First International, Volumes 1–5 (Moscow, 1964)

Dooley, Dolores, *Equality in Community: Sexual Equality in the Writings of William Thompson and Anna Doyle-Wheeler* (Cork, 1996)

Draper, Hal, *Karl Marx's Theory of Revolution, Volume 1* (New York, 1977); *Volume 2* (New York, 1978); *Volume 3* (New York, 1986)

Dudley Edwards, Owen, *The Mind of an Activist: James Connolly* (Dublin, 1971)

Dudley Edwards, Ruth, *James Connolly* (Dublin, 1981)

Eley, Geoff, and Keith Nield, 'Why does social history ignore politics?', *Social History*, vol. v, no. 2, May 1980

Elliott, Marianne, 'Irish republicanism in England: the first phase, 1797–99', in Thomas Bartlett and David Hayton (eds.), *Penal Era and Golden Age: Essays in Irish History, 1690–1800* (Belfast, 1979)

Partners in Revolution: The United Irishmen and France (New Haven and London, 1982)

Engels, Friedrich, *The Condition of the Working Class in England* (New York, 1973)

Socialism: Utopian and Scientific (New York, 1985)

Epstein, James, and Dorothy Thompson (eds.), *The Chartist Experience: Studies in Working Class Radicalism and Culture, 1830–1860* (London, 1982)

'Fathers of the Society of Jesus', *A Page of Irish History: Story of University College, Dublin, 1883–1909* (Dublin, 1930)

Fielding, Steve, 'Irish politics in Manchester, 1890–1914', *International Review of Social History*, vol. xxxiii, no. 3, 1988

Fitzpatrick, W.J., *The Life, Times and Contemporaries of Lord Cloncurry* (Dublin, 1855)

Fox, R.M., *James Connolly: The Forerunner* (Tralee, 1946)

Gallagher, Michael, 'Socialism and the nationalist tradition in Ireland, 1798–1918', *Éire–Ireland*, vol. xii, no. 2, Summer 1977

Garnett, R.G., *Co-operation and the Owenite Socialist Communities in Britain, 1825–45* (Manchester, 1972)

Garvin, J.L., 'A party with a future', *The Fortnightly Review*, 1 Sept. 1895

Garvin, Tom, *The Evolution of Irish Nationalist Politics* (Dublin, 1981)

'The anatomy of a nationalist revolution: Ireland, 1858–1928', *Comparative Studies in Society and History*, vol. xxxviii, 1986

Nationalist Revolutionaries in Ireland, 1858–1928 (Oxford, 1987)

Geary, Dick, *European Labour Protest, 1848–1939* (London, 1984)

Geoghegan, Vincent, 'Ralahine: An Irish Owenite community (1831–1833), *International Review of Social History*, vol. xxxvi, no. 3, 1991
'The emergence and submergence of Irish socialism, 1821–51', in D.G. Boyce, Robert Eccleshall and Vincent Geoghegan (eds.), *Political Thought in Ireland since the Seventeenth Century* (London, 1993)
George, Henry, *The Irish Land Question* (London, 1881)
Progress and Poverty (London, 1882 and 1889)
'England and Ireland: an American view', *The Fortnightly Review*, 1 June 1882
George, Henry, and H.M. Hyndman, 'Socialism and rent appropriation: a dialogue', *The Nineteenth Century*, no. 96, Feb. 1885
Gilley, Sheridan, 'The Catholic Church and revolution', in D.G. Boyce (ed.), *The Revolution in Ireland, 1879–1923* (Dublin, 1988)
Gilley, S. and R. Swift (eds.), *The Irish in the Victorian City* (London, 1985)
Glasier, John Bruce, *William Morris and the Early Days of the Socialist Movement* (London, 1921)
Goldstein, R.J., *Political Repression in Nineteenth-century Europe* (London, 1983)
Gonne-McBride, Maud, *Servant of the Queen* (London, 1938)
Gray, Robert, 'Class, politics and historical "revisionism"', *Social History*, vol. xix, no. 2, May 1994
Greaves, C.D., *The Life and Times of James Connolly* (London, 1961)
The Irish Transport and General Workers' Union: The Formative Years, 1909–23 (Dublin, 1982)
Grimshaw, T.W., 'A statistical survey of Ireland, from 1840 to 1888', *Journal of the Statistical and Social Inquiry Society of Ireland*, pt lxviii, 1889
Hamer, D.A., 'The Irish question and Liberal politics, 1886–1894', *Historical Journal*, vol. xii, 1969
Harris, Nigel, *National Liberation* (Harmondsworth, 1990)
Harrison, J.F.C., *Robert Owen and the Owenites in Britain and America* (London, 1969)
Harrison, R., 'The Land and Labour League (some new light on working class politics in the eighteen seventies)', *Bulletin of the International Institute for Social History, Amsterdam*, no. 3, 1953
Hazelkorn, Ellen, 'Marx, Engels and Ireland', *Teoric*, no. 10, Autumn 1980
'Reconsidering Marx and Engels on Ireland', *Saothar*, vol. 9, 1983
'Why is there no socialism in Ireland? Theoretical problems of Irish Marxism', *Science and Society*, vol. liii, 1989
Hepburn, A.C., 'Work, class and religion in Belfast, 1871–1911', *Irish Economic and Social History*, vol. x, 1983
Henderson, Philip, *William Morris: His Life, Work and Friends* (London, 1967)
Henderson, Philip, (ed.), *The Letters of William Morris* (London, 1950)
Hobsbawm, E.J., 'Bernard Shaw's socialism', *Science and Society*, vol. xi, Fall 1947
Industry and Empire: An Economic History of Britain since 1750 (London, 1968)
The Age of Capital, 1848–1875 (London, 1975)
The Age of Revolution: Europe 1789–1848 (London, 1977)
Labouring Men: Studies in the History of Labour (London, 1986)
Hobson, J.A., 'The influence of Henry George in England', *The Fortnightly Review*, 1 Dec. 1897

Hoffman, John, 'James Connolly and the theory of historical materialism', *Saothar*, vol. ii, 1975

Hogan, J.F., 'Early modern socialists, II', *Irish Ecclesiastical Record*, vol. xxvi, 1909

Hoppen, K. Theodore, *Elections, Politics and Society in Ireland, 1832–1885* (Oxford, 1984)

Ireland Since 1800 (London, 1989)

Howell, David, *British Workers and the Independent Labour Party, 1888–1906* (Manchester, 1983)

Hyndman, H.M., 'Irish needs and Irish remedies', *The Fortnightly Review*, 1 Feb. 1880

'The dawn of a revolutionary epoch', *The Nineteenth Century*, no. 47, Jan. 1881

England for All: The Textbook of Democracy (London, 1881)

The Record of an Adventurous Life (London, 1911)

Further Reminiscences (London, 1912)

Jeffares, A.N., *W.B. Yeats: Man and Poet* (Dublin, 1996)

Johnson, Andy, Laraggy, James, McWilliams, Edward, *Connolly: A Marxist Analysis* (Dublin, 1990)

Joynes, J.L., *The Adventures of a Tourist in Ireland* (London, 1882)

The Socialist Catechism (London, 1884)

Kapp, Yvonne, *Eleanor Marx. Volume II: The Crowded Years, 1884–1898* (London, 1976)

Kee, Robert, *The Laurel and the Ivy: The Story of Charles Stewart Parnell and Irish Nationalism* (London, 1993)

Keogh, Dermot, *The Rise of the Irish Working Class: The Dublin Trade Union Movement and Labour Leadership, 1890–1914* (Belfast, 1982)

Larkin, Emmet, 'Socialism and Catholicism in Ireland', *Studies*, vol. lxxiv, no. 293, Spring 1985

Lawrence, E.P., 'Henry George's British mission', *American Quarterly*, vol. 51, no. 3, 1951

'The reception of Henry George by British socialists', *American Journal of Economics and Sociology*, vol. ii, no. 63, Oct. 1951

Henry George in the British Isles (Michigan, 1957)

Lee, David, *Ralahine: Land War and Co-operative* (Dublin, 1981)

Lee, Joseph, *The Modernisation of Irish Society, 1848–1918* (Dublin, 1973)

Lemire, Eugene D., 'The Socialist League leaflets and manifestoes: an annotated checklist', *International Review of Social History*, vol. xxii, no. 1, 1977

Levenson, Samuel, *James Connolly: A Biography* (London, 1973)

Levy, Carl, 'Education and self-education: staffing the early ILP', in Carl Levy (ed.), *Socialism and the Intelligentsia, 1880–1914* (London, 1987)

Lichtheim, George, *Marxism: An Historical and Critical Study* (New York, 1965)

Lipmann, R.I., 'The progress of socialism', *Dublin University Review*, April 1886

Lynch, Patrick, 'William Thompson and the socialist tradition', in John W. Boyle (ed.), *Leaders and Workers* (Cork, 1966)

Lynd, Robert, 'Introduction', in James Connolly, *The Reconquest of Ireland* (Dublin, 1934)

Lyons, F.S.L., *The Fall of Parnell* (London, 1960)

Ireland Since the Famine (London, 1973)

Charles Stewart Parnell (London, 1977)

Culture and Anarchy in Ireland, 1890–1939 (Oxford, 1982)

McAteer, Shane, 'The "new unionism" in Derry, 1889–92', *Saothar*, vol. xvi, 1991

McBriar, A.M., *Fabian Socialism and English Politics, 1884–1918* (Cambridge, 1966)

MacCarthy, Fiona, *William Morris: A Life for our Time* (London, 1994)

McCarthy, Justin H., *England under Gladstone, 1880–1884* (London, 1884)

McClelland, K. and H.J. Kaye (eds.), *E.P. Thompson: Critical Perspectives* (Cambridge, 1990)

McClung, Bob, 'William Walker', *Labour Opposition*, Mar. 1925

  'Alex Stewart, Belfast', *Labour Opposition*, July 1925

  'Senator Bob Dorman', *Labour Opposition*, Aug. 1925

Macintyre, Stuart, *A Proletarian Science: Marxism in Britain, 1917–1933* (London, 1986)

MacKenzie, Norman (ed.), *The Letters of Sidney and Beatrice Webb. Volume One: Apprenticeships, 1873–1892* (Cambridge, 1978)

McKibben, Ross, *The Ideologies of Class: Social Relations in Britain, 1880–1950* (Oxford, 1991)

MacMahon, Joseph A., 'Catholic clergy and the social question in Ireland, 1891–1916', *Studies*, vol. lxx, no. 280, Winter 1981

Marx, Karl, and Friedrich Engels, *Selected Correspondence* (Moscow, 1965)

  Ireland and the Irish Question: A Collection of Writings (New York, 1972)

  Collected Works (50 volumes, London, 1975–95)

Metscher, Priscilla, *Republicanism and Socialism in Ireland* (Frankfurt am Main, 1986)

Mikhail, E.H., (ed.), *The Abbey Theatre: Interviews and Recollections* (London, 1988)

Miliband, Ralph, *The State in Capitalist Society* (London, 1969)

  Marxism and Politics (Oxford, 1977)

Mill, John Stuart, *Autobiography* (New York, 1924)

Miller, Martin A., *Kropotkin* (Chicago, 1976)

Mitchell, Arthur, *Labour in Irish Politics, 1890–1930* (Dublin, 1974)

Moody, A.D., 'Pound's Allen Upward', *Paideuma*, vol. iv, no. 1, Spring 1975

Moody, T.W., 'Michael Davitt and the British labour movement, 1882–1906', *Transactions of the Royal Historical Society*, vol. ii, 1953

  'Michael Davitt', in John W. Boyle (ed.), *Leaders and Workers* (Cork, 1966)

  Davitt and Irish Revolution, 1846–82 (Oxford, 1981)

Moran, Gerard, 'James Daly and the rise and fall of the Land League in the west of Ireland, 1879–82', *Irish Historical Studies*, vol. xxix, no. 114, Nov. 1994

  'The Land War, urban destitution and town tenant protest, 1879–82', *Saothar*, vol. xx, 1995

Morgan, Austen, *James Connolly: A Political Biography* (Manchester, 1988)

  Labour and Partition: The Belfast Working Class, 1905–23 (London, 1991)

Morley, John, 'England and Ireland', *The Fortnightly Review*, 1 April 1881

Morris, William, *Collected Works*, 24 Volumes (London, 1910–15)

Morton, A.L., (ed.), *Political Writings of William Morris* (London, 1979)

Munck, Ronaldo, *The Difficult Dialogue: Marxism and Nationalism* (London, 1986)

Murray, Peter, 'Electoral politics and the Dublin working class before the First World War', *Saothar*, vol. vi, 1980

Neale, R.S. (ed.), *History and Class: Essential Readings in Theory and Interpretation* (Oxford, 1983)

Nevin, Donal, (ed.), *Trade Union Century* (Cork, 1994)

Newsinger, John, 'A great blow must be struck in Ireland: Karl Marx and the Fenians', *Race and Class*, vol. xxiv, no. 2, Autumn 1982

'As Catholic as the Pope: James Connolly and the Roman Catholic Church in Ireland', *Saothar*, vol. 11, 1986

Nowlan, Kevin B., (ed.), *Karl Marx: The Materialist Messiah* (Cork, 1984)

O'Brien, C.C., *Parnell and his Party, 1880–1890* (Oxford, 1968)

O'Brien, William, *Forth the Banners Go: Reminiscences* (Dublin, 1969)

O'Brien, William, and Desmond Ryan (eds), *Devoy's Postbag, 1880–1928* (Dublin, 1979)

Ó Broin, Leon, *Revolutionary Underground: The Story of the Irish Republican Brotherhood, 1858–1924* (Dublin, 1976)

O'Connor, Emmet, 'The influence of Redmondism on the development of the labour movement in Waterford in the 1890s', *Decies*, no. 10, January 1979

A Labour History of Waterford (Waterford, 1989)

A Labour History of Ireland, 1824–1960 (Dublin, 1992)

O'Ferrall, Fergus, *Catholic Emancipation: Daniel O'Connell and the Birth of Irish Democracy, 1820–30* (Dublin, 1985)

O Gráda, Cormac, 'The Owenite Community at Ralahine', in E.T. Craig, *An Irish Commune* (Dublin, 1983)

Ireland: A New Economic History, 1780–1939 (Oxford, 1994)

O'Higgins, Rachel, 'Irish trade unions and politics, 1830–50', *Historical Journal*, vol. iv, 1961

'The Irish influence in the Chartist movement', *Past and Present*, no. 20, Nov. 1961

O'Malley, E., 'The decline of Irish industry in the nineteenth century', *Economic and Social Review*, vol. xiii, no. 1, 1981

Owen, Robert, *The Life of Robert Owen with Selections from his Writings and Correspondence*, vol. 1A (London, 1857)

Palmer, N.D., *The Irish Land League Crisis* (New Haven, 1940)

Pankhurst, Richard, *William Thompson, 1775–1833* (London, 1954)

Patterson, Henry, *Class Conflict and Sectarianism: The Protestant Working Class and the Belfast Labour Movement, 1868–1920* (Belfast, 1980)

Pelling, Henry, *America and the British Left: From Bright to Bevan* (London, 1956)

The Origins of the Labour Party, 1880–1900 (Oxford, 1965)

A History of British Trade Unionism (Harmondsworth, 1967)

Pierson, Stanley, 'Ernest Belfort Bax: 1854–1926, the encounter of Marxism and late Victorian culture', *Journal of British Studies*, vol. xii, 1972

Marxism and the Origins of British Socialism (London, 1973)

British Socialists: The Journey from Fantasy to Politics (Cambridge, Mass., 1979)

Plowright, John, 'Political economy and Christian polity: the influence of Henry George in England reassessed', *Victorian Studies*, vol. xxx, no. 2, Winter 1987

Quail, John, *The Slow Burning Fuse: The Lost History of the British Anarchists* (London, 1978)

Rae, John, 'The socialism of Karl Marx and the Young Hegelians', *Contemporary Review*, October, 1881

Contemporary Socialism (London, 1884)

Ransom, Bernard, *Connolly's Marxism* (London, 1980)

Rowlandson, H., 'The Socialist League and its poet', *Dublin University Review*, Aug. 1885

'Towards democracy', *Dublin University Review*, Apr. 1886

Ryan, Desmond (ed.), *Socialism and Nationalism: A Selection from the Writings of James Connolly* (Dublin, 1948)

Ryan, W.P., *The Irish Labour Movement* (Dublin, 1919)

Sargant, William Lucas, *Robert Owen and his Social Philosophy* (London, 1860)

Saville, John, 'Henry George and the British labour movement', *Science and Society*, vol. xxiv, Fall 1960

'Henry George and the British labour movement: a select bibliography with commentary', *Bulletin of the Society for the Study of Labour History*, vol. v, 1962

'The ideology of labourism', in Robert Benewick et al. (eds.), *Knowledge and Belief in Politics: The Problem of Ideology* (London, 1973)

Sexton, James, *Sir James Sexton, Agitator: An Autobiography* (London, 1936)

Shaw, James J., 'The nationalisation of the land', *Journal of the Statistical and Social Society of Ireland*, pt. lxii, July 1884

Sheehan, D.D., *Ireland since Parnell* (London, 1920)

Sheehy-Skeffington, Francis, *Michael Davitt* (London, 1967)

Sombart, Werner, *Socialism and the Social Movement* (London, 1909)

Stead, W.T., 'The Labour Party and the books that helped to make it', *Review of Reviews*, pt xxxiii, 1906

Steenson, Gary P., *Karl Kautsky, 1854–1938: Marxism in the Classical Years* (Pittsburgh, 1991)

Strauss, Erich, *Irish Nationalism and British Democracy* (London, 1951)

Thompson, Dorothy, 'Ireland and the Irish in English Radicalism before 1850', in James Epstein and Dorothy Thompson (eds.), *The Chartist Experience: Studies in Working Class Radicalism and Culture, 1830–1860* (London, 1982)

Outsiders: Class, Gender and Nation (London, 1993)

Thompson, E.P., *The Communism of William Morris* (London, 1965)

William Morris: Romantic to Revolutionary (New York, 1976)

Thompson, Paul, *Socialists, Liberals and Labour: The Struggle for London, 1885–1914* (London, 1967)

Thompson, William, *An Inquiry into the Principles of the Distribution of Wealth* (London, 1824)

Appeal of one Half the Human Race, Women, Against the Pretensions of the Other Half, Men, to Retain Them in Political, and Thence in Civil and Domestic Slavery (London, 1827)

Labor Rewarded: The Claims of Labor and Capital Conciliated or How to Secure to Labor the Whole Product of its Exertion (London, 1827)

Thom's Irish Almanac and Official Directory, 1886 (Dublin, 1887)

Thom's Official Directory of the United Kingdom of Great Britain and Ireland, 1882 (Dublin, 1882)

Thorne, Will, *My Life's Battles* (London, 1925)

Tsuzuki, Chuschichi, *H.M. Hyndman and British Socialism* (Oxford, 1961)

Tynan, P.J.P., *The Irish National Invincibles and their Times* (London, 1894)

Wallace, A.R., 'How to nationalise the land: a radical solution of the Irish land problem', *Contemporary Review*, Nov. 1880

Ward, Margaret, *Unmanageable Revolutionaries: Women and Irish Nationalism* (Dingle, 1983)

Warwick-Haller, Sally, *William O'Brien and the Irish Land War* (Dublin, 1990)

Waters, Chris, *British Socialists and the Politics of Popular Culture, 1884–1914* (Manchester, 1990)

Watmough, P.A., 'The membership of the Social Democratic Federation 1885–1902', *Bulletin of the Society for the Study of Labour History*, vol. xxxiv, Spring 1977

Webb, Sidney and Beatrice, *The History of Trade Unionism* (London, 1920)

Whelan, Kevin, 'Come all you staunch revisionists: towards a post-revisionist agenda for Irish history', *The Irish Reporter*, no. 2, 1991

Wilkins, M.S., 'The non-socialist origins of England's first important socialist organization', *International Review of Social History*, vol. iv, 1959

Willis, Kirk, 'The introduction and critical reception of Marxist thought in Britain, 1850–1900', *Historical Journal*, vol. xx, no. 2, 1977

Wolfe, Willard, *From Radicalism to Socialism: Men and Ideas in the Formation of Fabian Socialist Doctrines, 1881–1889* (New Haven and London, 1975)

Yeats, W.B., *Autobiographies* (London, 1955)

Yeo, Stephen, 'A phase in the social history of socialism, c.1885–1895', *Bulletin of the Society for the Study of Labour History*, vol. xxii, 1971

'A new life: the religion of socialism in Britain, 1883–1896', *History Workshop*, no. 4, Autumn 1977.

'Notes on three socialisms', in Carl Levy (ed.), *Socialism and the Intelligentsia, 1880–1914* (London, 1987)

Index